THE HITLER/HESS DECEPTION

Martin Allen was born in Caerphilly, South Wales, and spent his childhood in Cornwall before attending King's College, Cardiff in the 1970s. He is the author of *Hidden Agenda: How the Duke of Windsor Betrayed the Allies*.

By the same author

HIDDEN AGENDA: HOW THE DUKE OF WINDSOR
BETRAYED THE ALLIES

THE HITLER/HESS DECEPTION

British Intelligence's Best-Kept Secret
of the Second World War

MARTIN ALLEN

HarperCollins*Publishers*

HarperCollins*Publishers*
77–85 Fulham Palace Road,
Hammersmith, London W6 8JB

The HarperCollins website address is
www.harpercollins.co.uk

This paperback edition 2004
1 3 5 7 9 8 6 4 2

First published in Great Britain by
HarperCollins*Publishers* 2003

Copyright © Martin Allen 2003

9 8 7 6 5 4 3 2 1

ISBN 0 00 714119 X

Set in Stempel Garamond by
Rowland Phototypesetting Limited
Bury St Edmunds, Suffolk

Printed and bound in Great Britain
by Clays plc, St Ives

For Jeanie, without whose invaluable assistance
this book would not have been written

Contents

Illustrations

Rudolf Hess as a fighter pilot on the Western Front in 1918.
(© Bettmann/CORBIS)

Hess as a young political activist, October 1922. (Bildarchiv
Preußischer Kulturbesitz)

Hess, Hitler and Streicher at the 1927 Nuremberg rally. (© Bettmann/
CORBIS)

Martha and Karl Haushofer in the 1930s. (By kind permission of
Renata Haushofer)

Albrecht Haushofer and his brother Heinz at the end of the First
World War. (By kind permission of Renata Haushofer)

Hess with Karl Haushofer in the early 1930s. (Scherl/SV-Bilderdienst)

Hess discusses his latest flying adventure with his wife Ilse and
colleagues. (Popperfoto)

Hess, Goebbels, head of the Reichsbank Hjalmar Schacht and
Dr Robert Ley on board a cruise ship in the Baltic. Hitler snoozes
in the background. (The National Archives, Washington DC)

Hess greets the Russian Foreign Minister, Vyacheslav Molotov, during
a visit to Berlin. (Scherl/SV-Bilderdienst)

Albrecht Haushofer in the early 1930s. (By kind permission of Renata
Haushofer)

Hess amidst the ruling Nazi elite. (Hulton Archive)

Hitler attended by Albrecht Haushofer before a banquet at the Reich
Chancellery on 26 March 1935. (Photograph by Heinrich Hoffman.
Reproduced courtesy of Bayerische Staatsbibliothek, München)

Albrecht Haushofer delivers a lecture on European geography. (By
kind permission of Renata Haushofer)

Albrecht Haushofer with his niece and nephews. (By kind permission
of Renata Haushofer)

Sir Robert Vansittart and Sir Alexander Cadogan, 1937. *(Hulton Archive)*

Anthony Eden and Vansittart, 1937. *(Hulton Archive)*

Winston Churchill and Sir Samuel Hoare, 1937. *(Hulton Archive)*

Churchill, accompanied by Brendan Bracken, welcomes Harry Hopkins to London, January 1941. *(Hulton Archive)*

Ernst Bohle with Churchill in pre-war London. *(Scherl/SV-Bilderdienst)*

Bohle as head of the Auslandsorganisation in the 1930s. *(Scherl/SV-Bilderdienst)*

Lord Halifax and Anthony Eden in May 1940. *(Hulton Archive)*

Hugh Dalton in 1948 as Chancellor of the Exchequer. *(Hulton Archive)*

Woburn Abbey, the wartime headquarters of SOE. *(© The Marquess of Tavistock and the Trustees of the Bedford Estates)*

Hess boards his personal Me-110 in the months preceding his flight to Britain. *(Scherl/SV-Bilderdienst)*

The Messerschmitt-110. *(Hulton Archive)*

The Duke of Hamilton serenading the young Princesses Elizabeth and Margaret. *(The Imperial War Museum – HU 86241)*

The Duke of Hamilton in the early part of the war. *(Popperfoto)*

The Duke of Kent with RAF officers early in the war. *(Hulton Archive)*

The Duke of Kent views bomb damage in London in January 1941. *(Popperfoto)*

The wartime aircraft hangars, maintenance facilities and offices at Dungavel House. *(© Crown Copyright/MOD. Reproduced with the permission of the Controller of Her Majesty's Stationery Office)*

RAF personnel pose with the wreckage of Hess's plane. *(© Imperial War Museum – HU 71891)*

A haggard and weary Albrecht Haushofer in 1944. *(By kind permission of Renata Haushofer)*

'Rex' Leeper as Ambassador to Argentina in 1946. *(Hulton Archive)*

Hess questioned by US Army Colonel John Amen in autumn 1945. *(Bildarchiv Preußischer Kulturbesitz)*

Hess in the dock at Nuremberg, October 1946. *(Popperfoto)*

Maps

Acknowledgements

I would like to thank all those people who have helped with the research and logistical requirements behind the writing of this book. Some took the time and trouble to write to me, whilst others granted an interview; some assisted in translations, additional research, or by voluntarily providing information that it had not occurred to me to ask for.

I would firstly like to pay a tribute to Herr Gerd Ahlschwede, formerly of the 1st Panzer Division; Mr Steve Alexander; Mrs Felicity Ashtree; Mr Stuart L. Butler; Mr Roy Conyers-Nesbit; Senor Carlos Alberto Damas; Mrs Regina Davis; Dr Alfred Grupp of the Auswärtiges Amt; Mrs Cate Haste; Mr Oliver Hoare; Mr Masahiro Kawai of the IDS, Tokyo; Mr John M. Kelso of the FBI; Frau Christine Kislar and Herr Guido Knopp of ZDF; Mrs Brenda Levinson; Mr Lawrence H. McDonald; Mr Colin R. Macmillan; Mr A. Nikonov of the Russian State Archive; Ms Dunja Noack; Major T.W.F. Odell (retd); Franz-Dieter Paulsen; Mrs Penny Prior of the Foreign Office; Professor Robert K. Shaw; Mrs Amy Schmidt of the National Archives, Washington DC; Mr T. Sekiguchi; Frau A. Stocker of the Bundesarchiv; Mrs Hilary Sweet-Escott; Mrs Lucy Takezoe of the National DIET Library, Tokyo; Mrs Errol Trzebinski; Mr Steven Walton of the Imperial War Museum; Mr William J. Walsh; Mr Hitomi Watanabe, Second Secretary (Political Division) of the Japanese Embassy; Mrs Linda Wheeler; Herr Viktor Wolf of the Internal Division of the German Foreign Ministry; and Frau Zandeck of the Bundesarchiv.

I would also like to thank those persons, connected either by family relationship to or exceptional knowledge of the main personalities or events of 1940–41, who extended me their assistance: Rudolf Hess's son Wolf Rüdiger Hess; Adolf Hitler's secretary Frau Gertaud Junge; Joachim von Ribbentrop's Private Secretary Herr Reinhardt Spitzy; the Duke of Hamilton's son Lord James Douglas-Hamilton; Albrecht Haushofer's nieces, Frau Andrea Haushofer-Schröder and Frau Renata Haushofer; Albrecht Haushofer's assistant Herr Heinz Albers-Schonberg; Herr Hans Noebel, family friend of Albrecht Haushofer; and Sir Samuel Hoare's daughter, Mrs Verily Paget.

I am particularly indebted to the following institutions and government bodies for replying to my letters, or who otherwise gave me their time and assistance to aid my research: De Arquivo Historico, Lisbon; the Auswärtiges Amt (the Federal Foreign Office of Germany); the Bundesarchiv-Militärarchiv, Freiburg; Companies House, Cardiff; the *Daily Record*, Glasgow; the Federal Bureau of Investigation; the Foreign and Commonwealth Office; the Hoover Institution; the Imperial War Museum; the Japanese Embassy in London; the Japanese Foreign Ministry; the KGB Archives, Moscow; the National Archives and Records Administration of the United States of America; the National DIET Library of Tokyo; the National Institute for Defence Studies, Tokyo; the Public Records Office, London; the Royal British Legion; the University of Kiel; the US Department of Justice; and the Zweites Deutsches Fernsehen.

I would also like to pay tribute to those friends, colleagues and translators who assisted in the logistics of creating this book: Dr Olaf Rose, for his assistance as personal translator during my lecture tours and conferences in Germany, as well as his generous and unstinting assistance during my research and conducting of interviews; Dr Gerd Sudholt, of Verlag Gesellschafts Berg, who has been of great assistance in my search for testimony from eyewitnesses of Germany's past; Dr Michael Stenton for his considered and expert advise on SOE, SO1, the Political Warfare Executive, and Britain's political warfare and propaganda conducted during the early years of the Second World War; Mr D.R.

Brown for his knowledge about aircraft of the First and Second World War; Mr F.P. Creagh for his chauffeur and security services; M. Pierre Vial, Mr Nick Burzynski, Herr Alfred Gottlieb and Mrs Sabine Wickes for their hard work in translating the extremely large number of documents necessary to unravel the mystery behind the events of 1940–41; Mr David Prysor-Jones and Mr James Crowden for the many, many hours of late-night discussion as we pondered the subtleties of the British and German governments' political dilemmas and diplomatic priorities of the late 1930s and early 1940s.

Finally, I would like to pay a very special tribute to my wife, Jean. As my business manager and partner in research, she had a very major influence on the writing of this book, and I am indebted to her for her unstinting support through many worrying and difficult times that lay between the start and finish of this project.

Preface

One wet Friday morning in the spring of 2000, I found myself in the Dorset market town of Dorchester to give a radio interview about a book I had written on the politico-diplomatic events of 1939–40, called *Hidden Agenda*.

As I sat in the tiny broadcast studio staring at the microphone, my head clamped within a hefty pair of headphones, I little realised that within the next twenty minutes a question asked by a DJ tucked away in a BBC broadcast studio in Southampton would occupy my life for the next two years, cause me to collect many thousands of documents from as far afield as Germany, Japan, the United States and Russia, or travel many thousands of miles to interview experts and witnesses from as far afield as a nursing home in Glasgow, to a mansion in Bavaria, an apartment in Stockholm, and a townhouse on the outskirts of Washington DC.

I took a sip of water from a plastic cup, blissfully unaware that a mysterious element of the Second World War would soon prove so magnetic to my curiosity that before the end of the week I would begin a hunt for documents and people who might help me solve a mysterious affair that had taken place over sixty years ago . . .

Suddenly the headphones cracked into life and a disembodied voice greeted me jovially: 'Hello. Are you there, Mr Allen?'

After a brief acknowledgement from me, the voice pronounced 'Great! I'm cutting you in now . . .' and with that music that was being broadcast to the south of England burst loudly from the headphones for a few brief seconds, before almost immediately beginning to tail away again.

'Wasn't that nice, just the sort of thing for a wet summer's day,' the DJ announced to his audience. 'Now, as I mentioned earlier, I've been joined this morning by Martin Allen, who has just written a book on the Duke of Windsor which throws new light on events at the start of the Second World War. Hello Martin . . .'

And so the interview got under way, with much banter from the distant DJ, and some searching questions as well for he had evidently read the book and wanted the most out of the interview.

About halfway through the interview, whilst we were discussing the Duke of Windsor's time in Lisbon, where surreptitious communication had begun between the German government and Britain's former King at loose on a continent aflame with war, the DJ pointedly asked: 'Given that the Duke of Windsor knew Hess, is it correct to say he was connected to Hess's flight to Britain in May 1941?'

I paused, my immediate inclination was to answer yes, but in the nanosecond between the DJ asking his question and my considering the answer, I suddenly realised, *No, it can't be connected to Windsor. Hess's flight to Britain was nearly a year later, and the Duke of Windsor had been in the Bahamas for much of that time.* What then was the answer? I sidestepped the question, declaring that the Hess problem would not easily be solved until all the documents on the matter were released, and the interview duly progressed in another direction.

I do not really remember the drive home that day, for my mind was back sixty years in those dreadful dangerous days of 1940–41, when Britain had stood alone and fought desperately for her very survival. Ignoring the heavy traffic and pouring rain, I found myself mentally sifting through the considerable Foreign Office and Intelligence evidence I had accumulated to write my last book, sure that a clue to what took place was there somewhere, yet positive it would not be the full answer.

Rudolf Hess's flight to Britain had taken place on the night of Saturday 10 May 1941, 10 months after the Duke of Windsor had departed Portugal aboard the SS *Excalibur* bound for the Bahamas where he was to become the colony's new Governor. That the Windsors did not want to go, considered the Bahamas little more than a gilded cage with golden sands, a 'St Helena of 1940' as Wallis called it, was without a doubt. However, I also knew that despite still feeling himself deserving of some greater task in life, the Duke of Windsor had lost his importance to the Germans by then and become superfluous to their needs. In addition, with the Duke of Windsor's departure from war-torn Europe, Ribbentrop's potential as a man capable of delivering that illusive peace deal Hitler wanted had taken yet another severe knock as well, for the German Führer had finally realised that his Foreign Minister was not up to the job of ending the war with Britain. Therefore, I concluded, Ribbentrop, together with the Duke of Windsor, was unlikely to have been connected to Hess's flight to Britain in May 1941.

What, then, was the answer?

To uncover the facts behind a wartime event that is in many respects still secret is extremely difficult, for a substantial number of key documents on this element of the Second World War have never been declassified. Against such a climate of secrecy, this paucity of available evidence, it can be almost impossible to uncover the truth, and it has to be said that one eventually learns new ways to uncover the facts.

When I had written *Hidden Agenda*, a French-American named Charles Bedaux had proven to be the key to revealing the Duke of Windsor's secret activities during the Phoney War. I therefore concluded that what I needed was a new version of Bedaux; someone who had been privy to the events of 1941, but who might have escaped undue attention. Having given some thought to the Hess mystery, it occurred to me that there *had* been another such person, someone who had been privy to Hess's innermost thoughts during the 1940–41 period – his close friend and personal foreign affairs advisor, Albrecht Haushofer.

What made me realise that Albrecht Haushofer might become my key to unlocking the Hess mystery was the knowledge that at the end of the war the Haushofer family itself had become a source of mystery. Great efforts had been made by Allied intelligence to investigate both Albrecht Haushofer and his father Karl Haushofer, but more intriguing still was the knowledge that certain of their papers had vanished from Allied custody. A sure sign someone had something to hide.

And so I began the chase again – a search of the world's archives, the tracking down of persons who had worked for the British and German Foreign Ministries, associates of Haushofer, Hess, Hitler, and Ribbentrop too; those privy to certain other secret events of 1941, and finally, the not insubstantial task of reading many thousands of pages of evidence.

Slowly – by not only examining the obvious evidence, but also looking for the unobvious and spending a great deal of time pursuing dead-ends – the Rudolf Hess mystery began to give up its secrets, and what was revealed was not at all what I had expected . . .

Martin A. Allen
April 2002

Prologue

On a bright Saturday afternoon, 12 May 1945, the spring sunshine made harsh and uncompromising by the leaf-denuded trees and surrounding bombed-out buildings, a young German named Heinz Haushofer picked his way through the ruined shell of Berlin. He was largely ignored by the numerous Russian troops who now occupied the city, and those he stopped to question had little patience for any German after the terrible war that had ended a mere five days before.

Haushofer had arrived on foot in Berlin the previous evening and, after spending an uncomfortable night with an acquaintance in the suburbs, had ventured into the city centre to look for his missing brother Albrecht, who had spent the last eight months of the war as a prisoner of the SS at Berlin's Moabit prison.

After traversing the churned-up remains of the Tiergarten, almost treeless after a winter of Allied bombing and the Russian bombardment of April, Heinz managed to cross the River Spree by one of the few remaining bridges in Berlin. Quests like that being undertaken by Heinz were taking place all over Europe at the end of the war, particularly in Germany, as displaced persons travelled in search of missing loved ones. Sometimes these searches ended in the joy of reunion; but more often in sadness.

On reaching Moabit prison, Heinz managed to find someone with news. Albrecht, he was told, had been marched away by the SS on the night of 22 April in the direction of Potsdam Station, accompanied by fifteen other prisoners.

A little over an hour later, Heinz cautiously entered the bombed-out ruins of the one-time showpiece Ulap Exhibition Centre, just off Invalidenstrasse. After heavy Allied bombing, the vast building was almost completely buried under the shattered remains of the roof, which had collapsed. Following the directions he had been given, Heinz clambered over an enormous mound of rubble and twisted girders to get to the far side of the complex. There he was confronted by the last act of barbarism that the SS would ever commit on the direct orders of their leader, Heinrich Himmler. In the ruins of the exhibition centre, Heinz found the remains of the sixteen men who had been marched away from Moabit nearly three weeks before, to be murdered the same night. Steeling himself to the grim task, Heinz went from body to body, attempting to identify his brother.

There was a puzzle here that would not be solved by Heinz. What had led Albrecht Haushofer, one of Germany's foremost experts in foreign affairs, to such a dismal end with these fifteen other prisoners from such disparate backgrounds? A mechanical engineer, an Olympic athlete, a Russian PoW, an Argentinean, a German Communist, a Lieutenant-Colonel of the OKH (Germany's high command), a lawyer, a legal adviser to Lufthansa, an Abwehr officer, a merchant, a State Secretary of Germany's Foreign Ministry, an industrialist, an adviser to the Congregational Church, a professor of aviation, and, finally, a Councillor of State.

Eventually, after searching through the entwined husks of these men brought together in death, a jumble of arms, legs, overcoats, Heinz finally found his elder brother. To have been murdered in such circumstances by the SS was a terrible end for anyone, yet it was particularly so for a man who had been not only Secretary General of Germany's prestigious Society for Geography, the Geographie Gessellschaft, but a friend and adviser to Germany's Deputy-Führer, Rudolf Hess, and to the Führer himself, Adolf Hitler.

With his bare hands, Heinz dug a simple temporary grave for Albrecht out in the open air. It was now late afternoon, and he felt it prudent to hurry, for in the immediate aftermath of the war, Berlin was not a place to be out after dark, and he would have to find sanctuary for the night. After laying his brother to rest in a patch of ground outside the exhibition centre and saying a few simple words in farewell, Heinz set off for the suburbs.

He did not, however, leave all of Albrecht behind. Tucked safely within his overcoat he carried his brother's final words to posterity, written during his last months of captivity. Clutched in his brother's hand, Heinz had found a sheaf of papers: a set of sonnets, one of which Albrecht had titled *Schuld* – 'Guilt'.

As Germany settled down to post-war occupation under the Allied powers, Allied Intelligence began to make enquiries about Albrecht Haushofer. During the war French, British and American Intelligence had been largely bonded together by the common cause of defeating Nazism, but victory brought about a rapid unravelling of that cohesion, as different national priorities once again took pre-eminence.

By midsummer two distinct organs of Allied Intelligence, with two quite distinct agendas, were taking an interest in Albrecht Haushofer. The first was British Intelligence, the second non-British, primarily American. The main difference between the two was that while every document found by non-British Intelligence was registered and stored for future reference, those that fell into the hands of the British were comprehensively weeded, and certain sensitive pieces of evidence vanished completely, never to be seen again.

Throughout the summer of 1945, British Intelligence made extraordinary efforts to locate the private papers of both Albrecht Haushofer and his father, Professor Karl Haushofer, and it was at this time that a set of six of Albrecht Haushofer's diaries were found in Berlin. As they were located by the Americans, they were duly logged and their importance noted, for they covered the period of 1940–41 which had seen an extraordinary chain of events culminating in Rudolf Hess's flight to Britain in May 1941. However, within a few days of the diaries arriving in Britain, on 7 June 1945, an American Intelligence officer was forced to report to his superior that they had vanished. They have never been seen since.[1]

At the end of September 1945, consternation erupted amongst a select band of Whitehall civil servants when they learned that

American Intelligence officers from the Office of Strategic Studies (OSS) had managed to track down Karl Haushofer at his substantial home, Hartschimmelhof, deep in the Bavarian forests south of Munich. Why British Intelligence had not already located and interrogated the elderly Professor Haushofer is something of a mystery, but their activities may have been impeded by the fact that Haushofer resided in the American Zone of occupation. That he had not been more actively pursued was now bitterly regretted, for it was discovered that Albrecht Haushofer had sent his father copies of certain sensitive sections of his correspondence (hoping thereby to protect himself in the future); and the Professor was proving to be a veritable fount of information to his American interrogators.

Professor Karl Haushofer was a nineteenth-century-style imperialist who, after the end of the First World War, had been the leading academic promulgator of 'geopolitics' – the theory that in the future the world would be restructured into an age of great land-empires. He had also been Rudolf Hess's university tutor, and during the rise of the Nazis to power he had privately tutored Adolf Hitler on the rudiments of foreign policy and European ethnicity. He was therefore widely recognised as the man chiefly responsible for the Nazis' concept of *Lebensraum* – living space for the German people – which Hitler had used as his justification for wars of conquest. This was the man that three OSS officers tracked down to a house deep in the Bavarian forests on a late September afternoon in 1945.

When the interrogation began, the senior American Intelligence officer, Edmund Walsh, had merely looked meaningfully at Haushofer and said a single word: 'Hitler.'

According to Walsh, the elderly Professor's 'face assumed a pained expression'. He admitted that he had taught Hitler geopolitics, but then qualified his answer by declaring that Hitler had 'never understood'.[2]

If this had been the extent of Haushofer's knowledge, British Intelligence might not have subsequently taken much interest in him. However, during the course of the interrogation one of the Americans was intuitive enough to ask whether Haushofer's son

Albrecht's expertise in British matters had been connected to Rudolf Hess's mysterious flight to Scotland in May 1941. The OSS officers were surprised when Haushofer unhesitatingly replied: 'In 1941 . . . Albrecht was sent to Switzerland. There he met a British confidential agent – a Lord Templewood, I believe.' He then revealed that Hitler had wanted peace, and that 'we offered to relinquish Norway, Denmark, and France. A larger meeting was to be held in Madrid. When my son returned, he was immediately called to Augsburg to see Hess. A few days later Hess flew to England.'[3]

The OSS men listened to these revelations with shocked astonishment. Lord Templewood was Britain's former Foreign Secretary and later Ambassador to Spain, Sir Samuel Hoare.

Over the course of the next three hours, whilst Bavaria descended into darkness, the American agents struggled to digest all the elderly Professor Karl Haushofer told them. Yet this Aladdin's cave was not limited to verbal information. At the end of the interrogation they asked him to hand over any documents he possessed that related to his work. If they had thought they would be able to leave with a few boxes of papers piled into the back of their Buick staff car, they were in for a shock: Haushofer's archive of personal papers extended to nearly eighteen thousand documents, and the OSS men were forced to return the following morning with an army lorry.

During the late autumn of 1945, other documents began to appear. Of particular importance were the papers from the Geopolitical Institute in Berlin, where Albrecht Haushofer had kept some of his records.

On 27 November, an American Intelligence officer urgently dispatched to Washington 'letters and material from the files of Albrecht Haushofer, regarding peace feelers to England'.[4] He included a note drawing his superior's attention to:

Document No. 8.
A personal memorandum, datelined Obersalzberg 5 May 1941, is from Haushofer to Hitler, and concerns Haushofer's English

connections and the possibility of their being used as contacts for peace discussions.[5]

What was intriguing about this memorandum was that it was dated five days *before* Rudolf Hess had flown to Britain. This was at odds with the generally held belief that Hitler had not known what his Deputy was planning. Clearly, this document might have provided answers to some of the many questions which remain about what actually took place in 1941. Unfortunately, although the memorandum arrived safely in Washington DC on 11 December 1945, and an official of the US State Department signed for it, an unknown person removed it just three days later, scrawling 'Enclosure removed 12-14-45' across the receipt stamp.[6] It has never been seen since.

During the winter of 1945 the prosecution at the International Military Tribunal (IMT) in Nuremberg considered placing Karl Haushofer on trial with the leading Nazis, but concluded that it was not possible to prosecute an academic merely for putting forward theories, even theories as provocative as Professor Haushofer's. It was, however, seriously debated whether Haushofer should be called as a key witness for the prosecution of Hitler's Deputy Rudolf Hess and Foreign Minister Joachim von Ribbentrop, to explain his theories, which were at the core of Nazi foreign policy, and to give general evidence.

What occurred next cannot be viewed with anything but a sceptical eye. On Sunday, 10 March 1946, Professor Haushofer was discreetly visited at Hartshimmelhof by two Allied Intelligence officers. On this occasion the men were not Americans, but from British Intelligence. Several days later they wrote a brief memorandum to Ivone Kirkpatrick, a high-ranking official at the Foreign Office. They reported that Haushofer 'knew nothing further on the subject in question', and, curiously, concluded: 'In response to our instructions, the problem concerning this man and the IMT has been removed.'[7]

Two days later, on Tuesday, 12 March, Heinz Haushofer, puzzled by his inability to contact his parents on the phone, went to Hartschimmelhof. He found the house deserted, although the lights within were burning. With increasing concern, Heinz searched the substantial house, before moving on to the grounds and the surrounding forest. An hour later, deep within the woods in a hollow beside a stream about half a mile behind the house – a spot later described by an American Intelligence officer as the 'loneliest hillside in Bavaria' – Heinz Haushofer found his parents. Karl Haushofer was lying in a hunched position in the hollow, and his wife Martha was hanging from a nearby tree. It was later established that Professor Haushofer's death had been caused by cyanide poisoning.

The local police, together with the American authorities, investigated the matter in some detail, but after all the horrors of the war, and with the desperate state of Germany in the spring of 1946, resources and time were limited, and the Haushofers' deaths were officially recorded as suicides.

There is, however, a curious fact about the German police reports on the case, and the subsequent interest taken in the case by the American authorities. Nowhere, in any statement taken at any time, did anyone reveal, record or admit that the last people to see the Haushofers alive were almost certainly two British Intelligence agents. Agents who reported on their visit to Ivone Kirkpatrick, the Foreign Office official who in 1941 had been one of the very first men to interview Rudolf Hess after his unexpected arrival on British soil. Kirkpatrick was also, incidentally, later that year to land a plum appointment as Britain's High Commissioner to Germany.

Almost from the moment Rudolf Hess parachuted out of the night sky on 10 May 1941 to land on a remote Scottish hillside, the official British line on the arrival of Germany's Deputy-Führer on British soil was that he was mad. Intriguingly, within twenty-four hours Adolf Hitler would make much the same claim.

The two opposing parties had very different reasons to denigrate Hess's importance. British Intelligence may have been hiding an entirely different, and infinitely more dangerous, secret. The arrival of Hess was merely an unplanned offshoot of an operation intended to achieve a much more important end. Right up until the moment they were confronted by Germany's Deputy-Führer standing before them in a gleaming black flying-suit, British Intelligence had actually been expecting someone else.

In Germany, Hitler's reaction to Hess's flight was largely motivated by fear of losing face before his own people should they discover that their Führer, whilst exhorting them to fight on in his war of conquest, had actually been secretly involved in negotiations with certain top Britons to make peace and end the war. Indeed, he had even offered to withdraw all German forces from occupied western Europe in order to attain a deal.

The extraordinary truth is that, for sixty years, a potentially devastating political secret has been covered up by subterfuge. This secret was related to British fears in 1940 and 1941 that the country might go down to crushing defeat, and to how Britain's top political minds determined that Britain would survive. The means they used to accomplish this were ingenious and extremely subtle, but also unscrupulous. They were the acts of desperate men, faced with the options of either catastrophic defeat or national survival.

By its very nature, what was done became a secret that could *never* be revealed. The decision to promulgate the legend of the stand-alone nation – that Britain had survived through pure military endeavour and luck – meant that disclosure during the dangerous years of the Cold War would have resulted in the shattering of Britain's international credibility, and the ruin of many political careers.

Yet it could also be said that there was another, more noble, purpose to keeping this secret for all time. The impression has always been maintained that the Nazi leaders were a bizarre range of individuals, devoid of compassion for humanity – and, in many cases, evil personified. If, however, the truth should turn out to be that some of these men had considerable political acumen, but that the inexorable spread of the Second World War resulted largely from their inability to control the situation, the distinction between pernicious men of evil intent, and politicians unable to control the flames of war they had themselves lit, becomes less clear-cut.

CHAPTER 1

An Unlikely Triumvirate

If one were looking for some lasting important artefact of the Third Reich, one should not seek a swastika-adorned fighter-plane or medal-bedecked army uniform in a military museum, for these are really the vestiges of failure, items of hardware used by the Nazis to attain their empire when the politics broke down. For a more meaningful relic of Nazism, one intent on exploring the darker side of humanity need only look as far as *Mein Kampf*. In its pages, more than by any other means, one can gain an insight into National Socialism. Nazism was a concept, a radical if unwholesome ideology that sprang from the disasters of the First World War, the German right's patriotic yearnings for nationhood, and the fear of Bolshevism in the 1920s and thirties. The torchlit marches, the ostentatious neo-classical structures, the plethora of eagle-surmounted swastikas that adorned buildings, banners and uniformed breasts, were but a manifestation of thought, an ideology that powered National Socialism: the belief that Germany could rise phoenix-like from the ashes of Weimar mediocrity.

Nazism, history tells us, sprang from political theories implemented by a band of individuals who would have been regarded as social misfits in any other society, led by men such as Josef Goebbels, Heinrich Himmler, Robert Ley, Julius Streicher, Joachim von Ribbentrop and, of course, Adolf Hitler and Rudolf Hess. All were determined to create a new world where Aryan supremacy and mysticism became fact, and where humanity would be classified into the top-of-the-heap Aryans, followed by the lower orders – the Slavs, the Jews, and other sub-humans.

But what if some of these top Nazis were not so strange? If they were in fact extremely capable and competent politicians? Our present-day perception of Nazism would be very different. National Socialism would not have been any less terrible or objectionable, but the boundaries between the normal political mind and the bizarre would be less easy to determine.

Nazi rule was a tree whose roots lay initially in a defeated nation's fear and despair, and whose branches would eventually be strong enough to support the Gestapo, the SS and the 'final solution'. The leaders of the Nazi Party controlled the German Reich on many levels, but the political alliances, the expedient agreements and the bitter feuds were all directed towards one grand master-plan: the creation of a Greater Germany and Reich that would last a thousand years.

Behind the party leadership stood many important academics who shared a fear of Bolshevism and hatred of the Treaty of Versailles. Over many years they had developed academic theories that would shape the modern world that, they believed, had to come. They came from many disciplines – from physics and medicine, economics and geography, psychiatry, anthropology and archaeology – and the Nazi Party cherry-picked their work for ideas that fitted in with their objectives.

There was, however, one elderly academic whose involvement with the Nazis actually helped formulate National Socialist policy. This man's involvement with Adolf Hitler, through the intervention of Rudolf Hess, in 1921 would lead to his becoming the politico-foreign affairs tutor and adviser to the Führer and his Deputy.

Rudolf Hess was not a monumentally important personality in National Socialism, but it is certainly the case that had he never existed, or had he been killed during the First World War, the course of world history during the inter-war years may well have taken a very different path. His introduction of Adolf Hitler to Professor Karl Haushofer, Germany's leading expert on geopolitics, was to have profound consequences.

Haushofer would provide Hitler with the theoretical concepts of Nazi expansionism, German ethnicity and *Lebensraum*, or living space, for the German people. Furthermore, in the years to come his son Albrecht would provide important assistance to Hitler and Hess, inexorably advancing the Nazis' aims of territorial expansion within Europe, according to his father's plans for a Greater Germany. By the late 1930s Albrecht Haushofer would become the hidden hand of Hess and his Führer in pursuing the Nazis' foreign policy objectives.

However, Albrecht Haushofer would also unwittingly prove to be the key that would enable British Intelligence to unleash an overwhelming tide of disaster upon Hitler's entire war strategy. This is a secret that has remained hidden since the Second World War. Indeed, Hitler himself never knew that a situation deep in the Haushofer's past had been exploited to obliterate his hopes for victory, or that his own Deputy, Rudolf Hess, had himself set these destructive wheels in motion over twenty years before.

The story of how this occurred, of how Hitler, Hess and Haushofer, working towards ultimate German supremacy, in the end brought about their own undoing, is perhaps the strangest story of the whole war.

With the sudden end to the First World War in November 1918, many Germans, among them soldiers who had been fighting at the front without knowing what was happening at home, looked at the ruination of their country and asked themselves what had happened. How had Germany gone from a mighty imperial superpower in 1914, possessed of a superb army and the world's second-largest navy, to be laid so low a mere four years later? The last months of the war had seen enormous political unrest in Germany, and the suspicion was born that the nation had not been defeated militarily, but that she had been undone by sly, underhand, political agitators and revolutionaries at home. Taking their lead from the Bolshevik Revolution in Russia, many left-wing revolutionary factions had sprung up in Germany in 1918, intent upon changing Germany's political system. They demanded an end to the Kaiser, the aristocracy and the ruling classes, and power to the proletariat.

Just as in Russia, where sailors of the Imperial Navy had launched the revolution that had toppled the Tsar's regime, so did the spark of Bolshevik revolution ignite in Germany's Imperial Fleet. In October 1918, sailors of the German Navy had mutinied at Kiel, and large numbers of deserters quickly scattered inland to seek out fellow thinkers among the disaffected workers of Germany's industrial heartland. Here they fomented social unrest and insurrection, cutting Germany's supply of materials and power, and crippling the country.

Unable to restore order, and fearing the loss of his life in the same ghastly manner as had befallen his cousin Tsar Nicholas II four months previously, Kaiser Wilhelm II's nerve failed. He abdicated and fled the country within a few days, leaving a hastily propped-up Socialist government to cope with an internal situation that threatened to turn into full-scale revolution. Faced with this dilemma, and knowing that the Allied forces were growing steadily stronger, the new German government promptly declared that the war could not be sustained any longer, and sued for peace. Germany had lost the war not only militarily, but also economically and politically.

Thus, when the twenty-four-year-old fighter-pilot Rudolf Hess journeyed home by train to his parents in Bavaria in December 1918, he took with him the bitter depression of defeat and the deep feelings of betrayal shared by the millions of other men suddenly discharged from Germany's armed forces. However, Hess was not a typical German, and his background – for a man destined to hold high political office in 1930s Germany – was most unusual. He was what was called an *Ausländer*, an ethnic German born overseas.

Rudolf Walter Richard Hess had been born in a luxurious villa in the Egyptian coastal resort of Ibrahimieh, a few miles to the east of Alexandria, on 26 April 1894. His background was to have a profound effect upon the man he would become. Although recognised as a reasonably bright child, he would grow to be a frustrated young man, expected to take over the reins of the family business, the successful mercantile company Hess & Co., run by his domineering father, Fritz Hess.

Rudolf Hess's childhood with his younger brother Alfred and sister Margarete was an idyllic one. The Hess children played adventurous games in the substantial grounds of the family home. At night they would stand on the villa's flat roof, gaze up at the Egyptian night sky, and listen enraptured as their mother explained the wonders of the cosmos, the intricacies of the solar system.

Although Hess's parents were established and well settled in Egypt, seeming to have made a successful transition to expatriate life, they had not broken their ties with the mother country. Fritz Hess was proud of his German heritage, displaying a large portrait of the Kaiser in his office, and being most particular to ensure he took his family 'home' to the more temperate climate of southern Germany every summer. On these visits the Hess children re-established their German identities, wandering the countryside north-west of Nuremberg, enjoying family picnics, and establishing friendships that would last a lifetime.

This charmed life ended for the young Rudolf when he reached the age of fourteen. In September 1908, instead of returning to Egypt with his family after their summer holiday, Rudolf travelled to Bad Godesberg to attend the Evangelical School, where he was to receive his first formal education, having been educated at home since the age of six by a tutor. The young Hess showed an aptitude for mathematics and science, much to the concern of his father, who was hoping for a son who would take over the family business when the time came. In the hope of igniting the commercial spark that would turn his son into a young entrepreneur, Fritz Hess sent Rudolf to the École Supérieur de Commerce in Neuchâtel, hoping that some of the Swiss acumen for business would rub off on his son.

In 1912, after a year of high expense for the father, and comprehensive cramming by the son, the eighteen-year-old Rudolf left Switzerland to join the flourishing Hamburg trading company of Feldt Stein & Co. as an apprentice. As he took his first tentative steps as an adult in the heady atmosphere of pre-war Hamburg, Rudolf was blissfully unaware that the worst war the world had ever seen was about to erupt. Yet this was also a war that would give Hess his first great adventure, his chance to break free of the future his parents had mapped out for him as a middle-class businessman.

Far from the delights of *belle époque* Hamburg, in distant Sarajevo the course of European history was changed forever on 28 June 1914, when a young Serb named Gavrilo Princip shot dead the heir to the Austrian throne, Archduke Franz Ferdinand, and his consort Sophie Chotek, the Duchess of Hohenburg. Princip's were the first shots that would herald an unimaginably terrible war that would not only sweep away the flower of Europe's young men, but change forever the political complexion of the continent.

Rudolf Hess was among the very first bands of young men to volunteer, quitting his job in the summer of 1914 to join the German infantry. Over the next four years he would see action in many of the horror-spots of the war, from the Western Front at Ypres and Verdun to the Carpathian Mountains on the Eastern Front, where he was severely wounded. However, against all the odds, he survived – a remarkable testament not only to his luck, but to his mental strength as well. Eventually, with considerable persistence, he managed to get himself inducted into Germany's fledgling Air Corps, where he trained and became a fighter-pilot flying Fokker triplanes in Belgium during the last weeks of the war.

Now, as he returned home at the end of the war only to find turmoil and political unrest, he commented bitterly: 'I witnessed the horror of death in all its forms ... battered for days under heavy bombardment ... hungered and suffered, as indeed have all front-line soldiers. And is all this to be in vain, the suffering of the good people at home all for nothing?'[1]

Not only had Hess seen his once-glorious nation go down to crushing defeat, but his father's successful business in Egypt had been ruined by the war, and was eventually taken over by the victorious Allies. It was a loss Fritz Hess never really recovered from, psychologically or financially; his son's bitterness ran deep indeed, on both a national and a personal level.

The manner in which the First World War ended, and the deep sense of betrayal felt by the returning German soldiers, would dominate German politics for the coming twenty years. At this time were sown the seeds of bitterness that would be cultivated by the men who would rise to power in the 1930s – men just like Rudolf Hess, who believed that victory had been swindled from them by a devious gang of traitors at home: Communists, Socialists, wishy-washy liberals; and, worst of all, some of the more ultra-right wing declared, the Jews. It would become a dangerous and volatile cocktail of disillusionment and hate, just waiting to explode.

On returning to Bavaria at the end of November 1918, Hess found his country facing a peril he had only read about in newspapers – the threat of a Bolshevik revolution similar to that which had taken place in Russia a year before. A militant Bolshevik organisation called the Spartakusbund had taken over Bavaria, overthrown the legitimate Bavarian government, and set up its own Soviet Republic of Bavaria, the Räterepublik.

With the end of war, Germany had been plunged into political turmoil. On one side was the far left, predominantly led by militant workers and educated men well-versed in the works of Marx; on the other was the right wing, made up virtually without exception of the middle classes and war veterans determined that these Bolshevik troublemakers should be crushed completely before Germany descended into chaos. The country teetered on the very edge of an abyss that had the potential to mirror what was taking place in Russia.

Intent on taking his part in the struggle, Rudolf Hess quickly joined a right-wing band of veterans called the Thule Gesellschaft – the Thule Society – set up to counter the organised thuggery of the Spartakusbund. Over the course of the next five months, much bitter street-fighting ensued in the struggle to prevent the Spartakists consolidating their grip on power in Bavaria. The Thule Gesellschaft may be considered a forerunner of the Nazi Party, created before National Socialism became a concept; indeed, created even before Adolf Hitler became prominent. It was a nationalist anti-Bolshevik society, used the swastika as its emblem, and loudly proclaimed the motto 'Remember you are German. Keep your blood pure.' It was not as large an organisation as the Spartakists, and its struggle was hard, but events were about to turn in its favour.

In late April 1919, the Spartakists captured seven Thule Society members and an innocent bystander called Professor Berger, a Jewish academic who had the incredible bad luck to be swept up as a member of the anti-Semitic society. His luck was about to get worse, as all eight men were summarily executed. The Spartakists then made the fatal error of accepting three Bolshevik emissaries sent from Moscow by Lenin. These three Russian agitators promptly took over the Spartakusbund, and began to consolidate their power-base in Bavaria's new Räterepublik by instigating a Soviet-style purge.

This was all too much for the new German government. From Weimar in Thuringia they watched events in Bavaria and blanched, for the Spartakusbund had nailed its colours to the mast by declaring that its ultimate aim was to topple the legitimate government and set up a Soviet Germany. Prompted by a sense of self-preservation, the government sent troops in to restore order, gladly accepting help from the Freikorp Epp (a right-wing paramilitary organisation affiliated to the Thule Society), and succeeded in toppling the Spartakists. With the collapse of the Räterepublik most people in southern Germany breathed an enormous sigh of relief, and hoped that the natural order of predominantly conservative Bavaria would re-assert itself, and that they could now get on with their lives.

It was at this time, mid-1919, that Rudolf Hess first made the acquaintance of Professor General Karl Haushofer, the man who would instil in him the political awareness and the understanding of world affairs that he would apply to his as-yet unplanned career in politics. Twenty-five years later, in October 1944, an investigation by the FBI would take a statement that revealed: 'According to [Name Censored] Rudolf Hess ... brought Hitler and Haushofer together [and this] combination of Hess and Haushofer was, in the opinion of [Censored] the root of the Nazi Party.'[2] But this statement missed the crucial fact that Karl Haushofer and his son Albrecht became confidential advisers to Adolf Hitler and Rudolf Hess on their most important foreign policy matters – in effect an unofficial Führer's private office on foreign affairs.

On a balmy summer's evening in 1919 a man called Beck invited his friend and fellow member of Thule Gesellschaft Rudolf Hess to dine with him at the home of Professor Karl Haushofer, 'an old-time pan-Germanist'[3] who had commanded the Thirteenth Bavarian Infantry Division during the First World War. This first meeting between Haushofer and Hess, a purely social affair, was an immediate success. Long into the night, an enthralled Hess sat and listened intently to everything the eminent Professor had to say about the wrongs of the Treaty of Versailles, and his views on foreign affairs defined under the all-encompassing banner of *Welt-Politik* (world politics), as determined by his new theories of 'geopolitics'. For Hess it was the opening of an intellectual door, and he suddenly came to believe that there was a bigger picture to consider – that of the new age to come – which through science would redefine the world. Haushofer had himself undergone this intellectual revolution in the late 1890s.

Basically, geopolitics was the theory, as promulgated by Haushofer, that in the future the world would be restructured into an age of great land-empires, dominated by 'the Heartland', an area 'invulnerable to sea-power in Central Europe and Asia'.[4] This, Haushofer asserted, would revolutionise the world's balance of power, ushering in a 'new age' of stability, peace and prosperity for all.

In 1904, the eminent British geographer H.J. Mackinder had written a paper titled 'The Geographical Pivot of History',[5] which Haushofer had read avidly, particularly the paragraph that declared: 'The spaces within the Russian Empire and Mongolia are so vast, and their potentialities in population, wheat, cotton, fuel and metals so incalculably great, that it is inevitable that a vast economic world, more or less apart, will there develop inaccessible to oceanic commerce.' Mackinder went on to expound his theory that

> sea power alone, it if is not based on great industry, and has a great industry behind it, is too weak for offence to really maintain itself in the world struggle ... both the sea and the railway are going in the future ... to be supplemented by the air as a means of locomotion, and when we come to that ... the successful powers will be those who have the greatest industrial base ... [and] *those people who have the greatest industrial base* ... [will] *have the ... power of invention and science to defeat all others.*[6] [Author's italics]

Hess listened to all this and more, as Haushofer explained his theory that ethnicity should be added to this geopolitical formula. All Europe's current borders, he maintained, resulted from old-world wars and conflict dating back to the Dark Ages, the time of strife and confusion following the collapse of Rome. European peace would only truly come about when Europe was redefined according to ethnic background. And that meant, by happy coincidence, that Germany and the Germanic peoples would become the largest single bloc, dominating central Europe.

Hess quickly became a total convert to Haushofer's theories, and for his part the elderly Professor took a keen interest in the intriguing young man, who showed signs of considerable ability. A ready friendship soon developed between the two, Hess finding the genteel Haushofer a stark contrast to the authoritarian figure his own father had been. 'He is a wonderful man,'[7] wrote Hess, and within a few days of their first meeting the two would meet after Hess finished work to stroll in the park, often on their way to dinner at Haushofer's home. Here Hess found himself readily absorbed into the Haushofer family, developing a close affection for Haushofer's 'very nice' half-Jewish wife, Martha, and becoming firm friends with the Professor's sons, Albrecht and Heinz.

Hess got on particularly well with Haushofer's elder son, Albrecht, an intelligent young man of seventeen. A friendship swiftly developed that would last the rest of their lives. In a fore-taste of events to come, Hess would comment: 'I sometimes go for a walk with [Albrecht], and we speak English together.'[8] At the time, however, Hess could have had no concept of how entwined his and Albrecht's lives would become.

Had Hess not fallen under Adolf Hitler's spell in 1920, he would almost certainly have accompanied Albrecht into a life of academia. After five months of congenial friendship with Karl Haushofer – the relationship having quickly developed into one of devoted protégé and mentor – Hess quit his job at a Munich textile importers to enrol at Munich University as a student of geographical politics under Haushofer.

Who then, was this eminent Professor Karl Haushofer, the behind-the-scenes man of Nazi foreign policy, the sage figure consulted by the whole Nazi elite from Hess, Himmler, Göring and Ribbentrop, to Adolf Hitler himself?

In 1946 *Life* Magazine published an article, dramatically titled 'The Mystery of Haushofer', that declared:

> For something more than twenty years the voluminous writings and manifold activities of this German General, who later in life became a geographer on the faculty of the University of Munich, had engaged attention. He was discounted by many and dismissed by some as simply another obscure writer from Germany who exemplified the Teutonic passion for obscuring the obvious with unintelligible terminology. But by others he was considered a subtle and dangerous influence in the evolving challenge of National Socialism, a close collaborator with Rudolf Hess, Deputy-Führer, and the master genius of an organised movement designed to justify, by scientific argument, the Nazi gamble for total power.

The article went on to reveal that:

> Through Haushofer's pupil, Rudolf Hess, a vengeful philosophy of power and a technique for achieving it were communicated to Hitler, who avidly seized on the windfall and capitalised ruthlessly

on the half-truths popularised in the name of objective science. [This] venerable scholar thus became not only an elder statesman in the field of geographical strategy but developed into a companion and political Nestor of the ruling clique . . . He testified under oath that he had been consulted on Japanese affairs by von Ribbentrop and was frequently summoned to the Foreign Office in Berlin. His residence on Kolbergerstrasse in Munich was the rendezvous for conferences between Nazi leaders and Japanese statesmen during the courtship of Nippon by Nazi Germany.[9]

Karl Ernst Haushofer was born in 1869, at the time of the creation of Germany as a state, and thus during his early years he grew to see Germany develop, gain colonies, prosper, and become a major power on the world stage. After a brief period of military service with the First Bavarian Artillery Regiment in the late 1880s, he secured a position with the Auslandskommando (the Foreign Service), and was posted to Germany's distant Embassy in Japan.

The experience was a revelation to the young German, and after two tours of duty in Tokyo, during which he set himself the task of learning to speak fluent Japanese, and learned all he could about Japanese society, Haushofer returned to Germany in the early 1890s, taking up a post with the General Staff to teach at the Military Academy. He did, however, continue to conduct regular tours of the Far East, during which he almost certainly carried out some form of intelligence-gathering. Indeed, in 1942 British Intelligence would assert that Haushofer spent two years on attachment to the Imperial Japanese Army, and that during this time he also 'conducted several extensive tours Greater Asia – India, Japan, China, Korea, and Asiatic Russia'.[10] This was a region of great sensitivity to Britain at the turn of the century, a source of much wealth and power to the British Empire, and she would not readily accept German attempts to usurp her position here. Haushofer's trips were noted and logged away, but they were not forgotten.

In 1896 Haushofer courted and wed a certain Fräulein Martha Mayer-Doss, the half-Jewish daughter of a high-ranking Bavarian civil servant. The new Frau Haushofer's ethnic background raised few eyebrows in Germany at the time, for the country had one of the better records in Europe with regard to the treatment of its Jewish citizens. In the 1940s, however, British Intelligence would speculate that it 'accounted for the fact that Haushofer does not hold any official positions in the leadership of the National Socialist State'.[11] This was a misreading of Haushofer's situation in Nazi Germany. Haushofer's importance to the top Nazis protected him and his family from the fate that daily befell other Germans with Jewish connections. Indeed, Haushofer's eminence would cause Hitler to welcome his elderly adviser *and* his wife as visitors to Berchtesgaden, where, unknown to Germany's populace, the Führer always kissed Martha's hand on meeting her, and treated her with the greatest courtesy and respect. It was a feature of Nazi Germany that what took place behind the scenes was frequently at odds with public appearance and policy.

After his marriage, Haushofer abandoned his military career, determining to carve out a new niche for himself in academia as a geographer. In 1898 the Haushofers visited Britain, where Karl was to conduct a series of lectures on 'Internationalism'. It was during this tour that he first learnt of a theory that he would one day develop into geopolitics. During this trip, he also made several important contacts that would stand him in good stead in the coming years. In London he met the Colonial Secretary, Joseph Chamberlain (father of Neville Chamberlain), considered at the time to be very much the coming man of British politics. After this the Haushofers had planned to travel on to Cambridge, where Karl was due to give a lecture. However, they first went to Oxford, where Karl made the acquaintance of a young Scot by the name of Halford Mackinder, a geography don who was developing an exciting new theory concerning the Eurasian 'heartland' (Eastern Europe and interior Asia) which, he claimed, would by 'natural ascendancy eventually gain superiority' over the 'maritime lands'.

Mackinder was taking his first tentative steps in the new science of what Haushofer would one day adopt as his own and name geographical politics. It was from this meeting at the end of the nineteenth century between two men steeped in the application of

Empire that Karl Haushofer went on to develop his theories of a dominant Eurasia. It was a concept, he immediately realised, that could become the basis for a land-based German empire to mirror the British, which was based on maritime supremacy.

It was a very quiet and thoughtful Haushofer who left Oxford a few days later, for he knew that what Mackinder had told him was important. By the late 1890s, Germany was in an arms race with Britain, pouring millions of marks into building ever more sophisticated and powerful battleships to keep the sea routes to her colonies open in time of war. But what if Germany changed the rules? What if she threw away her overseas colonies in exchange for a land-based empire? In this way she could circumvent Britain's naval supremacy, rendering the British fleet largely impotent. It would take a great deal of theorising over the coming twenty years before Karl Haushofer's concepts on geographical politics would be completely formulated, but by then Germany had suffered defeat in the First World War, and as a result had already lost her colonies and an empire. Thus Haushofer's theories gained a disproportionate importance.

Following their visit to Oxford, Karl and Martha Haushofer travelled on to Cambridge. Here the Professor was due to complete his British tour with a lecture to the Cambridge Foreign Science Students Committee. The Secretary of this society was a Cambridge lecturer by the name of Herbert Roberts, and the Haushofers soon became firm friends with him, his wife Violet and their son Patrick, a brilliant young student at Eton.

Over the next forty years the two families would maintain their friendship, the Roberts visiting Germany to stay with the Haushofers at their Bavarian country home, Hartshimmelhof, and the Haushofers making return visits to Cambridge. Herbert Roberts and Karl Haushofer's friendship was to be mirrored by their sons, Patrick and Albrecht.

By 1919, following a brief wartime career as an artillery general in the service of the Kaiser, Karl Haushofer, now titled Professor General, had become a member of Munich University's Department of Geography. Here he lectured on his new science of geopolitics, defined as 'a science concerned with the dependence of the domestic and foreign politics of peoples upon their physical environment'.[12] He was already redefining his theories, adjusting them to explain why Germany's turn-of-the-century imperial and foreign policies had proven unworkable. His theories, which he was to postulate to the eager Rudolf Hess, had evolved in the following way: Imperial Germany's attempts at empire had been fatally flawed. Her colonies lay far overseas, and thus were not safe so long as Britain ruled the waves. Therefore, Haushofer declared, Germany should recognise that these colonies were of no practical use, and should be given up in exchange for the right to expand Germany's land-based European frontiers to re-absorb all Europe's ethnic Germanic peoples in western Poland, the Sudeten-land, Austria, the north-western extremity of Yugoslavia, Switzer-land, northern Italy and Alsace-Lorraine, together with sufficient territory to meet her new needs (*Lebensraum*). Germany's future prosperity lay in obtaining a land-based empire of connected terri-tory (safe from the dangers of the sea) to the east, a vast 'Eurasian Empire' that might one day stretch from the Baltic to the Pacific. Haushofer quietly ignored the small but significant fact that this territory currently belonged to someone else – Russia.

Whilst Hess was becoming ever more involved with Professor Haushofer, taken in like a long-lost member of his family and enormously enjoying his new role of university student, another force began to enter his life. Late in the spring of 1921, Hess persuaded Professor Haushofer to accompany him one evening to a working-class district of Munich to hear a man – Hess did not know his name – speak.

With some misgivings, Haushofer accompanied Hess to a rough-neck beerhouse called the Sterneckerbrau. Once inside, they took a seat at the rear of a dingy, smoke-filled back room, the air heavy with the scent of tobacco, beer and sweat. Soon a man stood up on a low platform at the front and began to talk. Haushofer would later recall how he noticed that once Adolf Hitler's harsh-toned voice began haranguing his audience, rising in tempo and ferocity against the injustices of the Treaty of Versailles, venting his spleen

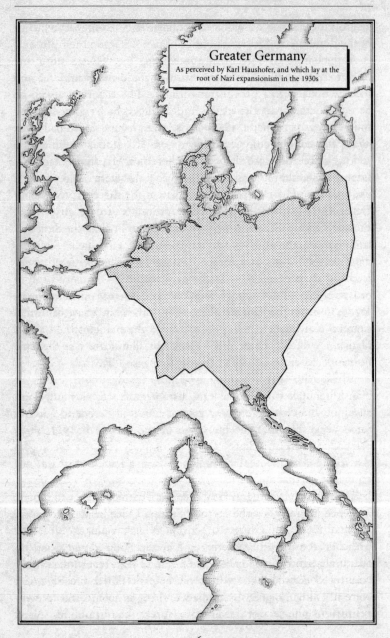

Greater Germany

As perceived by Karl Haushofer, and which lay at the
root of Nazi expansionism in the 1930s

against the evils of Communism and gesticulating wildly, Hess became mesmerised.

Karl Haushofer was not as immediately impressed with Hitler as Hess was. He thought Hitler's rantings crude and without form, basically echoing and amplifying the cry of the Nationalists who could be heard on any street corner in Munich, angry men decrying the way Germany had been defeated, denouncing the injustices of 1919, and condemning those villainous Communists who would see their beloved fatherland ruined. However, despite his first impression that Hitler's style was overly dramatic and noisy, the Professor of Geopolitics did pay attention to the evident way Hitler's oratory instilled enthusiasm in the crowd by sheer force of will. Here was a man of potential, a man who with guidance and support could become an important force. All he needed was a political education; tutoring in the use of protocol, political finesse and style.

Later that same night Hess persuaded his new girlfriend, Ilse Pröhl, to accompany him to another meeting at the Sterneckerbrau, saying: 'You must come with me to a meeting of the National Socialist Workers' Party. I have just been there with the General. Someone unknown spoke . . . if anyone can free us from Versailles he is the man – this unknown will restore our honour.'[13]

Adolf Hitler in 1921 was a case of a man with extraordinary speaking ability being in the right pace at the right time. What he said was on the whole well received because it was what the people wanted to hear. In 1920s Munich, the masses did not want to hear that Germany had lost the First World War through the ineptitude of its leaders; that the German military's yearning to flex its muscles had blinded it to the dangers of fighting Russia, France and Britain at the same time, with disastrous results. Hitler charged into the political arena and, with all the venom of a maniacal bible-belt preacher, screamed that Germany had been tricked and deceived, that underhand people had worked behind the scenes to cause the country's downfall. And worse yet, he proclaimed, those plotters were still at work against Germany and her people. With a powerful turn of phrase and a magnetism rarely seen in politics, Adolf

Hitler indoctrinated his audiences with the idea that anti-German plotters, Communists and, worst of all, the Jews, were to blame for all their woes. Germany's only saviours, he proclaimed, the only men willing to stand up against these evils, were the National Socialists – the Nazi Party.

With Hitler's arrival on the scene, a new phase of Rudolf Hess's existence began. Over the next two decades the lives of Hess and Hitler would become inexorably entwined as the Nazi Party struggled to find its feet, fought for the hearts and minds of the German people, strove for success at the ballot box, and ultimately took and held power. The first and most serious hiccup to Hitler's progression came a mere two years after Hess's first encounter with his Führer, or the Tribune, as Hess at first called him.

In 1923 Hitler mistakenly concluded that Germany's fragility as a democratic state led by a weak government made it ripe for a *coup d'état*, and he believed he could take a short-cut to power by instigating a *Putsch*. That Hitler, with the backing of only a small nationalist movement, took this enormous step might with hindsight seem to have been total folly. However, Hitler was a great digester of newspapers. He had developed a passion for news, for reading about politics and foreign affairs, and he could see the other strong men of Europe successfully taking power whilst Germany crumbled into economic ruin. Indeed, only the year before the man Hitler most admired, Benito Mussolini, had led his Fascists on Rome where, aged only thirty-nine, he had been placed in power by King Victor Emmanuel III.

At the beginning of 1923 Germany had defaulted on her reparations payments to France, as set down in the Versailles Treaty, and the French had invaded the Ruhr to enforce payment. Instantly Germany's inflation rocketed out of control – soon a single postage stamp would cost ten thousand marks. Hitler must have thought the time was ripe to do away with the old order, and took the bold step of attempting to usurp power before events took the initiative away from him.

Hitler's second-in-command for the *Putsch* was a powerful force within the Nazi Party, former flying ace Hermann Göring, who led the Sturmabteilung (SA) or Storm Troopers.* Hess too had an important role, for whilst he officially led only the student wing of the SA, Hitler by now relied heavily on him, giving him 'special orders' to capture key members of Bavaria's government, who would be attending a political gathering at Munich's Bürgerbräukeller. Hess would later recall that his meeting with Hitler just prior to the coup attempt had ended with 'a solemn handclasp . . . and we parted until evening'.[14]

That evening, Thursday, 8 November 1923, saw an extraordinary scene, even by German standards of the 1920s, as a sedate political meeting at the Bürgerbräukeller was interrupted by machine-gun-toting, steel-helmeted SA men, led by a fanatical individual in a long black overcoat – Adolf Hitler.

After bursting in, Hitler leapt up onto a chair, fired his pistol into the air, and as the speaker on the platform subsided into shocked silence, brazenly declared: A 'national revolution in Munich has just broken out.' To which he added untruthfully, 'the whole city is at this moment occupied by our troops. This hall is surrounded by six hundred men.'[15]

At this point Hess began picking out the politicians he wished to take into custody, taking them from their seats and ushering them from the hall to be sent away under armed guard to the home of a Nazi sympathiser, where they were to be held overnight.

In 1923, however, the thirty-four-year-old Adolf Hitler was still a novice at the taking and holding of power, and he quickly lost control of the situation. Within the Bürgerbräukeller a wave of patriotic anthem-singing, Nazi saluting and volatile speeches on everything from the incompetence of the Social Democrats to the evils of Communism took the initiative away from Hitler, and he failed to consolidate his position by sending his men to take over the key buildings and services of the city. By the following morning

---

* The Nazi Party's own private army, created to protect party meetings and oppose rival political parties. By 1932 the SA would have 400,000 members, and it would be a potent weapon in the Nazis' rise to power. In 1923, however, it was still a small organisation, numbering just a few hundred badly trained and ill-equipped men – roughneck bully-boys for the most part.

Hitler's *Putsch* lay in disarray, and it was at the Bürgerbräukeller that the *Times* correspondent in Munich found him still: 'a little man . . . unshaven with disorderly hair, and so hoarse that he could hardly speak'.[16]

During the course of the night, Hitler's failure to consolidate his position had been surpassed in naïveté by Göring, who, after eliciting promises from the captured Ministers (as officers and gentlemen) that they would not act against the *Putsch*, released all his leading prisoners. However, much to Göring's surprised consternation, and Hitler's absolute fury, they discovered that as soon as the politicians had been released, they promptly summoned the army to aid them in putting down the attempted coup. The final act of this fiasco was a gun-battle in central Munich that would soon enter Nazi folklore: fourteen Nazis died, Göring was wounded, and Hitler dislocated his shoulder when he tripped over and someone fell on top of him.

In the hours following the shoot-out, Hitler's sense of self-preservation led him to find sanctuary with Karl and Martha Haushofer in their flat on Kolbergerstrasse, where he hid out for some hours. During this time Hitler and Karl Haushofer undoubtedly discussed what had occurred, what had gone wrong, and what would now ensue, for by 1923 Karl Haushofer had become important to both Hess and Hitler – the sage old expert on politics, nationalism and German ethnicity regularly gave the two up-and-coming politicians private lectures and political tutoring.

One of the significant facts about the 1923 Munich *Putsch* is that it marked a watershed in the Hess–Hitler relationship. Hess would come to prominence as the loyal Nazi who followed his Führer to Landsberg prison, near Munich, for a year of confinement after the failed *Putsch*,* during which time he acted as Hitler's secretary whilst he wrote his vitriolic book on political ideology, *Mein Kampf*.

While they were incarcerated at Landsberg, Hitler and Hess

---

* Hitler was sentenced to five years' imprisonment, although he only served nine months. Hess was sentenced to one year.

were extensively tutored by Professor Karl Haushofer. Indeed, many of Haushofer's geopolitical theories on *Lebensraum*, German ethnicity and nationhood, became adopted as Hitlerisms in *Mein Kampf*. In effect, Hitler was quite literally a captive audience to Hess and his political guru Karl Haushofer, receiving tutorials on the European balance of power, the distribution of peoples, ethnicity, colonies and nationalism.

Hess's importance to Hitler at this time should not be underestimated. Their long conversations were not between Führer and obedient disciple, but rather between two close friends and political colleagues, and set the tone for Hitler's future reliance on his loyal friend. In private they were not 'Mein Führer' and 'Hess', but 'Wolf' (Hitler) and 'Rudi' (Hess); often seated with them in their enforced seclusion – a tight-knit political commune in a sea of criminality – was Karl Haushofer.

At the end of the Second World War Haushofer would resolutely deny that he had made any contributions to *Mein Kampf*. However, during the 1930s he was not nearly so reticent. Deep within the microfilmed records of America's National Archive in Washington DC are numerous Haushofer letters from the 1920s and thirties, in which the extent to which his theories influenced *Mein Kampf* is not concealed. Indeed, even in 1939, between a letter to the head of the Volksdeutsche Mitelstelle (German Racial Assistance Office), or VOMI, and a report on the exploitable resources of Poland, reposes a nine-point statement by Haushofer enumerating his credentials and his importance to the Volksbund für das Deutschtum im Ausland (the Committee for Germanism Abroad), known as the VDA, and listing amongst the accomplishments he was proud of his contributions to Hitler's thinking, which appeared in *Mein Kampf*.[17]

Rudolf Hess's input into *Mein Kampf* was not insubstantial either. During Professor Haushofer's interrogation by American Intelligence in 1945, he was asked: 'Isn't it true that Hess collaborated with Hitler in writing *Mein Kampf*?' The by now very elderly Haushofer replied unhesitatingly: 'As far as I know Hess actually dictated many chapters in that book.'[18]

Hess was very much Professor Haushofer's protégé, and as such had a keen understanding of the theories behind *Lebensraum*, the distribution of ethnic Germanic peoples across central Europe, and how this ethnicity could be mobilised in the future to create a Greater Germany and Reich.

Haushofer's original position had been that Germany's living space should stretch from the Baltic to the Pacific. Hitler, however, was more circumspect, and advanced the view that if Germany were to conquer the east, it should initially aim to occupy only western Russia, using the Ural Mountains as a natural buffer between the Reich and Asia. This territory, Hitler proposed, would take Germany a century to exploit. In the summer of 1941, while Germany's armies rolled ever eastward enjoying early successes under Operation Barbarossa, a relaxed Hitler became extraordinarily open about his aims in the east, and over dinner one evening confided to his guests:

> We'll take the southern part of the Ukraine, especially the Crimea, and make it into a German colony ... [Russia] will be a source of raw materials for us, and a market for our products, but we shall take care not to industrialise it ...
>
> If I offer [people] land in Russia, a river of human beings will rush there headlong ... In twenty years' time, European emigration will no longer be directed towards America, but eastward.

Finally, he added whimsically:

> The beauties of the Crimea, which we shall make accessible by means of autobahns – for us Germans, that will be our Riviera ... [for] we can reach the Crimea by road. Along that road lies Kiev! And Croatia, too, a tourists' paradise for us ... What progress in the direction of the New Europe. Just as the autobahn has caused the inner frontiers of Germany to disappear, so it will abolish the frontiers of the countries of Europe.[19]

This is a revealing insight into the world Hitler was attempting to create, a Reich that had been designed for him by Karl Haushofer.

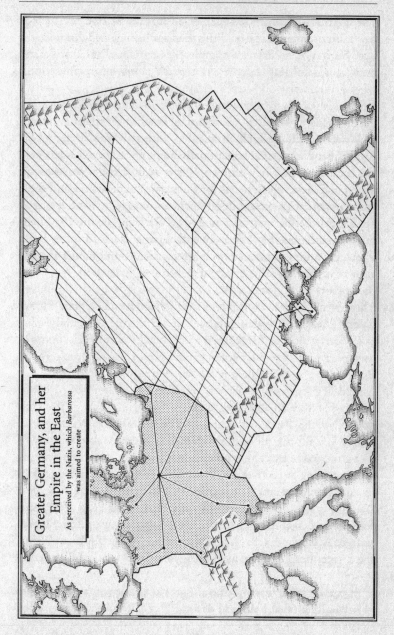

Greater Germany, and her
Empire in the East
As perceived by the Nazis, which *Barbarossa*
was aimed to create

The impression has always been given that the Second World War was Hitler's attempt at total European and then world domination, but this is not necessarily completely accurate. The above statement, allied to Map 2 (p.23), is a much closer approximation of what Hitler's war objectives really were.

The Nazis' rise to power took ten years of hard political struggle, during which the party grew into a membership that numbered well over a million souls disaffected with the Weimar Republic. From a handful of members of parliament, by 1933 the Nazis held the balance of power with over 70 per cent of the vote. Many of Hitler and Hess's aspirations for the party had been accomplished, and their theories, as laid down in *Mein Kampf*, were about to be applied to the German nation. In the Germany of the 1930s, the majority accepted the concept of authoritarianism, of a ruling party which promised to take your children and turn out model citizens who would in turn have safe, if controlled, existences, free from the horrors of economic decline and the threat of the Communism. Through all this, at Adolf Hitler's right hand stood Deputy-Führer Rudolf Hess, the upstanding, well-spoken, educated family man, who yearly took part in competition flying, and had no stigma of seediness – unlike other leading Nazis such as the drunkard Dr Robert Ley, or the appallingly anti-Semitic Julius Streicher.

Rudolf Hess's character was one that naturally instilled confidence. He was an unassuming man, frequently called 'the conscience of the Party', who annoyed his fellow top Nazis – ever attired in uniforms glittering with medals and bedecked with swastika armbands – by calmly going about his work in earnest fashion, often arriving at the Reich Chancellery dressed in a sports jacket, or neatly tailored suit. The image of the brown-shirt-wearing Hess standing at his Führer's shoulder and screaming '*Sieg Heil!*' was for public consumption. In private he was a very different man indeed. After the war, a close acquaintance of Hess's, Ernst Bohle, the former head of the Auslandsorganisation,* was asked whether

---

* The agency of the Nazi Party responsible for the supervision and political well-being of German nationals abroad.

Hess was a sincere Nazi. After mulling the question over for a few moments, Bohle replied: 'He was sincere as an idealist, in my opinion the biggest idealist we have had in Germany, a man of very soft nature, no uniforms with him or that sort of stuff, [and] he very seldom went into the public field.'[20]

Hess was therefore an earnest politician, content to toil behind the scenes for the advancement of National Socialism, and in many ways he quickly became the all-round acceptable face of Nazi government.

Importantly, the high regard in which Hess was held in the 1930s was not limited to Germany. Politicians and Foreign Office officials in many other European countries, including Britain, saw him as a moderating influence within National Socialism. Hess was viewed as a reliable, solid politician, a man who did not drink, lived modestly, had a model family life, and, most important of all, was a safe pair of hands. This last sentiment, particularly in light of the surprising level of disorganisation in the Nazi administration, placed Hess in a particularly strong position not only within government, but also with Adolf Hitler.

When Hitler became Chancellor in 1933, he quickly found that his long-sought position was an all-consuming task that affected his ability to interact with the party. He therefore appointed his trusted friend Rudolf Hess as Deputy-Führer of the Nazi Party, with the responsibility of leading the party as his direct representative. Hess proved so successful an administrator that within eight months, on Hitler's proposal, the elderly German head of state President Hindenburg appointed Hess to the position of Reich Minister without Portfolio in 1934.

Despite the ambiguity of this title, defined as 'a Minister without an office or papers of state', and the fact that his role during the 1930s has been largely overlooked, Hess's position as Deputy-Führer was an important one. Whilst he did not have a prominent Ministry which people could easily identify him with (such as the air force under Göring, or propaganda under Goebbels), Hess nevertheless held a position of great power, working behind the scenes, making sure that the National Socialist machinery of state worked.

Primarily, Hess's role was party–government liaison, ensuring that 'the demands of the National Socialist *Weltanschauung* [philosophy and ideology] were brought more and more to realisation'.[21] This was a very important and far-reaching role, perhaps best compared to that of a political commissar who has the responsibility of ensuring that the government's policies and state decisions follow the ruling party's ideology. With his promotion to Minister without Portfolio, the Deputy-Führer became a high-ranking member of the Cabinet, and with his remit to oversee implementation of the Nazi *Weltanschauung* in state policy, he quickly developed interests in internal and foreign affairs.

As Minister with interests in internal affairs, Hess had responsibility for applying Nazi theory to education, public law, tax policy, finance, employment, art and culture, health and 'all questions of technology and organisation'. It was a powerful empire, the tentacles of which could infiltrate all areas of government in the name of ensuring that policy and projects corresponded with Nazi ideology.

As Deputy-Führer with special interest in foreign affairs, Hess had responsibility for applying Nazi geopolitical theory to foreign policy. For this important and complicated role he built a sophisticated foreign affairs structure, creating three departments with which to pursue National Socialist foreign policy.

Firstly, there was the Auslandsorganisation (the Foreign Organisation) under Ernst Bohle, which looked after the political interests of party members abroad. In the 1920s and thirties the Nazis had divided Germany into many political districts, each called a *Gau* and under a regional leader called a *Leiter* – hence *Gauleiter*, or regional political leader (akin to a Soviet Commissar). The same concept was now applied to ethnic Germans resident abroad, each region becoming a pocket of National Socialism abroad, under a leader who in turn reported to *his* leader further on up the chain, in a pyramid-like structure, all the way up to Ernst Bohle. Ausland members were thus all party members, ordered to submit monthly reports on events and incidents in their resident countries, which were destined eventually to land on Bohle's desk in Berlin. Thus

Bohle became the recipient of valuable up-to-date foreign intelligence, and he guarded his territory jealously, gaining a great deal of influence because of it.

Next came the Aussenpolitisches Amt (the Foreign Affairs Office), under Alfred Rosenberg. This was controlled exclusively by and for the Nazi political machine to pursue National Socialist policy interests abroad, on its own and without deference to the Foreign Ministry.

Lastly, there was the VDA, created with the aim of strengthening ethnic German groups living in Germany's neighbouring regions such as Austria, the Sudetenland or the Polish Corridor which the Nazis intended one day to reintegrate into a Greater Germany.

Hess appointed his old Professor of Geopolitics, Karl Haushofer, as Honorary President of both the Auslandsorganisation and the VDA.

It was at this point that Hess's friend, Haushofer's son Albrecht, began to be increasingly involved in Hess and Hitler's foreign affairs interests, and he became an extremely important behind-the-scenes adviser to the Nazi leadership, with the ability to directly influence Hitler's foreign affairs decisions, even on occasion supplanting the opinions of Ribbentrop.* This brought him some powerful enemies (such as Goebbels, who hated him).

Geographer, foreign affairs expert and leading light within the English Section of the Dienststelle Ribbentrop (the private office of Ribbentrop, which advised Hitler on foreign affairs), Albrecht Haushofer was to play a very important role throughout Germany's time under Nazi rule. He frequented the Nazi social circuit, met, chatted and discussed foreign affairs matters with men like Himmler, von Neurath and Göring – yet Albrecht Haushofer's existence as a major player in European foreign affairs in the late 1930s is virtually unknown today. The question has to be asked,

---

* Ribbentrop had at this time not yet become Foreign Minister, but as head of the Dienststelle Ribbentrop – Hitler's own Foreign Ministerial advisory body based within the Reich Chancellery – he had a great deal of influence, at times more than that of Germany's actual Foreign Minister, Constantin von Neurath.

how did this mild-mannered, part-Jewish academic become so inexorably entwined in the foreign affairs machinery of the Nazi state? To be valued by Hitler and part-Jewish was no mean feat in Germany in the 1930s.

Regardless of the complications of an ancestry at odds with Nazi ideology, Albrecht Haushofer's talents as an expert in foreign affairs, with an extensive range of political contacts in many parts of the world, especially Britain, gave him an immunity from the more brutal side of life in Nazi Germany. While his father was a fervent supporter and theorist of the regime, all the evidence points to Albrecht Haushofer being a different sort of person.

Nine years Hess's junior, Albrecht Haushofer had been too young to be called to active service during the First World War. He had, however, been old enough to see his country take the terrible journey from imperial power to humiliating defeat in 1918, and subsequently be reduced to mayhem as the far left attempted revolution. Years later he would still recall that period as representing 'something to me which I shall never get rid of ... an inexhaustible source of hatred, distrust, anger and scorn'.[22] Even more importantly, it was also the time that Rudolf Hess first entered the Haushofer family home.

In 1920, at the age of seventeen, Albrecht enrolled to study under his father at Munich University, together with his close friend 'Rudi' Hess. Both were recognised as star pupils. But in 1923 Hess's participation in the abortive Bürgerbräukeller *Putsch* took him away from academia to a year's enforced seclusion with Hitler at Landsberg prison. Here he was visited and continued to be tutored by his mentor, Karl Haushofer. Albrecht too was a visitor to Hess and his fellow prisoner, the enigmatic man nicknamed 'Wolf'.

In 1924, while Hess was still assisting Hitler with *Mein Kampf* in prison, Albrecht Haushofer graduated from Munich University with a doctorate in geography. In a few weeks, after a quiet word from Haushofer senior to his old-boy network, Albrecht was appointed as personal assistant to the renowned Dr Penck of Berlin, a world-class geographer.

Within eighteen months Albrecht applied for, and was appointed to, the post of Secretary-General of Germany's prestigious Society for Geography, a Berlin-based foundation with a worldwide reputation. A year later he became editor of the prestigious *Periodical of the Society of Geography* (a similar publication to the *National Geographic*). With this position came a sumptuous apartment on the top floor of the society's central Berlin premises on Wilhelmstrasse.

Throughout the next fifteen years, as Secretary-General of the Society for Geography, Albrecht Haushofer travelled the world – to South America and the Andes one year, India and the Himalayas the next; home again for a season's lecturing at Berlin University, then off again, to China and Japan, Egypt or the Sudan. All this time he was making friends who would be invaluable to him in the 1930s, when the Nazi hierarchy suddenly realised that this quiet man had important political contacts in virtually every nation in the world. Thus, by the time Rudolf Hess approached Albrecht in 1931 to advise him on international matters, he found a man steeped in the art of diplomacy and foreign affairs.

Despite Albrecht's range of contacts across the world, the country that he – and also Hitler and Hess – had a predominant interest in cultivating was not an ocean or a continent away. It was a rather staid, old-fashioned, class-structured little nation a mere 350 miles from Germany's western frontiers. It did however possess one of world's great empires, and was one of the world's major powers. Albrecht Haushofer was Germany's foremost expert on Britain.

Haushofer was fascinated by Britain and her people. During the 1920s he had visited Britain extensively, becoming near-fluent in English and developing a wide range of important personal acquaintances that allowed him to mix in the highest political and social circles. His initial entrée into British society had been through his old friend Patrick Roberts, who introduced him to many of his friends and colleagues, young men who in the early 1920s were junior Foreign Office minions, young aristocrats and political acquaintances, but who by the latter 1930s would be Britain's top diplomats, civil servants and politicians.

Slightly older than Albrecht Haushofer, Patrick Roberts had

joined the Foreign Office, where he had an interesting, if slightly curious, career. His postings were numerous – ranging from Berlin, Warsaw and Addis Ababa through to Belgrade and Athens, ever hotbeds of Balkan discontent – with hardly ever enough time for him to become familiar with a place before he was transferred yet again. In 1937, Roberts would meet with a sudden and untimely end when he was killed in a bizarre road accident in a dusty, dead-end Greek village north of Athens. The question of whether his career was connected in some way to British Intelligence has remained unanswered ever since.

Among the men Roberts had introduced to his young German friend Albrecht Haushofer was Sir Owen O'Malley, who had subsequently risen through the Foreign Office to become Ambassador in Budapest and Lisbon. At the end of the Second World War, O'Malley panicked when an American newspaper published an account of how newly discovered German documents revealed details of his friendship with Adolf Hitler's private adviser on foreign affairs, and that he, together with other 'British subjects both inside and outside the Government Service' was being referred to at the Nuremberg trials in connection with the Rudolf Hess case. Keen to unburden his soul and protect his career, a flustered O'Malley swiftly wrote to a colleague at the Foreign Office: 'I knew Haushofer quite well. He was originally introduced to me many years ago by the late Patrick Roberts, who had got to know both the Haushofers and Hess first during the period when he was learning German in Germany and secondly during his period when he was at the British Embassy in Berlin.'

Keen to distance himself from his former friend, and apparently not at all loath to drop someone else in the mire, O'Malley went on: 'Haushofer was a great fat smelly German with the usual German rather academic outlook on politics. I liked him although [being rather overweight, he] broke two of my more fragile Hepplewhite chairs by merely sitting on them. He used to come and spend the weekend at my house in the country round about the years 1932–1935 during the period he had been in contact with Lord Clydesdale and, I think also Lord Lothian.'[23]

Intriguingly, Lord Lothian was the British Ambassador to Washington in the late 1930s whose sudden death in 1940 resulted in the former Foreign Secretary Lord Halifax's appointment to his post. Lord Clydesdale was the man Rudolf Hess allegedly flew to Scotland to see in May 1941, for he was none other than Douglas Douglas-Hamilton, who in 1940 became the Duke of Hamilton.

Thus Albrecht Haushofer's connection to the Roberts family was firmly entrenched. His friend Patrick had introduced him to all his friends and colleagues, up-and-coming young men who by the late 1930s would be Britain's top civil servants and politicians, and who in 1940 would be vital contacts to Haushofer in assisting the German leadership's elusive search for peace.

No less important was Patrick Roberts' mother Violet. The next time she made an appearance in Albrecht Haushofer's life, as an elderly widow in 1940, she would be the dab of honey at the centre of an intricately spun spider's web of intrigue that would lure Haushofer, Hess and Hitler to destruction; for there was an aspect to the Roberts family of which both Karl and Albrecht Haushofer remained totally ignorant – a fortuitous coincidence that British Intelligence would use to doom Hitler's hopes of winning the Second World War.

By the mid-1930s Albrecht Haushofer's range of aristocratic and political contacts had completely opened up British society to him, and he had dined and smoked after-dinner cigars with such pillars of the British establishment as Stanley Baldwin, Ramsay MacDonald, Neville Chamberlain, Lord Dunglass (Alec Douglas-Home), Sir John Simon, Anthony Eden, Lord Halifax and, perhaps most intriguingly of all, Winston Churchill. Haushofer's contacts were a veritable panoply of Britain's high and mighty, and thus it is not surprising that when the Nazis took power in 1933 both Hess and Hitler looked upon him as a trusted friend who could confidentially advise them on foreign affairs, particularly with regard to the British, and embraced him as a gift sent down from on high.

Despite Albrecht's rise to eminence in German academic circles, and his abilities as a geographer and expert on European politics, he himself carried out little political activity on behalf of the Nazi regime, which he would eventually consider evil. Rudolf Hess and Adolf Hitler may have wanted to make use of his considerable expertise on foreign affairs and international politics, but that does not explain why Albrecht went along with them. At any point after 1933 he could easily have packed his bags and decamped to the democratic West, fled to the bright lights of America, where he would undoubtedly have been welcomed by virtue of his academic talents. Despite the fact that, even with Hess's support, his part-Jewish ancestry prevented him from ever attaining his boyhood dream of becoming Germany's Foreign Minister, in the 1930s he was largely an advocate of National Socialist foreign policy on the European stage – a reserved supporter, using his expertise to further Germany's position as a major European power.

Yet Albrecht's correspondence with Hess tells a slightly different tale, in which he is on occasion shaky in his support of National Socialism, and in which Hess the politician undertakes a role as moderating force, and is himself occasionally flexible in his attitude to Nazism in order to persuade his friend to stay on side.

An early example of this occurred in October 1930, when Hess wrote to Albrecht asking him to project a favourable image of National Socialism during his forthcoming trip to Britain, saying: 'It is possible you will be asked in England about your opinion of us over state matters in Germany.' He asked Albrecht to explain that Bolshevism posed a considerable threat not only to Germany but to democratic Europe as well, and that without Nazi intervention it was possible 'that Germany could not be saved'. In what follows there is little sign of the ultra-Nazi Hess; in his place stands a pragmatic politician: 'I am not writing this in the interest of the Party – for this alone I wouldn't bother you, only I am sure that Germany is more important than the Party, and that its overall importance maybe for the whole of Europe [which] is threatened by Communism, is how [the party] in foreign countries, and especially England, is judged.' He ended his letter hopefully, 'I am sure you will meet with a lot of people with influence.'[24]

For Rudolf Hess, of all people, to declare openly to Albrecht that he was not asking for help purely in the interests of the Nazi Party, and that he believed Germany was 'more important than the Party', was remarkable. It is amongst these rare glimpses behind the façade that can be found clues to the curious and dependant relationship between Hitler, Hess and Haushofer (the Führer, the moderating Deputy-Führer go-between and the part-Jewish expert on foreign affairs) – a most unlikely and unsuspected triumvirate of men united in their desire to pursue National Socialist foreign policy. Politically, Albrecht Haushofer was a 'conservative-liberal nationalist'.[25] He supported German nationalism, and hoped 'to be able to exercise a moderating influence on Hess and Ribbentrop, and through them on Hitler. He saw himself as a sort of Talleyrand for the Third Reich.'[26]

Within a few months of the Nazis coming to power in 1933, Albrecht began to undertake increasingly important tasks for the party hierarchy, and Hess soon appointed him as his personal adviser on foreign affairs.[27] As well as providing the Nazi leadership with valuable political insight into the political mood of Germany's neighbours – France, Italy and Britain – Albrecht now began to assist the Nazis establish a Greater Germany encompassing all Europe's peoples of ethnic German origin.

Albrecht's first major assignment for the Nazi leadership came in 1934, when he travelled to Danzig,* where he acted on behalf of the VDA in a series of meetings intended to persuade Germans resident in Danzig and ethnic Germans in western Poland (over six hundred thousand of them) to participate in the powerful new cult of National Socialism. Everything went well, and a substantial number of ethnic Germans signed up to the Zapot Agreement,

---

* Under the terms of the Treaty of Versailles, eastern Prussia had been stripped from the Kaiser's former realm, and a vast swathe of territory known as the Polish Corridor, populated by over half a million Germans, was handed over to Poland. Marooned on the coast to the north, under League of Nations control, stood Danzig, an island of Germanism deep in Polish territory. The loss of this valuable land rankled in Germany and amongst the former German nationals living in the Corridor. It was a loss the Nazis were determined to rectify, come what may.

which supported a long-term policy of reunification with the Fatherland under the all-encompassing banner of the Nazi Party.

Hess was delighted by Albrecht's success, and sent Albrecht to Czechoslovakia to set up a similar arrangement with ethnic Germans in the Sudetenland, that area of Bohemia adjoining Germany that had been awarded to Czechoslovakia under the Treaty of Saint-Germain-en-Laye in 1919. So significant were these first tentative steps by the Nazis' foreign-political machine that 'from 1935 onwards Hitler based some of his formulations on *Volksdeutsch* politics on statements submitted to him by Hess and prepared by Albrecht Haushofer'.[28]

The expansion of Germany was not Hitler's only objective at this time: the Treaty of Versailles had not only stripped valuable German territory away, it had also reduced Germany's military to a skeletal force fit only for defence and internal security. This did not fit with Hitler's future plans one bit, and by early 1935 he determined it was time to solve this problem. If Germany was to become a major power once again, she would need appropriate military forces to match her status.

Consequently, it was announced in March 1935 that Germany would re-introduce conscription to meet her new military needs. Immediately, all Europe sat up and took notice, the press proclaiming dire warnings of future German aggression, causing a Europe-wide level of consternation and panic not seen since the First World War.

'Let them curse,' Goebbels commented. 'Meanwhile we rearm and put on a brave face.'[29]

Within a few days, Britain's Foreign Secretary and Lord Privy Seal, Sir John Simon and Anthony Eden, hurriedly flew to Berlin to ascertain exactly what the German Führer intended to do next. Hitler, for his part, was deeply worried by the British reaction, and was indeed 'putting on a brave face'. He absolutely did not want a conflict with the British, and made no secret of the fact that he considered the English to be Germany's 'Aryan cousins'. He therefore desperately wanted to persuade Britain's politicians to let him do exactly as he wanted, without a war which he knew Germany would lose at that time.

In a confidential meeting on Saturday, 23 March 1935, held at his Reich Chancellery office, Hitler met with Hess, Philipp Bouhler, the Chancellery head and party business manager, and Albrecht Haushofer, attending as a specialist on English affairs, to decide the course of action. It was concluded that an Anglo–German diplomatic banquet would provide the best low-key opportunity for Hitler to argue his case for Germany's need to throw off of the shackles of Versailles. To Haushofer fell the task of drawing up the guest list, devising the seating plan[30] and advising Hitler during his meeting with Simon and Eden.

At the banquet the guests were placed so that Eden was seated close to Hitler, separated from him only by Lady Phipps, the British Ambassador's wife, while Sir John Simon was placed opposite the German Führer. Other British guests included leading Tory politician Viscount Cranborne, the new Ambassador to Berlin Sir Eric Phipps and his predecessor Sir John Seymour, while the top Germans present included Göring, Hess, Goebbels and von Neurath. There were, however, no military men, no SS or Schutzstaffel, and certainly no one whose presence would have hinted at the darker side of Nazism, such as Himmler or Heydrich. This was a diplomatic dinner aimed at defusing a sensitive international situation, not an occasion for military intimidation. However, as Goebbels later noted, Hitler did speak 'out against Russia, [and] has laid a cuckoo's egg which is intended to hatch into an Anglo–German entente'.[31]

The event was a success, and further enhanced Albrecht Haushofer's standing at the Reich Chancellery. Within a few weeks he began to expand his reputation as an expert on foreign affairs by writing a report for Hess on the problems with 'Germany's Foreign-Political Apparatus'. The report concluded that in order to attain Germany's territorial aims, Hitler would have to take the lead in a two-pronged approach to further Germany's position in Europe.

Haushofer posed the question: 'How do we view this instrument in reality, and proceed in the direction of the Führer's difficult foreign policy [of territorial expansion]?'[32] He then proceeded to explain that there existed a complicated conflict within Germany's foreign ministry, which was split between the old guard – the stalwarts of the diplomatic service (mainly Weimar Republic appointees), who opposed National Socialist policy – and the new men, all party members who believed in a strong Nazi approach to attain the Führer's territorial aims. The main problem, Albrecht pointed out, was that these new men were inexperienced, and the older diplomats were the more effective body within the ministry. Foreign governments, politicians and diplomats, he asserted, were exploiting these differences to Germany's detriment. The problem would not be solved until a reorganisation of the Foreign Ministry took place.[33]

Over the next four years Haushofer's importance to Hess and Hitler continued to rise. His was often the hidden voice of reason that attempted to put a tone of mollification into Nazi foreign policy, his often the role of modest intermediary between the Führer and certain top Britons.

1935 was to be the high point of Hitler's *England-Politik*, complete with the signing of the Anglo–German Naval Agreement, whereby Germany was permitted to expand its fleet beyond the constraints of the treaty of Versailles. In achieving this, Hitler made the catastrophic error of believing that the British government could be wooed into permitting an expanded Greater Germany, that they would calmly stand back whilst he carved out an enormous new empire for Germany in the east.

In 1937, two years after Anthony Eden and Sir John Simon's visit to Berlin, Haushofer's connections and talent for mediation meant that he was still very much in the fore of German diplomacy, particularly when Lord Halifax visited Germany and it was arranged for him to meet Hitler. The two politicians, eyeing each other warily, discussed the central European situation with regard to the Nazis' increasing calls for unification of all ethnic German peoples – as defined by Albrecht's father, Karl Haushofer. The meeting was unreservedly deemed a success, and during his train journey home, Halifax would note: 'Unless I am wholly deceived, the Germans, speaking generally, from Hitler to the man in the street, do want friendly relations with Great Britain. There are no doubt many who don't: and the leading men may be deliberately throwing dust in our eyes. But I don't think so . . .'[34]

In 1940 and 1941 Hitler would think back on his meeting with Lord Halifax, and remember that this eminent British politician, a leading member of the Conservative Party, had spoken earnestly of his desire to see a lasting European peace. Indeed, their discussions had seemed so propitious that Hitler had 'talked of the possibility of disarmament', beginning with 'the possible abolition of bombing aeroplanes'. Halifax had later told the British Cabinet that he believed Germany would continue working towards ethnic unity, and that 'the basis of an understanding might not be too difficult as regards to Central and Eastern Europe'[35] – which would have been music to Hitler's ears. Following their meeting the German Führer had thought well of Lord Halifax, seeing him as a voice of reason in Britain, particularly after the declaration of war in September 1939. However, his opinion of this eminent man of British politics would later change radically. Feeling deceived and let down by fickle British politicians, he would comment bitterly, 'I regard Halifax as a hypocrite of the worst type, as a liar.'[36]

Albrecht Haushofer's pre-war influence was perhaps most strongly felt during the Munich Crisis of 1938, when he acted on behalf of the VDA in the Sudetenland advising the German delegation during the negotiations that would see Czechoslovakia stripped of her western territories. One of the keys to explaining Haushofer's participation in high-level German foreign affairs is that Hitler believed Germany's Foreign Ministry to be a slow, plodding beast, run by old-fashioned diplomats who took forever to negotiate a deal with any foreign nation. He therefore encouraged the use of alternative diplomatic means in the form of his own Nazi Party foreign-political machinery, the Aussenpolitisches Amt, the VDA and the Dienststelle Ribbentrop, all of which were run by men whose primary loyalty was to the Führer himself, men Hitler knew he could trust to give him what he wanted. This group included Albrecht Haushofer. In 1936 Haushofer and a diplomat named Graf Trauttmansdorf were sent to Czechoslovakia on Hitler's secret orders for private talks about the Sudetenland. However, 'they were forbidden to have any contact with the German diplomatic mission in Czechoslovakia, and the then German Foreign Minister, von Neurath'.[37]

The end of the 1930s saw the pressure-cooker of European politico-diplomatic tensions rise inexorably towards bursting point as the Nazis strained to expand Germany beyond her frontiers, to absorb every part of Europe containing ethnic Germans, as outlined by Karl Haushofer in the 1920s (see maps, pp. 16, 23). This objective closely followed Professor Haushofer's theories, and like his son he was very active throughout the 1930s, contacting Ukrainian nationalists and working extensively with the Ukrainian Hetman Organisation, which supported the freeing of the Ukraine from Soviet domination. All of this would come together in June 1941, for Hitler would not attack the Soviet Union merely out of political ideology, but because western Russia played a critical role in the Nazis' plans for their future Reich. The Nazis intended that the Ukraine would become the Reich's breadbasket, while the Caucasus became her source of oil. Karl Haushofer was very important to this plan, and within his theories, his extensive range of contacts and his knowledge of the region lay the key, the Nazis hoped, to the Reich's future success.

When Rudolf and Ilse Hess's son, Wolf Rüdiger, was born in 1938, one of the child's godfathers was Adolf Hitler; the other was Albrecht Haushofer. It may seem extraordinary that the co-signer of the infamous Nuremberg Laws (which removed German Jews' political and social rights) chose the part-Jewish Albrecht Haushofer as his child's godfather, despite the fact that he, Hitler, and all the top Nazis knew full well the Haushofer family's Jewish connections. Indeed, at the christening party held at Hess's Munich home in the affluent suburb of Harlaching, guest of honour Adolf Hitler mingled freely and happily with his and Hess's friends, chatting gaily to his long-time acquaintance Martha Haushofer, who was half-Jewish.

1938 was a time of great change. The zenith of Nazi foreign policy successes was passing, and the Hess christening party was marred towards the end by a disagreement between Karl Haushofer and Hitler. The by-now elderly Professor Haushofer, who had become used to being regarded as the Nazis' geopolitical guru, sought out for his wise counsel, now sensed that he too was passing his zenith. Hitler, like some Frankenstein's monster of his own creation, was showing increasing signs that he intended to pursue Nazi foreign policy in an aggressive manner that the old Professor felt increasingly at odds with, and which he felt might well lead to war. Needless to say, when he voiced his opinion to Hitler, it was not well received.

Hitler should have listened to his old friend, for there would soon be signs that Germany's European neighbours would no longer stand back and turn a blind eye to the Nazis' expansionist agenda.

Following the autumn 1938 Munich Conference to settle the Sudeten Question, which was to strip Czechoslovakia of her western territories and leave her open to German conquest a mere six months later, certain high-ranking British civil servants and politicians regretfully concluded that Poland was likely to be next on Hitler's agenda. He would demand the return of Danzig and the Corridor – the last remaining major strip of territory taken from Germany in 1919. However, what Hitler did next shocked everyone. Rather than sticking to Karl Haushofer's plan for expanding Germany to encompass all ethnic Germans (which the British Foreign Office was well aware of), the German Führer swallowed up the rest of Czechoslovakia as well, in direct contravention of the agreement he had signed with Britain's Prime Minister Neville Chamberlain in Munich the previous year.

Czechoslovakia proper had never been part of Germany, and there were few, if any, ethnic Germans living there. Yet Hitler had simply marched in and taken a foreign nation over. This raised the frightening prospect that no one was safe, if not from direct invasion, then from belligerent German aggression to protect their interests – and who could say where the Nazis might judge those to be?

British MP Sir Henry 'Chips' Channon summed up these feelings succinctly on the day Germany invaded Czechoslovakia, writing in his diary: 'Hitler has entered Prague, and Czechoslovakia has ceased to exist. No balder, bolder departure from the written bond has ever been committed in history. The manner of it surpasses comprehension and his callous desertion of the Prime Minister is stupefying ... The country is stirred to its depths, and rage against Germany is rising.'[38]

It was not only the democrats of western Europe who were concerned by Hitler's ill-judged departure from Karl Haushofer's geopolitical game plan, which although blatantly nationalistic, at least made it appear that the Führer's territorial ambitions were limited. No one could feel safe if Hitler could so easily tear up a treaty. Italy's Fascist Foreign Minister, Count Ciano, immediately perceived the dangers of the situation: 'The thing is serious, especially since Hitler had assured everyone that he did not want to annex one single Czech. This German action does not destroy the Czechoslovakia of Versailles, but the one that was constructed at Munich and Vienna. What weight can be given in the future to those declarations and promises which concern us more directly?'[39]

Hitler's move against Czechoslovakia also took Albrecht Haushofer by surprise. Despite his position close to the centre of Nazi geopolitical planning, he had remained largely unaware of Hitler's true strategy for attaining his Greater Germany. Haushofer thought in terms of discussion, negotiation and plebiscite. Hitler, on the other hand, was running to a different timetable. He was aware that Germany would not be able to sustain her military superiority for very long before Britain and France attained parity.

Back in November 1937, Hitler had held a secret conference at the Chancellery to discuss this very situation, with War Minister Field Marshal Werner von Blomberg, commander-in-chief of the army General Werner von Fritsch, commander-in-chief of the navy Admiral Erich Raeder, Reich Minister for Air and commander-in-chief of the Luftwaffe as well as President of the Reichstag Hermann Göring, Foreign Minister von Neurath, and a certain Colonel Hossbach, who took the minutes. Hitler had begun by 'stating that the subject of the present conference was of such importance that its discussions would, in other countries, certainly be a matter for a full Cabinet meeting, but he – the Führer – had rejected the idea of making it a subject of discussion before the wider circle of the *Reich* Cabinet just because of the importance of the matter'.

After much debate on the subject of a Greater Germany, and how the nation was to attain *Lebensraum* for its people, Hitler declared: 'Germany's problem could only be solved by means of force and this was never without attendant risks ... If one accepts as the basis of the following exposition the resort to force with its attendant risks, then there remain still to be answered the questions of "when" and "how" ...'[40] The 'when' and 'how' were then divided into three criteria.

Firstly, Hitler judged that after 1943–45 Germany's military position would become increasingly unfavourable, as 'our relative strength would decrease in relation to the rearmament which would by then have been carried out by the rest of the world'.

Secondly, he declared it was hoped that 'internal strife' would occur in France (indeed, the Nazis began covertly financing the right-wing Cagoulards, who were gearing up to attempt a *coup d'état*[41]), precipitating a crisis that would absorb the French army completely and 'render it incapable of use in a war against Germany'.

Thirdly, it was hoped that France might become 'so embroiled by a war with another state that she cannot proceed against Germany'.

The implication was clear to the men seated around the conference table at the Reich Chancellery: Hitler was gearing up the German economy, as well as her politico-military bodies, for war.

Finally, Hitler revealed that he intended to absorb the Czech state into the Reich. Thus, what in the spring of 1939 appeared to be a belligerent Hitler whim was in fact part of his overall long-term strategy, for as he explained in November 1937:

the annexation of Czechoslovakia and Austria would mean an acquisition of foodstuff for five to six million people ... The incorporation of these two states ... means, from a politico-military point of view, a substantial advantage because it would mean shorter and better frontiers, the freeing of forces for other purposes, and the possibility of creating new units up to a level of about twelve divisions, that is, one new division per million inhabitants.[42]

In a last-ditch effort to preserve the European peace, whilst at the same time pursuing a line that would enable Germany to settle her grievances over her eastern territories lost to Poland in 1919, Albrecht Haushofer wrote to his old friend, the British MP Lord Clydesdale, in July 1939: 'My Dear Douglo, I have been silent for a very long time . . .' After some brief introductory pleasantries, he quickly got down to business, explaining the difficulties faced by Germany after the end of the First World War. He expanded upon the fact that Germany had been unfairly stripped of much territory that she now wanted back, despite the terrible danger of war, and that Germany had a need – both politically and psychologically – to regain her formed territories. He continued:

> I cannot imagine even a short-range settlement without a change in the status of Danzig and . . . the Corridor . . . (people in England mostly do not know that there are some 600,000–700,000 Germans scattered through the inner parts of Poland!) – but if there is to be a peaceful solution at all, it can only come from England and it must appear to be fair to the German people as a whole . . .
>
> Last September Mr Neville [Chamberlain] had the trust of the majority of Germans. If you want to win a peace without – or even after – war, you need to be regarded as trustees of Justice, not partisans. Therefore – once more – if you can do anything to promote a general British peace and armaments control plan – I am sure you would do something helpful.[43]

Clydesdale decided to discreetly show Haushofer's letter to a few of his top-ranking political acquaintances. But rather than the Foreign Secretary or the Prime Minister, the first person he approached was Winston Churchill. After carefully reading the letter, Churchill handed it back to Clydesdale with the comment: 'There's going to be a war very soon.'

'In that case,' replied Clydesdale, 'I very much hope that you will be Prime Minister.'

'What a hell of a time to become Prime Minister,' Churchill responded with a resigned shake of his head.[44]

Clydesdale next showed the letter to the Foreign Secretary, Lord Halifax, before taking it on to the Prime Minister, Neville Chamberlain. Yet neither felt compelled to act or reply.

It is noteworthy that even before war was declared, and indeed ten months before Chamberlain's resignation, Clydesdale, like many other Britons, already knew who was going to become important in the terrible times to come; and it wasn't going to be Neville Chamberlain.

Haushofer's letter, which did nothing to deflect the progression to war, is important, if for no other reason than that it set the pattern for the line of communication that would begin just over a year later, and that again involved key men who all knew each other well – Albrecht Haushofer, Clydesdale (by then Duke of Hamilton), Winston Churchill and Lord Halifax.

Back in Germany, Rudolf Hess added his voice to the Nazi assertions of peaceable intent, giving a speech in Berlin in August 1939. Germany had already absorbed Austria, the Sudetenland and, worst of all, Czechoslovakia by intimidation and force of arms. Now Hess tried to legitimise the invasion of Poland, which he knew was just days away. Decrying Polish aggression, he publicly requested Neville Chamberlain to inspect German refugee camps and see with his own eyes the horrors of Poland's terror campaign. 'There is bloodshed, Herr Chamberlain!' he declared. 'There are dead! Innocent people have died.' He went on to state that 'England has point-blank refused all the Führer's proposals for peace throughout the years.'[45]

Hess's pleas, however, fell on deaf ears. In London no one was listening any more. The time of appeasement had passed, and diplomatic deals were busily being done to bolster an Anglo–French partnership to support Poland.

CHAPTER 2

Peaceable Attempts

At dawn on 1 September 1939, Hitler's powerful new armies poured across the Polish frontier in a pre-emptive strike that would see Poland obliterated in under a month, and the Second World War begin. It would, however, be wrong to assume that the German Führer actually wanted an all-encompassing European war that was destined to become a world war, or that he realised that this would be the consequence of his actions. Over the next year, Hitler, increasingly aware of the Pandora's Box of horrors he had unleashed – that Germany was now pitted in a life-or-death struggle against Britain and her empire – would repeatedly try to open a secret line of communication to the British government in the hope of undoing the disastrous situation he had himself created.

These secret peace moves, of which only a very select handful of top men in Britain and Germany were aware (and which were kept secret from their people for very different reasons), became known by Britain's Foreign Office and War Cabinet as the 'peaceable attempts'; petitions made by Hitler and certain other leading Nazis to open negotiations that would culminate in an armistice. As time went by these peaceable attempts would take on an ever-increasing urgency, reflecting Hitler's mounting concern (despite his belligerent public stance for home consumption) that he was losing control of events.

In the first week of September 1940, whilst the skies above London thundered to the sound of the Battle of Britain, Britain's Ambassador to Sweden, Victor Mallet, would send a 'most secret' encrypted telegram for 'special distribution' to the War Cabinet.

In his telegram, an astounded Mallet reported that he had been contacted by a Berlin barrister named Dr Ludwig Weissauer, who 'is understood to be a direct secret emissary of Hitler ... [Furthermore, he wishes] me to meet him very secretly in order to ... talk on the subject of peace.'

Dr Ludwig Weissauer was in fact not only chief lawyer to the Nazi Party, but also Adolf Hitler's own private legal adviser. The Ambassador went on to reveal that this most eminent emissary 'wished conversations, if they took place, to be known to nobody but His Majesty's Government and Hitler to whom he intimated that he would report direct. Talks could begin at once ... [if a Swedish, and therefore neutral,] judge might be present in order to avoid any suggestion of trickery. Weissauer realised that peace might not yet be attainable but nevertheless felt that conversation would be useful.'[1] Mallet concluded his report by asking whether he should go ahead and meet Weissauer, before ending hopefully, 'of course [I will] say nothing to encourage him but it might be of interest to listen'.

This was an unusual and, until recently, unsuspected situation. That Hitler should make this secret approach to Britain – and it is worth noting that the initiative was kept secret from other top Nazis, as well as the German people – is indicative that something extraordinary was taking place behind the scenes. Hitler's use of his own lawyer was the culmination of a year's peace moves by the German Führer that had seen him attempt mediation through many avenues, ranging from neutral citizens and governments, to royalty and the Vatican. All had failed, undone, in Hitler's eyes, by a political faction in Britain that was determined to continue the war, come what may. This had not prevented him, during the final months of 1939 and the first half of 1940, from pursuing an aggressive military strategy tied to his private attempts to make peace – a carrot and stick policy that he hoped would free him from a war in the west he did not want.

Despite all the evidence that Hitler wanted to flex his military muscles, and was willing to obtain by force what he was unlikely to gain at the diplomatic table, a full-blown war with Britain and

France, supported by their substantial empires, was certainly not something he wanted in 1939. His primary objective had been to make the first moves in a politico-military game of chess that would see him expand and consolidate a Greater Germany, thereby placing Germany in the ideal position to expand her territories into an Eastern Empire. A substantial proportion of the responsibility for Hitler's total miscalculation of the British and French reaction to the formation of a German super-state at the expense of her smaller neighbours, such as Czechoslovakia and Poland, has to be laid firmly at the door of his Foreign Minister, Joachim von Ribbentrop.

In the months prior to the outbreak of war, Ribbentrop forcefully counselled Hitler that Britain would not come to the aid of Poland but would, bar the diplomatic protests and the fist-waving of a frustrated nation led by a weak government, flinch and stand back from outright war.[2] This view was in direct contrast to what Germany's other foreign affairs experts, such as Albrecht Haushofer, were advising Hitler. In the late spring of 1939, Hess had commissioned Haushofer to write a report for him on the British reaction to German expansion. Within weeks the Deputy-Führer was alarmed to read Haushofer's prophetic comments that:

> many British politicians . . . [are] thoroughly friendly towards Germany . . . [and] would consider discussing border changes to Germany's advantage . . . But a violent solution . . . would be a *casus belli* for England . . . In such a war the entire nation would support the government. England would wage the war as a crusade for the liberation of Europe from German nationalism. With the help of the USA (on which London could count) they would win the war against Germany [and] regrettably the actual winner in Europe would be Bolshevism.[3]

On its way to Hitler, the report was first shown to Ribbentrop, who disdainfully scrawled in the margin: 'English secret-service propaganda!'[4] But he was wrong.

*   *   *

On 3 September 1939, an utterly dejected Neville Chamberlain, worn out and disillusioned by his failure to deal with the dictator of Germany, stood before his colleagues in the House of Commons. He had seen his hopes for European peace blown away by the dry, hot wind of war. History is harsh, and Chamberlain's twenty-five years of honest public service would be forgotten in an instant. His name would forever be linked to the appeasement of Nazism, the pandering to a dictator who was plunging Europe into war even as he addressed the House.

A hush descended amongst the MPs, and Chamberlain began to speak, his sonorous tones echoing around the chamber as he declared:

> When I spoke last night to the House I could not but be aware that in some parts of the House there were doubts and some bewilderment as to whether there had been any weakening, hesitation, or vacillation on the part of His Majesty's Government. In the circumstances, I make no reproach, for if I had been in the same position as hon[ourable] members not sitting on this Bench and not in possession of all the information which we have, I should very likely have felt the same.

After informing the House that the British Ambassador in Berlin had delivered an ultimatum to the German government demanding that German armed forces 'suspended all aggressive action against Poland and were prepared to withdraw their forces from Polish territory', Chamberlain went on to disclose that: 'No such undertaking was received from [the German government] by the time stipulated, and, consequently, this country is at war with Germany.'

Finally, Chamberlain opened up slightly, expressing his own feelings of personal failure: 'This is a very sad day for all of us, and to none is it sadder than to me. Everything that I have worked for, everything that I have hoped for, everything that I have believed in during my public life, has crashed into ruins. There is only one thing left for me to do; that is, to devote what strength and powers I have to forwarding the victory of the cause for which we have to sacrifice so much. I cannot tell what part I may be allowed to play myself; I trust I may live to see the day when Hitlerism has been destroyed and a liberated Europe has been re-established . . .'[5]

Chamberlain's wish was not to be fulfilled – he would be dead in little over a year.

In Berlin, Britain and France's determination to stand by Poland and declare war on Germany left Hitler stunned. However, he quickly convinced himself and his intimates at the Chancellery that 'England and France had obviously declared war merely as a sham, in order not to lose face before the world.' Having given the Poles an assurance of protection, they could do little else. Hitler asserted that 'there would be no fighting',[6] and ordered Germany's forces in the west not to provoke the Allies, but to remain strictly on the defensive. 'Of course we are in a state of war with England and France,' Hitler would confide to his dinner guests a few days later, 'but if we on our side avoid all acts of war [against France and Britain], the whole business will evaporate. As soon as we sink a ship and they have sizeable casualties, the war party over there will gain strength.'[7]

However, events in Britain were about to deal a bad hand of cards to Hitler: within a short time of the British declaration of war, he received news that Winston Churchill had been appointed First Lord of the Admiralty, and joined the War Cabinet. An eyewitness recalled that on hearing the news, Hitler 'dropped into the nearest chair, and said wearily "Churchill is in the Cabinet. That means that the war is really on. Now we have war with England." '[8]

Regardless of the British and French declarations of war, and Hitler's fear of a conflict in the west that he did not want, Germany maintained her relentless attack on the ever-weakening Polish forces. On 17 September Poland's determination to fight off the German invaders turned to anguish when Soviet Russia attacked her rear, and as the Red Army poured into eastern Poland, Polish resistance began to disintegrate. A mere ten days later, on 27 September, Warsaw fell to the German army, and the following day saw what was left of Poland partitioned between Germany and Russia. Technically, Poland had ceased to exist.

Despite the military posturing that now took place on the Franco–German border, between the British and French armies on the one side and Germany's forces on the other, a sort of peace did appear to settle uneasily over Europe. This was the time of the 'phoney war', described in Germany as the *Sitzkrieg*, the sitting war.

It was during this period that Hitler developed hopes that some form of accommodation could be found to end the conflict, with Germany retaining her conquests, and the Allies, having made their protests and metaphorically waved their fists at a belligerent Germany, backing down and agreeing to peace.

On 6 October, the fighting in Poland having finished and there being only a minimal level of conflict in the west, Hitler made his first public appeal for peace, giving an unrepentant yet placatory speech to the Reichstag. To many in the west, Hitler's speech sounded like mere rhetoric. But, unbeknownst to the Reichsleiters and Reichsministers seated before him, the Führer had been making a concerted behind-the-scenes effort to negotiate an accord with Britain.

Ten days prior to Hitler's appearance at the Reichstag, he had had a confidential meeting in his office at the Chancellery with a man named Birger Dahlerus, a prominent Swedish businessman who was also a close friend of the British Ambassador in Oslo, Sir George Ogilvie Forbes. Dahlerus informed Hitler that Ogilvie Forbes had told him that 'the British government was looking for peace. The only question was: How could the British save face?'

'If the British actually want peace,' Hitler had replied, 'they can have it within two weeks – without losing face.'[9] He informed Dahlerus that although Britain would have to be reconciled to the fact that 'Poland cannot rise again', he was prepared to guarantee the security of Britain and western Europe – a region he had little interest in, for despite some concerns about German access to the North Sea, German expansion into western Europe was not part of the Karl Haushofer plan for the Greater Germany.

Also present at this confidential meeting with Dahlerus was Hermann Göring, who suggested that British and German representatives should meet secretly in Holland, and that if they made progress, 'the Queen [of Holland] could invite both countries to armistice talks'. Hitler finally agreed to Dahlerus's proposal that he 'go to England the very next day in order to send out feelers in the direction indicated'.

'The British can have peace if they want it,' Hitler told Dahlerus as he left, 'but they will have to hurry.'[10]

Now, ten days later, Hitler stood before the Reichstag and proclaimed Germany's justification for taking back her former territories from Poland. For over an hour he discoursed on the history of the region that had led to the present state of affairs. Then, having taken this belligerent position, so that any placatory utterances he now made would not be seen as weakness, Hitler began to make his overtures for peace. First, he declared:

My chief endeavour has been to rid our relations with France of all trace of ill will and render them tolerable for both nations ... Germany has no claims against France ... I have refused even to mention the problem of Alsace-Lorraine ... I have always expressed to France my desire to bury forever our ancient enmity and bring together these two nations, both of which have such glorious pasts.

He then went on to speak about his greater cause for concern:

I have devoted no less effort to the achievement of Anglo–German understanding, nay, more than that, of an Anglo–German friendship. At no time and in no place have I ever acted contrary to British interests. I believe even today that there can only be real peace in Europe and throughout the world if Germany and England come to an understanding ... Why should this war in the west be fought? ... The question of re-establishment of the Polish state is a problem which will not be solved by war in the west but exclusively by Russia and Germany.

After touching on a whole range of European problems that would in the end, Hitler felt, have to be resolved at the conference table, not on the battlefield, including the 'formation of a Polish state', Germany's colonies, the revival of international trade, 'an unconditionally guaranteed peace', and a settlement of ethnic questions in Europe, Hitler proposed that a conference should be arranged to 'achieve these great ends'. He concluded:

> It is impossible that such a conference, which is to determine the fate of this continent for many years to come, could carry on its deliberations while cannon are thundering or mobilised armies are bringing pressure to bear upon it. If, however, these problems must be solved sooner or later, then it would be more sensible to tackle the solution before millions of men are first uselessly sent to death and billions of riches destroyed.
>
> One fact is certain. In the course of world history there have never been two victors, but very often only losers. May those peoples and their leaders who are of the same opinion now make their reply. And let those who consider war to be the better solution reject my outstretched hand . . .[11]

The following morning the Nazi Party mouthpiece, the *Völkischer Beobachter* newspaper, blared the headlines:

GERMANY'S WILL FOR PEACE.
NO WAR AIMS AGAINST FRANCE AND ENGLAND –
NO MORE REVISION CLAIMS EXCEPT COLONIES –
REDUCTION OF ARMAMENTS – CO-OPERATION WITH
ALL NATIONS OF EUROPE – PROPOSAL FOR A
CONFERENCE.[12]

The olive branch had been proffered. Would it be taken up?

There followed nearly a week's stony silence from Britain and France, prompting the German Führer to once again officially announce his 'readiness for peace' in a brief address at Berlin's

Sportpalast. 'Germany,' he declared, 'has no cause for war against the Western Powers.'[13]

On 12 October 1939, Neville Chamberlain finally responded to Hitler's offer, terming his proposals 'vague and uncertain', and making the comment that 'they contain no suggestions for righting the wrongs done to Czechoslovakia and Poland'. No reliance, Chamberlain asserted, could be put on the promises of 'the present German government'. After the humiliating defeats of Munich and Hitler's move against Poland, Britain's Prime Minister now suddenly exhibited a strength few thought him capable of. If Germany wanted peace, 'acts – not words alone – must be forthcoming', and he called for 'convincing proof' from Hitler that he really wanted an end to the conflict.

The following day, 13 October, Hitler responded by issuing a statement which declared that Chamberlain, in turning down his earnest proposals for peace, had deliberately chosen war. Such was the public face of the events at the time.

Yet what about the private face? What about the travels of Mr Dahlerus, which few people in Britain, including the House of Commons, ever got to hear about?

It was one thing for Chamberlain to turn down some airy peace proposal made by Hitler, presumably aimed at home consumption. In the world of diplomacy, much more credence would have been given to such a proposal if it had been made in writing, or delivered by an official emissary. It is not suggested that peace would have suddenly erupted on the receipt of an official communiqué more clearly outlining Germany's peace proposal – but it would certainly have been a starting point, from which an accord approaching the Allied demands could have been discussed, even if those negotiations subsequently failed.

Incredibly, such a communiqué is exactly what the British government, in the form of Neville Chamberlain and Foreign Secretary Lord Halifax, had secretly received as far back as August 1939.

In the spring of 1941, Hjalmar Schacht, the head of Germany's Reichsbank, approached the then non-combatant American government to ask if they would be prepared to act as intermediaries to help negotiate a peace between Germany and Britain. Soon a positive flurry of urgent memos were flying between Foreign Office mandarins in Whitehall querying what should be done, for they were not at all keen for America to interfere in Britain's foreign policy decisions. Eventually the Permanent Under-Secretary at the Foreign Office, Sir Alexander Cadogan, sent a 'most secret' memorandum to Lord Halifax, who was by then British Ambassador in Washington, that stated:

> Many thanks for your letter of 17th June about Schacht's peace feeler.
>
> We recently prepared for our own use a memorandum summarising the various peace feelers which have reached us since the beginning of the war. The Germans are obviously now attempting to interest certain circles in the USA in the possibility of an early peace ... It therefore occurred to us that you might like to see a copy of this memorandum and to communicate it very confidentially to the President for his own personal and secret information. In suggesting that you should do this we do not mean to suggest for a moment that the President is in any need of advice as to how to handle any such German approaches, but he may find details of our own experiences useful in helping him to handle the 'weaker brethren' in the USA ...[14]

The memorandum then went on to disclose details of *sixteen* peace attempts that had been made by the Germans since the outbreak of war. These included the Dahlerus peace initiative, about which it was revealed: '[Dahlerus] was convinced that Göring genuinely regretted the outbreak of the war and short of actual disloyalty to Hitler would like to see a truce negotiated. The unwillingness of the Polish government to treat in earnest about Danzig and The Corridor, coupled, perhaps, with deliberate malice on the part of Ribbentrop, had unleashed the conflict.'[15] The memorandum went on to explain that on 18 September 1939 a confidential meeting had taken place in London between high-ranking officials of the

Foreign Office, including Cadogan, and Dahlerus, who 'reported that the German army were now approaching a position in Poland beyond which they would not go and that the German government were seeking an early opportunity to make an offer of peace.'[16]

At this meeting Dahlerus was informed that the British Foreign Secretary Lord Halifax 'could conceive of no peace offer likely to come from the German government that could even be considered ... and that the British government could not ... define their attitude to an offer of which they did not know the nature'.

On 12 October 1939, the report went on, Dahlerus had transmitted the final details of Germany's very comprehensive peace offer. These included the information that Hitler was prepared to discuss the Polish situation, non-aggression pacts, disarmament, colonies, economic questions and frontiers. Indeed, Dahlerus even communicated that 'Hitler had taxed the patience of the German people over the Soviet Union, Czechoslovakia and Poland, and that if Göring, as the chief negotiator, secured peace, Hitler could not risk acting counter to these national undertakings.'[17]

This comprehensive peace initiative was kept secret in both Germany and Britain. However, even while admitting these details for 'President Roosevelt's Eyes Only' in 1941, the British government was still sensitive enough about the subject to conceal certain details about what had taken place. To the uninitiated, Dahlerus's efforts at peace in 1939 appeared a damp squib that had fizzled out. Yet there had been much more to them than the British government was prepared to admit to the American President.

During 1938, Neville Chamberlain had, with much effort, negotiated comprehensive deals with Hitler. Hitler, however, had shown a dangerous penchant for negotiating agreements and then reneging on them as soon as it suited his purposes. He wasn't, as one diplomat later remarked, a gentleman. Chamberlain had therefore, not unnaturally, developed a marked sensitivity about being seen to negotiate again with the Nazis, whilst at the same time exhorting the British people to prepare themselves to make great sacrifices. Thus the report to Roosevelt, at a time when

America was still neutral and Britain could not afford even to hint at the possibility of negotiating with the Nazis, for fear of losing American support, concealed the fact that Dahlerus had been involved in Hitler's attempts to prevent war *before* the conflict had started. As consummate politician and diarist, close friend of Britain's high and mighty, Sir Henry 'Chips' Channon commented two days before Germany's invasion of Poland, on 28 August 1939: 'Mr D[ahlerus] and a Mr Spencer have it appears been negotiating secretly here ... I doubt the validity of the Walrus's [Dahlerus's] credentials, but he is taken seriously by Halifax, and a secret plane transported the two emissaries here, with special facilities at the airport.'[18]

Exactly one month later, on 28 September, Channon recorded that Dahlerus, having been to Berlin to consult with Hitler, was back in London for another secret meeting – a meeting that would not be mentioned in the information released to Roosevelt: 'Very Secret. "The Walrus" is in London. He arrived today by plane and this time his visit is known to Hitler. Halifax and others are seeing him this afternoon. No-one knows of this. What nefarious message does he bring?'

The following day, Channon noted:

The fabulously mysterious 'Walrus' ... was interviewed secretly yesterday ... This morning he walked about the Foreign Office openly. Also Cadogan had a talk with him and a report of their conversation was given to Lord Halifax, who read it I believe, at the War Cabinet ... The French, always realistic, say 'we had better make peace as we can never restore Poland to its old frontiers, and how indeed should we ever dislodge the Russians from Poland even if we succeeded in ousting the Germans?'[19]

However, in the atmosphere of diplomatic and international distrust that had developed by October 1939, British contemplation of negotiating peace with Hitler quickly began to evaporate. Dahlerus's initiative failed, and the war continued unabated.

* * *

This, however, did not mean that Hitler gave up on the idea, and he continued secretly trying to find a negotiated end to the simmering conflict in the west before it came to the boil, ruining his timetable for eastern conquest. In truth he had no choice. He had found himself fighting the wrong war.

This situation led, between the summers of 1939 and 1941, to the British government receiving a great many German peaceable approaches. A substantial number of these can be discounted, for they included such low-level attempts as the German Chargé d'Affaires in Washington contacting the British Ambassador to inform him that 'if desired he could obtain from Berlin Germany's present peace terms'.[20] On another occasion the British Legation to the Holy See reported that the Vatican would be prepared to arbitrate between Britain and Germany 'through the Apostolic Delegate on the subject of Germany's peace offer'.[21]

Indeed, reports on the possibilities of peace were submitted back to London from far and wide – even from distant Angora, where Ambassador Sir Hugh Knatchbull-Hugessen reported that the 'Netherlands Minister has sent me the following information regarding a conversation between Herr von Papen and Herr Hitler during the former's recent visit to Berlin'. He went on to tell his seniors at the Foreign Office that 'Herr Hitler discussed [with von Papen his] possible terms of peace'.[22]

Each one of these reports required the attention of an Under-Secretary at the Foreign Office and the creation of its own file, and so became counted in the plethora of peaceable attempts made to the British government by German nationals or well-meaning neutrals. There were so many of these little snippets of peaceable intent that the whole matter of peace in 1939, 1940 and 1941 becomes rather a jumble, and to a large extent the important – *real* – peaceable moves made at this time have become hidden amongst all these lesser ones. However, it is possible to refine the plethora of peaceable initiatives down to just a few nuggets of gold – those that were stamped with the hallmark of Hitler.

There were basically three distinct strata to the peaceable attempts. The vast majority were low-level suggestions made by neutrals, junior German diplomats or the odd German official at loose in a neutral state. The second stratum, which was of some interest to the Foreign Office, emanated from respected neutrals, such as the King of Sweden, and upper-echelon German nationals, such as former War Minister Otto Gessler and even top Nazis such as Goebbels. These pitches for peace were made with an eye to the credit that would accrue to their originators, particularly with Hitler, if they brought Germany peace.

There was however, a third stratum of peaceable attempts, and these were of a different ilk altogether. They were top-grade offers that received the personal attention of the Foreign Secretary, and frequently the Prime Minister as well. Furthermore, there were occasions when these attempts were of such importance that they required the Prime Minister to consult the dominion heads of government in Canada, Australia, New Zealand and South Africa before they could be rejected.

The most intriguing fact about these top-grade offers is not only that they clearly emanated from Adolf Hitler himself, transmitted to the British authorities through his own personal emissaries, but that there was a discernible pattern to them. As each attempt failed or began to flounder, a new one was immediately initiated through another avenue to replace it, thereby creating an almost unbroken chain of peaceable attempts from the summer of 1939.

It was a situation that caused much interest and speculation within Britain's Foreign Office and Intelligence Services. By the summer of 1940 it was realised that these secret Hitler-initiated attempts at peace mediation revealed a psychological flaw deep within the Führer's character that Britain could, with skill and guile, exploit to Germany's disadvantage.

Even as it became clear to Hitler that Birger Dahlerus's attempts at mediation in September–October 1939 would fail, moves began to open another channel to the British government. However, the German Führer was still a relative novice at the art of opening secret lines of communication to Britain's leadership, and rather than stepping back to assess the situation, calling upon expert

Schedule of Main (i.e. Führer-Initiated) Peace Attempts from Summer 1939 to Summer 1941

DAHLERUS
VENLO
WINDSOR
WIESSAUER
OP. HHHH
SCHACHT

1939   1940   1941

J A S O N D J F M A M J J A S O N D J F M A M J J A S O N D

advice before dispatching an eminent diplomat or well-respected neutral, he accepted the services of the SS. That was not a good idea.

On 17 October 1939 SS Colonel Walter Schellenberg was summoned to a meeting with the head of the Sicherheitsdienst (SD), Reinhard Heydrich, at RSHA (Reichssicherheitshauptamt – the Directorate General of Security for the Reich) headquarters on Prinz Albrechtstrasse in Berlin – a building it shared with the Gestapo, which reveals much about the RSHA's interests. Ushered into the presence of this extremely dangerous man, second only to Himmler in the SD–SS chain of command, Schellenberg was surprised to find Heydrich in congenial mood. 'For several months,' Heydrich confided, 'one of our agents in the Low Countries ... has been in contact with the British secret service.'[23] He went on to inform Schellenberg that this agent, a man named Morz, had made several important contacts with British Intelligence, including two agents based in Holland. These were Major Richard Stevens, the Passport Control Officer at the British Embassy in The Hague (all Passport Control Officers were members of Britain's intelligence service MI6, better known as SIS), and Captain Sigismund Payne-Best, who ran the Z Network in Holland (an intelligence-gathering unit which reported to Passport Control Officers). Schellenberg's orders were to use these two men to 'get in touch with the English government'[24] in order to initiate Anglo–German peace negotiations.

Within a few days of his meeting with Heydrich, Schellenberg found himself in Holland, under the alias of Captain Schaemmel of the Oberkommando der Wehrmacht (OKW) Transport Service, pretending to Stevens and Payne-Best that he represented a group of leading Wehrmacht officers who wanted peace. This pretence was almost certainly adopted not only to protect Heydrich and Himmler should anything go wrong, but also because the British would have blanched at finding themselves negotiating with the SS. Schellenberg offered the very tempting bait that his faction might even be prepared to accept conditions that limited Hitler's position within Germany, although he stressed that it was desirable that Hitler remained head of state – which in Nazi terms meant that in public Hitler would have remained the German head of state in a purely ceremonial capacity, while in private he continued in charge. This curious suggestion was not as improbable as it might first appear, for the SS was all-powerful in Nazi Germany, and Himmler secretly harboured great ambitions for it, planning that it would eventually supplant the Nazi Party as the controlling power in Germany.

Within hours of his meeting with Schellenberg, Stevens dispatched a 'most secret' telegram to London, putting forward the German peace proposals and relating the remarkable suggestions concerning Hitler's future status. He soon received a reply that stated:

> In the event of the German representatives enquiring whether you have had a reply to the questions which you said ... you would refer to H.M.G., you should inform them as follows (*not*, however, handing them anything in writing):-
>
> Whether Hitler remains in any capacity or not (but of course more particularly if he *does* remain) this country would have to see proof that German policy had changed direction ... Germany [would not only] have to right the wrongs done in Poland and Czechoslovakia, but she would also have to give pledges that there would be no repetition of acts of aggression ...[25]

The message concluded:

> It is not for H.M.G. to say how these conditions could be met, but they are bound to say that, in their view, they are essential to the establishment of confidence on which alone peace could be solidly and durably based ...
>
> Neither France nor Great Britain, as the Prime Minster said, have any desire to carry on a vindictive war, but they are determined to prevent Germany continuing to make life in Europe unbearable.[26]

On receiving the bulk of this communication via Stevens, Schellenberg promptly reported to Heydrich: 'The British officers [have] declared that His Majesty's Government took great interest in our attempt which would contribute powerfully to prevent the spread of war ... They assured us that they were in direct contact with the [British] Foreign Office and Downing Street.'[27] He concluded by informing Heydrich that the British had invited him to secret peace negotiations in London, and that Stevens had even given him a transmitter (call sign ON4) with which he could covertly contact the British directly.

Heydrich's response was most interesting, indicating that there was a great deal more going on behind the scenes than Schellenberg ever knew about. 'All this seems to me a little too good to be true,' the head of the SD commented. 'I find it hard to believe that it's not a trap. Be very careful going to London. Before making a decision I shall have to talk not only with the Reichsführer [Himmler] but more particularly with the Führer. Wait for my orders before proceeding.'[28] Evidently from the German side the negotiations emanated from the pinnacle of Nazi government.

Events, however, were about to take a bizarre and unexpected twist. In distant Munich, on the night of Wednesday, 8 November, there was an attempt on Hitler's life when a bomb blew up the Bürgerbräukeller just twenty minutes after he had cut short a speech and unexpectedly departed early. Outraged that this assassination attempt might have been prompted by the British, the SD took immediate action.

The very next afternoon, Stevens and Payne-Best, who were waiting to meet Schellenberg at the little Dutch–German frontier post at Venlo, were kidnapped by SD agents who dashed across the border, shot up the Dutch customs post, grabbed the two startled British Intelligence officers and made off with them across the frontier into Germany. Stevens and Payne-Best were intensively interrogated by German Intelligence, and after the German conquest of the west in 1940 the whole of Britain's secret service network in western Europe would be brought crashing down, leaving it with virtually no intelligence-gathering assets. On the

German side, the Venlo Incident, as it became known, ended any possibility of Schellenberg negotiating an end to the war.

As far as the British were concerned, this had been a true peace negotiation. The fact that Britain's participants in the secret discussions were headed by Lord Halifax and Neville Chamberlain reveals the seriousness with which they were regarded by the British side, for Chamberlain was still keen to restore European peace. The Prime Minister was motivated by the desire to restore his reputation, but wanted to keep his failure hidden if he did not.

Although Halifax and Chamberlain had thought they could still negotiate an end to the conflict, the manner of the Venlo snatch by the SD finally impressed upon London that the Nazis were beyond the pale. How could Britain engage in meaningful peace negotiations with the Nazis when they reacted to an internal security problem by kidnapping peace negotiators?

When Winston Churchill discovered the truth behind the incident shortly after Stevens and Payne-Best's kidnapping, his fury knew no bounds. Not only had Halifax and Chamberlain secretly engaged in a dangerous peace initiative, they had done so behind the back of the Cabinet. In Churchill's eyes the appeasement of Nazism had led to the obliteration of the Czech state, the invasion of Poland, and to Britain and France facing a war just as they had in 1914. Yet Chamberlain had apparently not learned the lessons of appeasement, and had attempted mediation again. This was bad enough, but what Churchill also realised – which had apparently escaped Chamberlain – was that Chamberlain had unwittingly placed the alliance itself in dire peril. If the Germans were to leak details of the negotiations to the French, it would utterly shatter France's confidence in Britain's resolve to stand firm, ensuring victory to the Germans.

That German Intelligence did not leak the Venlo details to the French, however, is a clear indication that they too had much to hide, for it was no part of Hitler's plans for the German *Volk* to hear that top Nazis were attempting secretly to negotiate peace with Britain until it was a done deal.

The Venlo Incident was not a clear-cut peace negotiation, for much double-dealing occurred behind the scenes, primarily organised by those masters of Machiavellian deceit, Reinhard Heydrich and Heinrich Himmler. To call it instead an 'SS peace move' might be more accurate. But Venlo was important because it involved Britons and Germans at the highest level; it also set in motion a chain of events that would give the first seeds of an idea to British Intelligence that they might conduct a similar 'sting' of their own.

It is entirely possible that the Stevens/Payne-Best–Morz operation pre-October 1939 was originally an SD 'sting' aimed at crippling British Intelligence's network in western Europe, but Heydrich's participation in the operation post-Dahlerus indicates that a change in priorities had taken place. Moreover, Schellenberg's reports on the affair were passed through Heydrich directly to Himmler.

On the British side, much of the remaining evidence suggests that the subsequent writing-off of Venlo as a 'sting' was primarily intended to protect Chamberlain from being caught holding secret peace talks with the Germans at the same time that he was condemning Nazi expansionism – a position he would have found hard to explain not only to Parliament, but to the Poles and the French. Intriguingly, in the Foreign Office's 'President Roosevelt's Eyes Only' communication of June 1941, Sir Alexander Cadogan would confidentially remark to Britain's Ambassador in Washington that 'the only important omission from our memorandum is the story of the Venlo incident in November 1939'.[29] Thus, within Whitehall, Venlo was classified as amongst the 'peaceable attempts', and not as an intelligence operation that went disastrously wrong.

Given what is known about Hitler's desperation to end the war with Britain, it is possible that had the SS found a possible route to peace, Himmler would have ordered Heydrich to explore it, for he too was well aware of the extremely dangerous situation Germany was falling into. In 1942 Count Ciano would record that 'Himmler, who now feels the real pulse of the country, wants a compromise peace',[30] for his 'plans for expansion into Russia were based on his hopes of coming to an understanding with the West'.[31] Indeed, when the tide of war had finally turned inexorably against

Germany in 1944, Himmler would earnestly engage in his own secret peace negotiations, this time without Hitler's knowledge, and would attempt to use Albrecht Haushofer to do this. It is therefore likely that Himmler was inclined to attempt to restore peace with Britain in 1939, at a time when it would have secured both the fortunes of the Reich and his own position at the top of the Nazi hierarchy.

The collapse of the Venlo/SS peace attempt unnerved Hitler, for he undoubtedly did believe that the Bürgerbräukeller attempt on his life had been connected in some way to the negotiations taking place in Holland. But unbeknownst to Himmler, Heydrich or anyone else in the SS, Hitler was already pursuing yet another entirely private avenue to peace – his own short-cut to European domination. Hitler was a great believer in auguries, mysticism, and what he liked to call his 'destiny'. It is therefore little wonder that he took his salvation from the Bürgerbräukeller bombing very seriously indeed, and was sure fate had played a hand in saving him from being blown to bits. The reason Hitler had left the Bürgerbräukeller early was to travel back to Berlin to meet another emissary. Only this emissary wasn't offering peace mediation, but a victory that would enable him to dictate peace terms to a defeated foe.

The important peaceable attempts (i.e. those that could be directly connected to Hitler's interests) between 1939 and 1941 fall into a clearly discernible pattern. As soon as one of them began to falter or fail, so keen was Hitler to have peace in the west that another was instantly begun through some other medium – be it by banker, businessman, diplomat or royal – in an attempt to keep the dialogue going.

There were, however, two exceptions to this rule.

The first occurred from mid-November 1939 to July 1940, directly following the failure of Venlo. It was a time when, through a French-American named Charles Bedaux, and later through Baron Oswald von Hoyningen-Huene, Germany's Ambassador in

Lisbon, Adolf Hitler attempted to open a line of communication to the former King Edward VIII, now the Duke of Windsor, whom he mistakenly believed was still an influential personality in British politics.

The other period of inactivity lasted from the second half of 1940 until mid-1941. At this time Hitler believed that the best opportunity for peace was through the efforts of Albrecht Haushofer and Rudolf Hess, whose high-level negotiations were aimed at permanently removing Britain from the war.

What this reveals is that Hitler repeatedly engaged in secret and complex efforts to negotiate his way out of a war in the west he did not want, *except* when he believed he had found an inside track to undermining the Allies' (i.e. Britain's) resolve and ability to continue the conflict – a carrot-and-stick approach to persuade or force Britain to the negotiating table. Two attempts to proffer the carrot – Dahlerus and Venlo – had failed, so now Hitler determined to use the stick.

Hitler's first attempt to force Britain to the table involved a French-American businessman named Charles Bedaux, a close friend of the Duke of Windsor, who (according to documents in British, German and American archives) offered to act as an intermediary carrying messages between Germany and the former King Edward VIII.[32]

Charles Bedaux was no novice in the world of espionage. He had been a spy for Germany in the United States during the First World War,[33] and had, in boom-time America of the 1920s, prospered to become a multi-millionaire. By the 1930s he was back in Europe, where his home, the Château de Candi, swiftly became known as a hotbed of Nazi intrigue and plotting.[34] During the 1930s Bedaux had played a key role in the reorganisation of German industry which enabled Hitler's rearmament programme to take place. He thus moved in very high Nazi circles indeed, knew Hitler personally, and even had a villa at Berchtesgaden within sight of the Führer's Berghof.[35]

In 1937 Bedaux had hosted the wedding of the abdicated King

Edward VIII to the American divorcee Wallis Simpson, at the Château de Candi. Having firmly insinuated himself into the Windsors' lives, he swiftly became responsible for their tour of Nazi Germany, which although well received in Germany, was a public-relations disaster in Britain, where Edward had hoped to restore his standing. Thereafter the relationship had cooled, but in October 1939 Bedaux reported exciting news to Hitler concerning the Duke of Windsor, with whom he was back on friendly terms.

What had occurred was that in late September 1939, Reichsleiter Alfred Rosenberg, head of the Aussenpolitisches Amt, received a postcard from an old friend, purporting to be in neutral Switzerland and asking for a meeting. The friend, a Balt named Baron 'Bill' de Ropp of east Prussian stock, was also an old acquaintance of Group Captain Winterbotham, who was near the top of British Air Intelligence. De Ropp also had close associations with British Intelligence, and had been of considerable assistance to the British secret service during the 1930s.

After checking with Ribbentrop, Rosenberg travelled to Switzerland at the beginning of October. He was soon rubbing his hands in glee at what de Ropp told him, reporting back to Berlin that: 'Because of the war psychology prevailing in England and the weak position of Chamberlain it was [currently] beyond to power of the [Air] Ministry [to move] in the desired direction of a termination of hostilities.' However, he commented that de Ropp had also informed him that certain top men within the Air Ministry felt that Britain would agree to peace if 'considerable losses on the part of the British Air Force and the related effects on the Empire [occurred]. It is believed then that the views represented by the Air Ministry would have to be taken into account, since the Empire could not permit its air strength to be reduced beyond a certain point.'[36]

At a meeting held a week later de Ropp went further. He informed the Germans that the British Air Ministry, whom he was now clearly claiming to represent, was extremely concerned about the possible politico-economic damage Britain and Germany would sustain if the conflict became a protracted war. This, it was claimed, would lead to 'the decline of the West, of the Aryan race, and the era of the Bolshevization of Europe, including England'. De Ropp's next statements caused the surprised German official to report back to Berlin that the British Air Ministry did not support its own government's policy regarding a continuation of the war, and that the Air Ministry was 'convinced that the war would be decided by the Luftwaffe'. He went on to state that it would 'therefore depend on the Air Ministry to explain to the British government that, in view of the losses it had sustained, it no longer found itself in a position of being able to continue the war'.[37]

What de Ropp had intimated to the Germans was that if Britain suffered a swift military defeat in western Europe, Chamberlain might well loose his nerve and negotiate an end to the hostilities before any further damage to Britain – particularly to her ability to control the Empire – could take place. This idea would germinate in the Führer's mind, and would become a strategy for the next seven months of conflict.

It also saved his life, for on the evening of 8 November 1939 Hitler left the Bürgerbräukeller early in order to travel back to Berlin for a meeting with Charles Bedaux at the Reich Chancellery the following morning.[38] He was thus mightily impressed both by the providence that had saved his life and by all that Bedaux was about to tell him.

With the coming of war the Duke of Windsor had been given the honorary rank of Major-General, and attached to the British Military Mission in Paris. His official role was to conduct a morale-boosting tour of the French front. However, the Chief of the Imperial General Staff, General Sir Edmund Ironside, also gave Windsor other secret orders. He was covertly to observe the strategic details of France's defences, and submit a series of reports to London. The objective of this covert intelligence-gathering operation was to give Britain's military planners a clearer picture of France's defensive strengths and weaknesses, which they could use to formulate tactics to counter any potential German offensive in the west. The Duke's mission was therefore important and very secret. As the head of the British Military Mission in Paris, Major-General Howard Vyse, declared: 'It will be realised that to give the French any sort of inkling of the source of this information would probably compromise the value of any missions which I may ask HRH [the Duke of Windsor] to undertake subsequently.'[39]

Unfortunately, however, Charles Bedaux also gained access to this highly confidential intelligence, apparently with the Duke of Windsor's connivance. This occurred because Windsor believed that a war between France, Britain and Germany was a disaster that would lead to the Soviet domination of Europe; and the Duke hated and feared Communism very much indeed.

Throughout the 1930s the Duke of Windsor – or the Prince of Wales, as he had been then – had been a leading proponent of closer Anglo–German relations. Not the least of his reasons for this stance were his close blood ties to Germany's aristocracy. However, he also saw Fascism in Italy and National Socialism in Germany as bastions against the Communist menace from the east.

There were many high-ranking Britons, even within the upper echelons of government, who shared these views. Indeed, up until the latter 1930s the government's official stance towards the Nazis had been placatory and somewhat accepting of the new political situation in Germany, perceiving National Socialism as a stabilising force in central Europe. It was the evidence of Hitler's increasingly expansionist ambitions – the *Anschluss* with Austria, the Sudetenland crisis in 1938 and the taking of Czechoslovakia in early 1939 – that changed the British government's position.

Throughout the 1920s and thirties the Duke of Windsor, first as Prince of Wales and then briefly as King, received frequent foreign policy briefings from the government. These ended on the day he abdicated in December 1936, and he soon became out of touch with the British government's stance towards the swiftly deteriorating European situation. He could not comprehend why Germany was suddenly considered a threat. If the royal family's intransigence against him had been relaxed, if he had received an occasional briefing on the government's position, he may have understood the reasons for British fears more clearly. As it was, by late 1939 the Duke of Windsor was still thinking in the terms of 1936, when Nazism had been regarded as acceptable.

On Sunday, 3 December 1939, the first hints about the Windsor/ Bedaux relationship began to surface in London when an Intelligence officer named Hopkinson, serving in The Hague, reported on a confidential meeting he had had with a member of Dutch Intelligence called Beck. Hopkinson reported that Beck 'informed me of an incident that might well be of interest to us concerning an American engineer named Charles Bedaux ... On November 9 [the Dutch] M[ilitary] A[ttaché] in Berlin was delivering a note from de With [the Dutch Ambassador] to the Reich Chancellery, when he recognised B[edaux], who he's met before ... but B[edaux] ignored him, got into an official car (a Luftwaffe vehicle) and was driven off.'[40]

From November 1939 to April 1940, Britain's Field Security Police and Military Intelligence watched with mounting concern as Charles Bedaux and the Duke of Windsor resurrected their friendship. Repeatedly throughout this period, as soon as Windsor returned from a tour of the French lines, he would meet Bedaux for dinner, following which Bedaux would take a train to Holland, where he would call on Count Julius Zech-Burkesroda, the German Ambassador in The Hague.[41] A spy at the German Embassy who 'had an opportunity to see the transcribed information that B[edaux] brings verbally' reported to British Intelligence in Holland that the information was 'of the best quality – defence material, strengths, weaknesses, and so on'.[42] In early April 1940, the agent reported that 'Z[ech-Burkesroda] accidentally referred to B[edaux]'s source as "Willi".'[43] 'Willi' was the German codename for the Duke of Windsor.

The information passed on by Bedaux enabled Germany to successfully circumvent France and Britain's defences, aiming for the weak point at Sedan, and almost certainly caused the Allied rout that culminated in Dunkirk.

Throughout this period, the seven months from November 1939 to June 1940, there was an unusual cessation in the high-echelon, Hitler-originated peace moves. Because of the information passed on by de Ropp and Bedaux, Hitler had come to believe that if Germany could inflict a sudden crushing defeat on the Allied armies, the British and French governments' resolve would evaporate, and they would sue for peace. There was only one flaw to this plan, but it was a devastating one. The plan was based on the character of Neville Chamberlain, and the assumption that he would wilt in the face of unrelenting military pressure. Unfortunately for Hitler, in May 1940, dogged by ill-health and the ruination of his credibility as a war leader, Chamberlain resigned, and was replaced as Prime Minister by Winston Churchill.

It immediately became clear that, despite Dunkirk and the withdrawal of British forces from continental Europe, Britain would fight on. And so Hitler's 'top-grade' peaceable attempts began all over again – only this time he would not use dubious Swedes like Dahlerus, or the SS.

On 16 June 1940, two days after the German army entered Paris, and a little more than a week after Britain's Expeditionary Force had managed its miraculous escape from Dunkirk, Hitler met General Juan Vigon, head of the Spanish Supreme Army Defence Council and Minister for Air. Vigon was a man of much influence in Spain's Fascist government, and would play an increasingly important role in the Anglo–German peace discussions of 1940–41. His introduction to the complicated world of peace mediation began with a simple request from Hitler, who informed him that 'the Duke of Windsor would shortly be travelling to Spain, and suggested that Germany would have a substantial interest if the Spanish government could use its influence to have the Duke and his wife delayed long enough for contact to be established once more'.[44]

During the fall of France, the Duke of Windsor had fled south to his home on the French Riviera. When Italy entered the war in June 1940, and it became clear that even here he and the Duchess might not be safe, the Ducal pair, together with a small retinue of servants in a convoy of vehicles, joined the refugee trail for neutral Spain. Here the Duke went straight to Madrid and the new British Ambassador to Spain, his old friend Sir Samuel Hoare.

In Hoare, the Duke of Windsor hoped to find a like-minded political ally, attuned to his concept of a European peace in which a strong Germany acted as a bastion against the danger posed by Soviet Russia. However, there was an element to Hoare's appointment of which, like the vast majority of people, the Duke of Windsor was completely unaware, and which has remained secret until relatively recently.

For sixty years, the impression has been that after Churchill became Prime Minister in May 1940, any prominent dissenter from his belief that the war against Nazism should be fought to the bitter end would be promptly demoted, and often speedily appointed to a posting far from British shores and out of harm's way. This was apparently what had happened to Sir Samuel Hoare, devisor of the notorious Hoare–Laval Pact* and, one would believe, an arch appeaser who was totally out of step with Churchill. Sure enough, within days of Churchill attaining the premiership, Hoare was ousted from his post at the Air Ministry and dispatched with indecent haste to the ambassadorship in Madrid, the existing Ambassador, Sir Maurice Peterson, being relieved of his post to make way for Hoare.

On 13 May, 'Chips' Channon had attended Churchill's first appearance at the House of Commons as Prime Minister. After noting that 'the House today was absurdly dramatic and very Winstonian', he commented: '[I] feel that Winston will not move Rab [Butler], who is "down" and depressed – today. Poor Sam Hoare is out . . .'[45]

The implication was clear: Hoare had been a Churchill opponent during the final catastrophic days of appeasement, and was being banished to Spain, out of Churchill's sight and mind.

---

* Under which Mussolini was allowed to keep a vast slice of territory in Abyssinia – newly invaded by Italy – in exchange for a large, useless tract of Italian Somaliland.

However, as is so often the case in this curious tale, not everything was quite as it seemed. Channon's comments demonstrate that there were two strata within the British government: those in the know, and those – politicians, civil servants, even Ministers – who were not. It has only recently been revealed that Sam Hoare was not banished to Spain, but was sent there to conduct a very important and secret mission for Churchill. It was one for which he would never receive any public credit (although before the war's end Churchill would reward his efforts with a peerage, Hoare becoming Lord Templewood), his name remaining tarnished until his dying day as one of the pre-war appeasers, when in reality he had played an important role in ensuring that Britain survived the Second World War.

Within days of Churchill coming to power, a secret scheme was hatched to encourage newly Fascist Spain to remain neutral. At a briefing attended by Lord Halifax, it was proposed that: 'General Franco's undoubted desire for neutrality should be fortified by a substantial economic bribe ... through some triangular arrangement with Portugal ... financed by us.' Hidden behind this economo-strategic façade, it was further suggested that 'the ostensible purpose of Sir Samuel Hoare's journey should be to review the working of the commercial and financial agreements recently concluded between the United Kingdom and Spain, [by which] sufficient cover would then be provided for any political work which Sir Samuel Hoare is able to do'.[46]

Therefore, while it publicly appeared that Sam Hoare had been banished from British politics to conduct menial commercial work in Spain, in reality he had been placed in extremely sensitive neutral territory to conduct 'political work' for the government. Furthermore, Hoare's new and powerful position was emphasised to Franco's government by the granting to him of the special title 'Ambassador Extraordinary and Plenipotentiary on Special Mission in Spain'. The meaning was obvious. Sir Samuel Hoare was no ordinary Ambassador, but was a direct representative of the British government, with the power to negotiate or take treaty-based decisions.

It was to this 'Ambassador Extraordinary' that the Duke of Windsor now turned; to his undoubted puzzlement, Hoare was not very forthcoming.

That Hoare indulged the Duke during his week-long stay in Madrid in June 1940 is without doubt – he even ordered British Intelligence in Madrid to suspend its activities for the duration of the Duke and Duchess's visit. The Duke spent much of his time busily engaged in private business, contacting Count Zuppo, the Italian Chargé d'Affaires in Madrid, to ensure that his French Riviera villa would be protected by the Italians, and arranging with the German government that his Parisian home would be protected during the occupation. He also made it clear to anyone he thought of importance that the war was a catastrophe of the first degree, and that Germany should not be deflected from her role as a buffer against Soviet Russia.

Despite hints in the Italian press that some form of peace discussions had taken place while the Duke was in Spain, it is unlikely that any took place at this time, for the Duke was only in Madrid for seven days before he decamped to Lisbon at the beginning of July.

The Germans' peaceable attempt in Lisbon would be unsuccessful for several reasons. Firstly, they made the error of believing that the Duke of Windsor was still an influential figure in Britain. Just as the Nazis had pandered to the Duke's ego during his tour of Germany in 1937, so they were still dazzled by the fact that they could so easily gain access to this formerly important person. The key word here is 'formerly'. If they had considered the situation, they would have realised that the Duke of Windsor did not have his government's ear. He may have been Britain's former King, at loose on a continent aflame with war, yet his very freedom of movement, his ability to make loose-lipped statements to anyone who would listen, was as strong an indication as possible that his importance had gone forever. Members of British royalty are invariably apolitical in their conversation, and the Duke of Windsor's freedom to make unguarded and insensitive political comments revealed just how out of touch and unimportant he had become.

Why, then, did the German leadership flock to the Duke like moths to a candle? Ribbentrop should have realised that the British had created a very subtle situation in the Iberian Peninsula. The Duke of Windsor – all glitz and show, and taking the attention – was politically unimportant. It was the starch-collared new Ambassador, Sir Samuel Hoare, who really mattered.

Hoare had the ear of both the Prime Minister and the Foreign Secretary, and despite the illusion of friction between him and Churchill, the experts at the German Foreign Ministry should have realised that Churchill would not have sent someone he did not trust to such a strategically important place as Spain. If Spain joined the Axis, Britain would lose Gibraltar, and thus her access to the Mediterranean, and with it possibly Malta and eventually Egypt as well. It could quickly become a disastrous chain reaction.

There are two reasons why the Germans mistakenly chose to woo the Duke of Windsor. The first is that the main peace protagonist on the German side this time was von Ribbentrop, who was not known for his politico-diplomatic acumen or intellectual capacity. The second is that it was probably felt by some within the German hierarchy that despite his reduced circumstances, the former King still retained his access to the decision-makers within the British government. He was a personal friend of Churchill and had eminent connections in the House of Lords, so he might yet be able to further moves towards a peaceable accord.

A week after the Duke's arrival in Lisbon, Ribbentrop received a telegram from his Ambassador in Madrid, von Stohrer, informing him that the Spanish Foreign Minister, Colonel Beigbeder y Atienza, 'told me today that the Duke of Windsor has asked that a confidential agent be sent to Lisbon to whom he might give a communication for the Foreign Minister [Ribbentrop]'.[47]

Within a few days of receiving von Stohrer's telegram, Ribbentrop summoned Walter Schellenberg, Germany's peace emissary to the British government a mere six months before, to a meeting at the Foreign Ministry. Schellenberg realised that his mission to

Lisbon was not merely to act for the Foreign Ministry when Ribbentrop telephoned Hitler to report on the meeting. As Schellenberg sat listening on an extension to Ribbentrop's call to the Führer, he heard Hitler periodically interject, 'Yes – certainly – agreed.' Towards the end of the call Hitler declared: 'Schellenberg should particularly bear in mind the importance of the Duchess's attitude and try as hard as possible to get her support. She has great influence over the Duke.' After a few more words from Ribbentrop, Schellenberg heard the Führer conclude: 'Good. He has all the authority he needs. Tell him from me that I am relying on him.'[48]

Within a few days Ribbentrop received a message from the German Ambassador in Lisbon, Hoyningen-Huene, who reported: 'The Duke paid tribute to the Führer's desire for peace, which was in complete agreement with his own point of view. He was firmly convinced that if he had been King it would never have come to war.'[49]

Over the course of the next two weeks much dialogue was undertaken with the Duke, primarily through a Portuguese intermediary named Santo y Silva (nicknamed 'The Holy Ghost' by the Intelligence community). At the end of July, Hoyningen-Huene reported:

> The Duke intends to postpone his departure for the Bahamas Islands [where he had been appointed Governor] as long as possible, at least until the beginning of August, in hope of a turn of events favourable to him . . . He is convinced that if he had remained on the throne war would have been avoided, and he characterised himself as a firm supporter of a peaceful arrangement with Germany.[50]

Whilst these negotiations were proceeding in Lisbon, on 19 July 1940 Hitler made a simultaneous effort to placate the British and open the door to peace by giving a speech at the Reichstag that, apart from some sniping at Churchill, was modest in tone and urged that no benefit could be gained from continuing the conflict. The immediate response from Britain was a loudly proclaimed 'No' broadcast by the BBC on all wavelengths.

There have never been any British disclosures of the details of what the Duke of Windsor was negotiating with the German government. The only clues to have surfaced allude to a seven-point plan, which was of sufficient importance for Hess secretly to meet the Duke in the privacy of the Sacramento a Lapa home of the German Ambassador to Portugal, Hoyningen-Huene, on Sunday, 28 July 1940, for a series of secret meetings. Unfortunately, the Duke was spotted by an expatriate Briton living nearby, Mrs Judith Symington, who recalled:

> I was driving home one day when I caught sight of a man in the car in front. I thought I recognised him. 'Isn't that the Duke of Windsor?' I asked, nudging my husband. The car stopped some distance from the German residence, and sure enough, it was he who got out. He was wearing a navy suit, and he walked along the street, up the steps and into the house. Obviously he didn't want to be seen. It wasn't the only occasion, either, that I spotted him going to see Hoyningen-Heune.[51]

Indeed, David Eccles, a high-ranking member of the diplomatic staff at the British Embassy in Lisbon, later recalled that the Duke of Windsor 'spent his days intriguing. We wanted to get him out. We knew once we had him on the other side of the Atlantic, we could watch him.'[52]

On 1 August the Duke, under increasing pressure from the London, departed for the faraway Bahamas. His endeavours to negotiate a peaceable accord proceeded not one jot further, for the British government refused to countenance any more interference from the man who had caused such constitutional turmoil less than four years before. Also, unbeknownst to the Duke of Windsor, peace with Germany was the last thing on Winston Churchill's mind.

Unsuccessful as they were, the Windsor negotiations – for that is undoubtedly what they were – in Lisbon in 1940 played a key role in what was to come. By August 1940, what had taken place in Lisbon would be added to the sum of knowledge gathered by British Intelligence on the Dahlerus Initiative and the Venlo

Incident. This would, to the British government's surprise, be added to significantly by a fourth peaceable move.

This fourth peace offer would emanate directly from Hitler himself, and it would be so secret that the Führer told no one in Germany about it at all, not in the diplomatic service, the government, or the party; not even his inner circle.

This latest attempt to open peace discussions caused considerable consternation in Whitehall. The very few men in the British Foreign Office who knew about it feared that the more impressive these peaceable attempts became, the greater the likelihood that they might dent Lord Halifax's determination to stand by Churchill and his 'no surrender' policy, and the resolve of those in the government who might be tempted to accept a quick fix today, and worry about a Europe dominated by Nazi Germany tomorrow. There was concern that the British government might split between those determined to defeat Germany, and those who might vote against Churchill in the House of Commons for peace, to save Britain from any further suffering. This new initiative came at the height of the Blitz, those crucial weeks of the Battle for Britain, which made the situation all the more worrying.

Hitler's offer on this occasion indicated that he was now approaching peace from a geopolitical, rather than military, point of view, revealing the continuing influence of his long discussions with Karl Haushofer in the 1920s and thirties. It also perhaps indicates that the intellect and the foreign affairs interests of Rudolf Hess lay behind the offer now being proposed to the British Ambassador in Stockholm, Victor Mallet, via Swedish High Court Justice Dr Ekeberg, once again through Hitler's personal legal adviser, Dr Ludwig Weissauer. Mallet duly reported back to London that:

> Hitler, according to his emissary [Weissauer], feels responsible for the future of the white race. He wishes for sincere friendship with England. He wishes for the restoration of peace, but the ground must be prepared: only after such careful preparation can official

discussions begin. Up till then it must be a condition that conversations be quite unofficial and secret . . .

The Führer's basic ideas [are that] economic problems are quite different from those of the past . . . In order to achieve economic evolution one must calculate on a basis of wide territories and consider them as an economic unit. Napoleon had attempted this, but in his day it was not possible because France was not in the centre of Europe and communications were too difficult. Now Germany is in the centre of Europe and has the means of providing communication and transport services.

England and America now have and will naturally continue to have the biggest navies and they need the oceans for their maintenance. Germany has the continent. As for Russia, Weissauer gave the impression that she should be considered as a potential enemy.

Mallet reported Hitler's peace terms as follows:

1 The Empire remains with all the colonies and mandates.
2 The continental supremacy of Germany will not be called into question.
3 All questions concerning the Mediterranean and the French, Belgian and Dutch colonies are open to discussion.
4 Poland. There must be 'a Polish State'.
5 Czechoslovakia must belong to Germany.

Weissauer did not go into detail, but Ekeberg understood by implication that the other European States occupied by Germany [Norway, Holland, Belgium and France] would have their sovereignty restored. It was only owing to the present military situation that Germany now has to continue to occupy them until the peace.

Dr Ekeberg . . . is convinced that Weissauer is very close to Hitler. He thinks he may have been one of the men sent secretly to Moscow last year to prepare underground for the German–Soviet Pact.

Finally, Mallet commented: 'I am naturally rather uncomfortable at having become even to this small extent involved in this mysterious proceeding . . . If you want any more questions asked I can easily get them put by Ekeberg . . .'[53]

Just before dispatching his report to London, Mallet received news that Weissauer had imparted further vital details to Dr Ekeberg concerning Hitler's plans for Europe. He typed an additional note for enclosure with his report, as 'the [diplomatic] bag never left last night after all':

> It appears that last night [Ekeberg] again met Dr Weissauer, and took the opportunity of asking him for more details about Hitler's plans for the occupied countries . . . Weissauer said that Hitler wished to re-establish the sovereignty of all the occupied countries 'auf die dauer' [i.e. on a permanent basis]. He has no interest in the internal affairs of these states. Germany's interest is to prevent a fresh war as Europe needs 100 years of peace. In the economic sphere, however, the occupied countries must be part of the European continent, but with complete political liberty . . .[54]

This latest peaceable attempt by Hitler was by no means insubstantial, especially in the context of the period. By the summer of 1940 Germany had conquered Poland, Norway, Denmark, Luxembourg, Holland, Belgium and France. The British Army had been defeated and only just escaped from Dunkirk, the Battle of Britain was raging in the skies over London and the Home Counties, and Britain's cities were suffering a ferocious blitz both night and day. Nevertheless, on receiving news of Hitler's overtures, the Foreign Secretary's Chief Diplomatic Adviser Sir Robert Vansittart rejected them outright.

Sixty years on, Vansittart's letter to Lord Halifax still makes uncomfortable reading, for it makes it clear that the mandarins of Whitehall had a totally different perception of what Britain was fighting for than did the majority of politicians, or the population at large. Britain's leading civil servants and politicians, including Vansittart and especially Churchill, had viewed Germany – and not particularly Nazism – as a threat for a very long time. This emanated from the nineteenth-century German policy of 'Drang *nach Osten*', which came with the fall of the Ottoman Empire, when Moltke and later the Kaiser became convinced that Germany could fill the resultant power-vacuum. In the eyes of men like Vansittart, Britain had been constantly pitted against German efforts to encroach into the Middle and Near East – 'the German Reich concept' – ever since the 1890s. Now, with the Nazis at the helm, the dangers were far greater.

Vansittart's letter read:

> Secretary of State. URGENT.
>
> I hope that you will instruct Mr. Mallet that he is on no account to meet Dr. Weissauer. The future of civilisation is at stake. It is a question of we or they now, and either the German Reich or this country has got to go under, and not only under, but right under. I believe it will be the German Reich. This is a very different thing from saying that Germany has got to go under; but the German Reich and the Reich idea have been the curse of the world for 75 years, and if we do not stop it this time, we never shall, and they will stop us. The enemy is the German Reich and not merely Nazism, and those who have not yet learned this lesson have learned nothing whatsoever, and would let us in for a sixth war even if we survive the fifth. I would far sooner take my chances of surviving the fifth. All possibility of compromise has now gone by, and it has got to be a fight to the finish, and to a real finish.
>
> I trust that Mr Mallet will get the most categorical instructions. We have had much more than enough of Dahlerus, Goerdeler,* Weissauer and company.[55]

Despite Vansittart's vehement rejection of any peace proposal emanating from Berlin, Weissauer's secret offer was still considered of sufficient importance for Churchill to put it, by ciphered telegram, before the heads of government of Canada, Australia and New Zealand, and the High Commissioner of the Union of South

---

* Carl Goerdeler, Lord Mayor of Leipzig, had unsuccessfully attempted low-echelon peace mediation in 1939.

Africa. Hitler's proposal was eventually rejected on the grounds that Germany's forces would have to be withdrawn from all occupied territory *before* Britain was prepared to discuss peace – a demand that Hitler was sure to reject.

It was at this point that Hitler's repeated peace moves over twelve months of war came under the scrutiny of British Intelligence. They were soon perceived as evidence of a weakness in the German Führer that might be exploited.

In mid-August 1940, Reginald 'Rex' Leeper, the head of Special Operations 1 (SO1), a branch of Britain's newest weapon, the Special Operations Executive (SOE), wrote a letter to Hugh Gaitskell, then a civil servant at the Ministry of Economic Warfare. The letter was primarily to apologise for failing to send Gaitskell the minutes of a previous meeting. However, Leeper went on to comment conversationally:

> You may be interested to know that following Ingrams' B[lack] P[ropaganda] suggestion, I took the idea to the P[rime] M[inister] who felt the German Leadership was now ripe for exploitation. I am sure the key to this B.P. lies within [Hitler's] recent attempts to find an accord. Ingrams and Crossman are going to look into this idea as any below the belt Ops we can initiate at this critical time can only help.[56]

Within a year, Leeper's seed of an idea would germinate into one of the most successful and best-kept British Intelligence secrets of the Second World War. It was an operation that would grow to encompass the top men of SO1, four Cabinet Ministers, two Ambassadors, and the Prime Minister. It would result in the complete ruination of Hitler's war strategy, causing him to make the fatal blunder that would cost him the war. It would also, incidentally, result in one of the strangest events of the Second World War – the unexpected arrival of Rudolf Hess on British soil in May 1941.

Destiny, however, can turn on a very small pivot indeed, and by an incredible turn of good fortune Leeper's SO1 just happened to possess a crucial asset that would give them access directly into the Nazi leadership's foreign affairs structure. With the coming of war, an unremarkable City of London stockbroker had been recruited to become SOE's Director of Finance and Administration. He was also by coincidence one of the few men in Britain who could communicate personally with Albrecht Haushofer in such a manner that the German foreign affairs adviser would never suspect it was anything but genuine. Through Haushofer, Leeper and his men at SO1 realised, they could penetrate the German leadership's inner sanctum – the Führer, Adolf Hitler, and his deputy, Rudolf Hess. And their objective would not be peace.

CHAPTER 3

Flag-Waving

The summer of 1940 was to be a pivotal moment in the Second World War. It was a time which could have seen Britain, assailed on all fronts by the overwhelming might of Germany's armed forces, forced to accept a bitter armistice that left Hitler master of Europe. The Battle of the Atlantic was beginning to bite; Norway, Denmark, Holland, Luxembourg, Belgium and France had all fallen; and Britain's armed forces, having suffered a severe mauling, had been forced to flee the continent in an armada of little ships.

Within weeks of Dunkirk, once the Luftwaffe's support infrastructure had moved up to occupy French airfields, Operation Adlerangriffe (Eagle-raids) had been launched, dispatching wave after wave of Stukas, Heinkel 111s and Junker 88s to obliterate all the RAF's bases in the south of England. This was clearly a prelude to invasion, and many predicted Britain's defeat within not months, but weeks. The forecasters of impending disaster were not limited to the foreign press, diplomats or panicky civilians, but included some of the top men within the War Cabinet itself. This was a cause of as much concern to Churchill as the conduct of the war itself.

Churchill was the constitutionally appointed leader of a democratic country, the head of a coalition government assembled in a time of exceptional peril. If events went badly, he himself was not immune to the vagaries of politics. Had he ever lost a vote of confidence in the House of Commons – and he was to survive several during the war – he could have found himself ousted from power, his premiership taken by someone who might be more inclined to reach a deal with Hitler and negotiate Britain out of the war. The Nazis, who were after all politicians too, realised this as well.

With this political situation taken into consideration, alongside Hitler's attempts to negotiate a peace and disentangle Germany's forces from a war with the British he did not want, it is now possible to reappraise the events of the summer of 1940, and to gain a clearer perspective on what was really taking place.

The Battle of Britain was primarily Germany's attempt to destroy Britain's air cover. To accomplish this the Luftwaffe began by concentrating its efforts upon establishing complete 'local air superiority over the straits of Dover', before quickly moving on to the next phase of the operation, attacking 'Fighter Command's airfields ... with the intention of crippling it on the ground, or provoking it into a major battle in which it would be destroyed in the air'.[1] However, just at the moment when this strategy seemed about to work, the carefully laid plans for the German air campaign against Britain were suddenly abandoned. Much to Fighter Command's relief, and British Intelligence's puzzlement, the Luftwaffe suddenly switched to attacking civilian targets such as London and other major cities.

One factor behind this change in German tactics, which kept Fighter Command operational, was almost certainly Hitler's response to Britain's night bombing of German cities, including Berlin.[2] However, that was not the entire story. It is no coincidence that the German change of strategy occurred at the very moment when Dr Ludwig Weissauer's secret attempt to negotiate peace with the British government began to flounder.

The Luftwaffe's bombing of Britain's ports, airports, RAF airfields and rail and road links was a strategic military campaign aimed at establishing complete air superiority and obliterating the enemy's infrastructure. The switch to bombing London and Britain's other major cities, however, can only have been intended to create terror, for it served little strategic purpose, save murder, mayhem and the destruction of civilian morale. The objective of such a strategy was to make the price of continuing the war exceedingly high for Britain's coalition government. A price, it was hoped, that it might think twice before paying. Hitler, therefore, changed the objectives of the Luftwaffe's campaign in an attempt to force the British government to the negotiating table. He wished to focus British political minds on his latest peace initiative, as proposed in Sweden by his own private emissary, Dr Ludwig Weissauer.

However, Hitler's hopes that such a terror campaign would aid his cause were sorely disappointed, for he completely failed to realise that Britain's top politicians were not in talking mood. Winston Churchill, with a keen sense of history and the moment, correctly discerned that if the fight against Nazism and the German 'Reich idea'[3] was to be won, it had to be fought here and now. Cutting a deal with Hitler, however tempting the offer, would almost certainly only postpone an eventual European conflict for a few years, by which time Germany would have become a continental superpower that Britain and the other democracies of western Europe would stand little chance of resisting. Thus, however hazardous the road of continued war against Nazi Germany was in the summer of 1940, there was no option. Churchill knew that if European democracy was ever to flourish again, the war must continue, whatever the immediate collateral damage or the danger of defeat.

The British government was therefore not at all receptive to Hitler's latest covert appeals for peace. Instead of forcing the British government to the negotiating table, the Luftwaffe's campaign of creating civilian terror only served to press home the dangers of appeasing German militarism.

Hitler had his own problems too, which by the summer of 1940 he was becoming increasingly mindful of.

In early June, Stalin took the opportunity of Germany's west European commitments to pour Russian troops into the Baltic states of Lithuania, Latvia and Estonia. This caused Hitler immediate concerns about Germany's eastern defences, where a mere ten German divisions were outnumbered ten to one by the Russians. Then, at the end of June, Stalin had moved again. This time he demanded that Romania restore Bessarabia and northern Bukovina, which had been Russian territory prior to 1918, to Soviet ownership. The Romanian government, given just twenty-four hours to answer, yielded, and Stalin's forces immediately swarmed into northern Romania to take possession of the two regions. This placed the Russians ominously close to the Baku oilfields, on which Hitler had been counting for his own supply.[4] Extremely concerned by this latest development, Hitler asked his Chief of General Staff, General Alfred Jodl, what would happen if a Russo–German conflict ensued over the oilfields. Jodl's answer resulted in an order to immediately dispatch two full armoured divisions and another ten infantry divisions to the east, more than doubling the German forces in the region.

By the beginning of September 1940 Germany had been committed to war for almost exactly a year. German forces had successfully overcome all the west European democratic nations with the exception of Britain, and presently occupied all of western Europe from the Arctic Circle to the Pyrenees, with the exception of Vichy France. But now an eastern war of conquest beckoned. Hitler did not want his objective of German expansion eastward to be jeopardised by a Russian offensive that would throw all his carefully worked-out plans into disarray. He was therefore highly motivated to find a politico-diplomatic solution that would bring an end to Germany's war with Britain.

It was at this point that a unique situation began to manifest itself, weaving an intricate web about the German Führer.

It is a golden rule of diplomacy never to allow your opponent to become aware of your true plans, or to know what you fear most, for it can become a very effective weapon to hold over you. But Adolf Hitler was not an expert diplomat, and his independent style of leadership had led him into several grave blunders in his dealings with Britain.

Firstly, he had openly revealed that Germany intended to expand eastward, even telling the head of Britain's Air Intelligence, Group Captain Freddy Winterbotham, during a frank discussion in 1934, that Germany intended one day to 'take Russia and together [with Britain] . . . decide the policy for China and the Far East'. He had also declared: 'All we ask is that Britain should be content to look after her empire and not interfere with Germany's plans for expansion.'[5] Thus Britain was aware of the Führer's plans even before he made his first expansionist moves in Europe.

Hitler's second mistake lay within his peaceable attempts. During his latest appeal he had confided many of his innermost thoughts to Ludwig Weissauer, believing that the British would regard this as a sign of sincerity, and would therefore be more inclined to see reason and negotiate a truce. But it only served to make British Intelligence more aware of the Führer's personality, and his aims, hopes and fears. Worse yet, he had told Weissauer that only two men in Germany knew of this latest appeal, as he wanted to keep it completely secret. This told the British a great deal. They now knew that the Führer of Germany, with the vast panoply of experts and advisers at his disposal, in addition to his circle of Nazi associates and Ministers, and able to call upon a vast range of specialists on international law, economics and diplomacy, had – through fear of losing face if he were rebuffed – reduced himself to a lone and far from expert individual pitted against another nation's most sophisticated politico-diplomatic minds.

Thus Adolf Hitler was alone and vulnerable, perhaps able to call on the advice only of one or two very close and trusted friends, such as Rudolf Hess and Albrecht Haushofer. The situation was, as Rex Leeper termed it, 'ripe for exploitation'.[6]

On the last day of August 1940, Rudolf Hess visited his old mentor, Professor Karl Haushofer. That Hess was aware of Hitler's desire to negotiate Britain out of the war as a prelude to a German campaign of eastern expansion is not in doubt. Indeed, the Deputy-Führer had helped formulate many of those plans, and he had certainly been party to the high-echelon discussions that had determined Germany's overall war strategy. In addition to this, Hess knew of Hitler's top-secret efforts to negotiate an end of the war with Britain. Indeed, Whitehall had been intrigued to learn from

Victor Mallet not only that 'Weissauer was acting at the instigation of Hitler in person', but that 'only two men in Germany knew of his mission'.[7]

Given Hitler's obsessive fear of losing face, he is unlikely to have spoken to Ribbentrop, Göring or Himmler about this matter. He would, however, have had few qualms about taking his old friend 'Rudi' Hess into his confidence. Hess had been a trusted colleague for twenty years, he was educated in foreign affairs, and he understood the intricacies of politico-diplomatic negotiations. He was also extremely knowledgeable about the many hurdles that lay in the path of placating Britain. However, perhaps Hess's most important virtues from Hitler's point of view lay in the facts that he was almost the only top Nazi who was trusted by Professor Karl Haushofer, and that he would give realistic advice without fear of reprisal for stating the truth, however unpalatable that truth might be.

As it became clear that the Weissauer initiative was not going to succeed, a decision seems to have been taken between Hitler and Hess that a fresh approach now had to be taken. They had spent a year floundering between one failed peaceable attempt and the next. What they needed was to proceed with care under the expert guidance of Karl and Albrecht Haushofer.

Following his meeting with Hess over the weekend of 31 August and 1 September 1940, the excited Professor Haushofer immediately sat down to write to his son, who was in Vienna. After some brief family chit-chat, the elderly Haushofer immediately got down to business and told Albrecht about his recent most interesting discussion: '. . . with Tomo [Haushofer's code name for Hess] from 5:00 o'clock in the afternoon until 2:00 o'clock in the morning, which included a 3-hour walk in the Grunwalder Forest, at which we conversed a good deal about serious matters. I have really got to tell you about part of it now.'[8] Haushofer then hinted that a subtle but important shift had taken place in Hitler's approach to seeking peace with the British:

As you know, everything is so prepared for a very hard and severe attack on the island in question [Britain] that the highest ranking person [Hitler] only has to push a button to set it off. But before this decision . . . the thought once more occurs as to whether there is really no way of stopping something which would have such infinitely momentous consequences. There is a line of reasoning in connection with this which I must absolutely pass on to you because it was obviously communicated to me with this intention.

Haushofer went on reveal that Hess had asked him: 'Do you . . . see no way in which such possibilities [for peace] could be discussed at a third place [neutral territory] with a middle man, possibly the old Ian Hamilton or the other Hamilton?' He replied that 'there would perhaps have been an excellent opportunity for this in Lisbon at the Centennial [celebrations on 2 June 1940], if, instead of harmless figureheads, it had been possible to send well-disguised political persons there'.[9]

Haushofer's comments are very revealing. The first possible contact, General Sir Ian Hamilton, had not only been a very close friend of Churchill's since the 1900s, but had invited Hess to stay with him in Britain in the summer of 1939, just prior to the outbreak of war. 'The other Hamilton' was Albrecht's close friend Lord Clydesdale, now the Duke of Hamilton, who was politically and socially acquainted with many of Britain's leading men, from Lord Halifax and Winston Churchill to King George VI.

Haushofer went on to expand upon what Hess had told him, before telling Albrecht: 'that the larger stage [has] suddenly called for you again does not astonish me. Indeed Tomo, too, on Saturday and Sunday expressed a wish to the same effect.' The elder Haushofer now became very discreet, almost resorting to code:

As little as you did I desire to bear the responsibilities for decisions which are historically very important. But the time is certainly not wasted if it brought you a wonderful flight over the Salzkammergut directly over the Traunstein, close to the Schafberg, and an unexpected reunion with the 'Butzelware'.

As the author of three Roman plays, the political subject matter of this conference must have moved you very strongly from the human angle – I do not mean like 2 years ago; but, like a year ago, you would have been interested in the strange show, the curious behaviour [*Gebahren*] – which, being an old-fashioned person, I spell with an 'h', and, in your place, even this year, I would have gone to Halls somewhat oftener.[10]

To understand what Haushofer was carefully attempting to impart to his son is not easy. The Haushofers had long realised that it was necessary to be extremely discreet in Nazi Germany, for an unguarded comment picked up by the postal censors or the Gestapo could be very dangerous indeed, perhaps fatally so. They had therefore invented a code for themselves to protect their correspondence from unwanted attention.

At its most basic level, the Haushofers gave all the leading Nazis Japanese code-names: Hitler became 'O'Daijin', meaning Master Great Spirit; Hess became 'Tomodachi', shortened to 'Tomo', meaning 'friend'; and Ribbentrop became 'Fukon', which translates literally as 'I will not deviate' – a private Haushofer joke at the expense of the Foreign Minister's ineffectual posturing on the world stage. Beyond this level, the code became considerably more complicated, and knowledge about the two men's backgrounds is often required to fathom out what was being communicated.

To take, for example, Karl's comment that Albrecht would soon be taking a journey 'over the Salzkammergut directly over the Traunstein, close to the Schafberg, and an unexpected reunion with the "Butzelware" '. If their co-ordinates are plotted on a map, Traunstein, the Salzkammergut, and the mountain known as Schafberg all triangulate in a small fifty-square-mile region in the vicinity of Salzburg – just to the north of Berchtesgaden.

'*Butzelware*' is a little more difficult to fathom out, but if we take note of Karl's comment that he is an old-fashioned sort of person who spells with an 'h', something rather interesting occurs. Pronounced phonetically, and with the inclusion of an 'h', '*Butzelware*' becomes '*Botselwahr*'. In an old German dictionary published in Stuttgart in 1893, '*Bote*' means messenger, and '*wahr*' means 'faithful' or 'genuine'. Thus Albrecht was being discreetly told to return for a meeting near Berchtesgaden, for an 'unexpected reunion' with the genuine/faithful messenger – someone who could be trusted to deliver a truthful message. Karl Haushofer was in effect telling his son that the Führer finally wanted a genuine peace with the British, and that he should go to a meeting near Berchtesgaden with Hess to give his assistance.

The last paragraph of Haushofer's letter, taken in the light of the foregoing, becomes of paramount interest, referring as it does to Albrecht's authorship of 'three Roman plays'. In the 1930s Albrecht had written a rather complicated trilogy of five-act plays on themes from Roman history: *Scipio*, *Sulla* and *Augustus*. All three of the subjects were Roman politicians who were skilled negotiators and manipulators of foreign policy. It is known that Albrecht saw himself as being very much in the mould of Scipio (c.243–183 BC), the patrician Roman who became Consul and ended the Second Punic War. Hitler himself also made comparisons between Nazi Germany and ancient Rome. National Socialism, he claimed, was heralding in a new age, an end to old nations created by the Dark Ages and medieval conflict. A new world of empire, with the Reich taking the predominant place in Europe, emulating the power and majesty of Rome. Thus in Albrecht's eyes he would be representing an empire, burdened with the heavy responsibility of negotiating with enemy powers to end a second major war.

Finally, there is Karl's statement that 'the political subject matter of this conference must have moved you very strongly from the human angle – I do not mean like 2 years ago; but, like a year ago'. This is intended to make Albrecht understand that the matter Karl had discussed with Hess was not that of two years before – when Albrecht had been part of the German negotiating team at Munich intent on tearing the Sudetenland from Czechoslovakia – but rather 'like a year ago'. He was thus drawing his son's attention to the previous summer, of 1939, when Albrecht had tried so hard to avert war with Britain by sending his letter to Lord Clydesdale, who had since become the Duke of Hamilton.

Therefore, Albrecht was being told in the plainest possible language, given the circumstances, that his father's meeting with Hess had been concerned with negotiating a peace with Britain, that Albrecht was required for a meeting with the Reich's high and mighty, and that he would be required to fulfil a key role, in the vein of Scipio. He would become the Führer's quasi-diplomatic emissary for peace.

Within a few days of receiving his father's letter, Albrecht Haushofer was back in southern Germany for a confidential meeting with Hess. Albrecht talked frankly to the Deputy-Führer about the problems that now faced any German negotiator who wished to persuade the British to enter peace negotiations. Albrecht's notes of this discussion, which took place on Sunday, 8 September 1940, are titled 'Are there still Possibilities of a German–English Peace?'

Albrecht didn't pull any punches, and bluntly told Hess that if a solution to the conflict was to be found, 'it was necessary to realise that not only Jews and Freemasons, but practically all Englishmen who mattered, regarded a treaty signed by the Führer as a worthless scrap of paper'.

That Albrecht felt emboldened to talk so frankly – and, more importantly, that Hess was receptive to such plain speaking – is a clear sign of the seriousness Hess attributed to attaining peace, to finding some way of disengaging Germany from its unwanted conflict with Britain. The timing of this meeting was also extremely important, coming as it did within days of Weissauer's peaceable attempt in Sweden being firmly rebuffed. It is thus a clear indication that Hitler, having spent a year in ineffectual secret peace manoeuvres, finally recognised that if he were to succeed in attaining peace, his leading expert on England and the English was needed, together with a strategy considerably more subtle than the crude attempts that had been made hitherto.

Not unnaturally, Hess was somewhat taken aback by Albrecht's forthright comments about his Führer. Yet he realised that what was being said was very important. He did not become angry, nor did he attempt to defend Hitler's actions. Instead, he asked his old friend why Hitler was held in such disdain and distrust by the British.

Albrecht counted off Germany's ten-year treaty with Poland, the 1939 Non-Aggression Pact with Denmark, and, most importantly of all, the Munich Agreement. Hitler had reneged on every single one of these treaties. Endeavouring to make Hess understand the extent of Britain's distrust of Germany, Albrecht declared: 'What guarantee [does] England have that a new treaty would not be broken again once it suited us? It must be realised that ... in the Anglo-Saxon world, the Führer is regarded as Satan's representative on earth, and has to be fought. If the worst came to the worst, the English would rather transfer their whole Empire bit by bit to the Americans than sign a peace that left to National Socialist Germany the mastery of Europe.'[11]

Above all, Albrecht explained, it came down to feelings of self-preservation and national security. Just as Germans feared having 'no security as long as provision is not made that the Atlantic gateway of Europe from Gibraltar to Narvik [in Norway] are free of any possible blockade i.e. that there must be no English fleet ... [so the British] under the same condition, argue [they] have no security as long as anywhere within a radius of 2,000 kilometres from London there is a plane that [they] do not control. i.e. there must be no German air force'.[12] Enthusiastically, if perhaps with a degree of utopian idealism, Albrecht went on to declare: 'There is only one way out of this dilemma: friendship intensified to fusion, with a joint fleet, a joint air force, and joint defence of possessions in the world – just what the English are now about to conclude with the United States.'

At this point Hess, trying to be level-headed and to keep up with all his brilliant friend was telling him, asked why the British were prepared to seek a relationship with America, rather than with Germany.

Albrecht considered Hess's question for a moment, realising he would have to express his answer in a very strong fashion to impress upon Hess the seriousness of his argument. Finally he replied:

Roosevelt is a man, and [he] represents a *Weltanschauung* [a philosophy and ideology] and a way of life that the Englishman thinks he understands, to which he can become accustomed, even where it does not seem to be to his liking. Perhaps he fools himself, but at any rate, that is what he believes. A man like Churchill – himself half American – is convinced of it. Hitler, however, seems to the Englishmen the incarnation of all he hates, what he has fought against for centuries – this feeling grips the worker no less than the plutocrats. In fact, I am of the opinion that those Englishmen who have property to lose – that is, precisely those portions of the plutocracy that count – are those who would be readiest to talk peace. But even they regard a peace only as an armistice.[13]

Hess now asked Albrecht whether he was of the opinion that the prior peace approaches might have failed because the right language had not been used.

Albrecht saw that Hess was beginning to understand what he was saying – that merely emphasising the high-level origin of peace offers, or making those offers extraordinarily attractive, was not enough. The whole endeavour required very careful consideration and planning, and, most important of all, needed to be conducted through the best intermediaries that could be found. He replied: 'To be sure – if certain persons [primarily meaning Ribbentrop], whom we both know well, were meant by this statement – then certainly the wrong language had been used.'

Hess then asked bluntly why the English distrusted Ribbentrop.

'In the eyes of the English,' Albrecht explained, 'Herr R[ibbentrop], like some other personages, played . . . the same role as Duff Cooper, Eden, and Churchill in the eyes of the Germans. In the case of R[ibbentrop] there was also the conviction . . . that – from completely biased motives – he had informed the Führer wrongly about England and that he personally bore an unusually large share of the responsibility for the outbreak of the war.' However, Albrecht stressed 'the fact that the rejection of peace feelers by England was today due not so much to persons as to the fundamental outlook'.[14]

Who on the British side, Hess asked, did Albrecht think might be amenable to negotiations, might still have a relatively open mind, and might listen to a reasonable offer?

After considering his answer, Albrecht eventually replied that he believed the initial contact should be a diplomat, amongst whose ranks several of his acquaintances sprang to mind. Firstly, he suggested his old friend Owen St Clair O'Malley, Britain's Ambassador in Budapest, 'the former Head of the South-Eastern Department of the Foreign Office, a clever person in the higher echelons of officialdom, but perhaps without influence precisely because of his former friendliness to Germany'.

Another, whom Albrecht suggested was 'most promising', was Britain's Ambassador to Washington, Lord Lothian, 'with whom I have had a close personal connection for years, who as a member of the highest aristocracy and at the same time as a person of independent mind, is perhaps best in a position to undertake a bold step – provided that he could be convinced that even a bad and uncertain peace would be better than the continuance of the war'.

Yet the person Hess and Albrecht eventually selected was not perhaps the most obviously suitable. He was, however, easily accessible, was situated in a neutral European country, and his credentials would immediately be understood by those top British politicians capable of reading between the lines. Albrecht suggested Sir Samuel Hoare, 'who is half-shelved and half on watch in Madrid, whom I do not know well personally, but to whom I can at any time open a personal path'.[15]

Finally, Albrecht suggested one more possibly useful person, his own best contact in the British hierarchy, but a man who had little interest in pandering to Nazi peaceable approaches. Unable to resist using the most eminent of his connections, Albrecht proposed 'the closest of my English friends: the young Duke of Hamilton, who has access at all times to all important persons in London, even to Churchill and the King'.[16]

At the end of their two-hour discussion, Albrecht recorded: 'The upshot of the conversation was H[ess]'s statement that he would consider the whole matter thoroughly once more and send me word in case I was to take steps. For this extremely ticklish case, and in the event that I might possibly have to make a trip alone – I asked for very precise directives from the highest authority.'[17]

For Albrecht Haushofer to have asked Germany's Deputy-Führer for 'precise directives from the highest authority' was an unusual request. Albrecht's notes are very clear, and not prone to inaccuracy. They are therefore a reliable record of some of the most confidential discussions ever to take place in Germany on the subject of foreign affairs and diplomacy. If he had requested a directive from Hess, he would have said so. Therefore he must have asked for 'precise directives' from Adolf Hitler himself.

This is supported by Albrecht's final comment that 'from the whole conversation I had the strong impression that it was not conducted without prior knowledge of the Führer, and that I probably would not hear any more about the matter unless a new understanding had been reached between him and his Deputy'.[18]

However, Albrecht was to hear more about Hess and Hitler's desire for peace very quickly. When his father had written to him the previous week to reveal his recent meeting with Hess, and to summon Albrecht back to Germany, he had also imparted an extraordinary piece of news. By some miraculous means in time of war, Karl Haushofer had just heard from a very old acquaintance living in Britain:

> it seems to me a stroke of fate that our friend, Misses [sic] V. R[oberts], evidently, though after long delay, finally found a way of sending a note with cordial and gracious words of good wishes not only for your mother, but also for Heinz and me, and added the address. Address your reply to: Miss V. Roberts, c/o Postbox 506, Lisbon, Portugal . . .
>
> I have the feeling that no good possibility should be overlooked; at least it should be well considered.[19]

Even as Albrecht was travelling home from his meeting with Hess, the Deputy-Führer was writing his account of it to his old

Professor. The matter of Mrs Roberts had undoubtedly also been discussed, for Hess wrote: 'Under no condition must we disregard the contact or allow it to die aborning. I consider it best for you or Albrecht to write to the old lady, who is a friend of your family, suggesting that she try to ask Albrecht's friend whether he would be prepared if necessary to come to the neutral country in which she resides, or at any rate has an address through which she can be reached, just to talk to Albrecht.'

Finally, the Deputy-Führer added hopefully: 'Meanwhile, let's both keep our fingers crossed. Should success be the fate of the enterprise, then the oracle given to you with regard to the month of August would yet be fulfilled, since the name of the young friend and the old lady friend of your family occurred to you during our quiet walk on the last day of that month. With best regards to you and Martha.'[20]

Despite this optimism, Hess and Haushofer's peaceable aspirations were already undermined, for Mrs Violet Roberts' apparently innocuous and well-meaning letter was nothing of the sort, and her reply address – 'Postbox 506, Lisbon' – although officially registered to Thomas Cook's travel, was in fact a drop address used by British Intelligence operating out of the British Embassy in Portugal. Added to this, Thomas Cook ran British Intelligence's Lisbon agency during the war, and its secretarial staff serviced SO1.[21]

It is widely acknowledged that British Intelligence's contribution to the war effort from September 1939 until the autumn of 1940 was largely ineffectual, and in several key areas its presence virtually non-existent. This resulted partly from the British government's complacency and a chronic underfunding of intelligence since the end of the First World War, partly from the appointment of various directors who were out of tune with the demands of modern intelligence, and partly from the virtual destruction of the SIS's presence in western Europe after the Venlo Incident in November 1939.

During the First World War Britain's Secret Intelligence Service had fulfilled an important role, reflected by its very substantial budget, which in 1918 amounted to nearly £250,000 per annum. However, after the Armistice the British government rewarded SIS's considerable contribution to the war effort by slashing its budget to the bare bone. In 1920 the SIS received £125,000, yet the Foreign Office proposed to reduce this further, to a mere £65,000.[22] In 1922, after much acrimonious wrangling, the annual budget was eventually set at £90,000. Throughout the 1920s and thirties SIS repeatedly petitioned to have its budget increased, but their pleas for realistic funding largely fell on deaf ears. As a result the Passport Control Officer and Z Network system, first devised in the 1900s, had by 1939 become virtually obsolete. This antiquated system had been quite sufficient against the Kaiser's men in those far-off days of the *belle époque*, but it was totally inadequate against the modernised Abwehr and Sicherheitsdienst, granted vast yearly budgets by the Nazis, who recognised the importance of intelligence.

By the latter 1930s SIS realised that a thorough overhaul of its entire intelligence-gathering system was vital – but that would cost money. In the end, and symptomatic of the malaise that dogged Britain at the time, the money was eventually found, but from a most unorthodox source. SIS, in a manner more akin to the twenty-first century than the 1930s, looked to the private sector to make up its funding shortfall.

In 1938, an SIS officer named Major Lawrence Grand was ordered to set up a new department that would not only supersede the old Passport Control Officer and Z Network, but would have the capability to undertake sabotage against an enemy. To create such an organisation required money that SIS did not possess; the problem was solved when an acquaintance of Grand's, an American entrepreneur named Chester Beatty, offered financial assistance. Beatty's company, the Selection Trust Group, owned vast mining interests worldwide, and had just acquired a mine in Serbia called Trepca, one of the richest mineral deposits in Europe.

In exchange for 'technical assistance' (which included intelligence on the political situation in Yugoslavia, for the Balkans was as ever a boiling-pot of discontent), Beatty began to make substantial investments in Lawrence Grand's new project.[23] Grand was delighted, for he now had the means to fund his new organisation, the remit of which was officially designated as intelligence and sabotage in enemy territory. Its name was Section D – 'D' for destruction.

However, Grand's unusual source of finance was soon to fall foul of the British government officials responsible for intelligence, for the mine at Trepca had only one real customer, a mystery buyer who took over 70 per cent of all its production. In the late autumn of 1939, as a result of enquiries by the British Embassy in Belgrade and an investigation by the Ministry of Economic Warfare, it was discovered that virtually Trepca's entire production of zinc and lead – munitions minerals – was, after shipment via Thessalonika to Antwerp, ending up in the Ruhr. Trepca's output was effectively supporting the German war effort.[24]

In the resultant outcry, Section D was stripped from SIS in the spring of 1940 and attached to Britain's newest secret service organisation, the Special Operations Executive – SOE. Lawrence Grand, despite his innocence, paid a high penalty. With a complete disregard for his good intentions under the constraints of inadequate funding, his loyalty was questioned, and he was soon dispatched to distant India, where he was stationed at a radio listening post near the Himalayas for the duration of the war.

Despite its curious and unconventional origins, Section D was to become a key component of SOE, being closely identified with SOE's sabotage role. SIS, for its part, was extremely angry to have lost this new and very useful tool, and the situation would breed much enmity between the two organisations throughout the war years.

SOE was a very remarkable organisation, and from its inception was destined to become controversial. Created by the War Cabinet in July 1940, and known ever since as being charged by Churchill with the task of 'setting Europe ablaze', it was, for the first year of its existence, really two organisations, each having a very different role.

One side, designated Special Operations 2, or SO2 for short, was the cloak-and-dagger unit charged with sabotage and fomenting revolt, perilously parachuting undercover agents into occupied Europe to set up resistance and sabotage cells. It was created out of an amalgamation of Lawrence Grand's Section D and the MI(R), the Military Intelligence directorate of the War Office.

The other side, operating out of offices in Electra House, on London's Embankment, was altogether more sinister, and was so secret that few people ever got to know about it. This unit, initially known as Department EH, was soon designated Special Operations 1, or SO1. It was steeped in the art of psychological warfare, involving enemy subversion through covert or 'black' propaganda, and had a brief to conduct 'political warfare' by whatever means available. SO1 became so important to Britain's war effort that it was soon removed from the dangers of the blitz to Woburn Abbey, the country seat of the Duke of Bedford, deep in the Bedfordshire countryside.

It is important to know a little about SOE's creation, for within the political infighting at its birth lay the seeds of much political animosity, which was to increase as its deception operation against Hitler progressed.

Many Labour members of Britain's wartime coalition government were extremely suspicious of MI5 and SIS, and the creation and control of any new intelligence service appeared to them a new cause for distrust. Labour's suspicion of British Intelligence dated back to the Zinoviev affair of 1924, when a forged letter purporting to be signed by Soviet Politburo member Grigori Zinoviev contributed to the general election defeat of Ramsay MacDonald's Labour government. The mistrust had been strengthened by the surveillance of trade unions and left-wing politicians carried out by the security services in the 1930s. Indeed, a former head of MI5, Sir Vernon Kell, had even threatened to destroy all MI5's files rather than let them fall into the hands of a Labour government. In 1940 many Labour politicians believed that MI5 and SIS had to some extent been compromised by their acceptance of a strong Germany as a bulwark against Soviet Russia, and their dealings with Nazi Party officials. Add to this the fact that in the summer of 1940 MI5 came under the remit of the Home Secretary, Sir John Anderson, and SIS under that of the Foreign Secretary, Lord Halifax, both Conservatives, and it is understandable that the Labour Party wanted SOE be placed under a Labour Minister. This led to an impasse, for Churchill wanted to place his own man, Lord Swinton, a long-time colleague and fellow-thinker who had supported him during his 'wilderness years' and over the call for rearmament in the 1930s, in charge of SOE. Swinton was another Conservative.

The situation was further complicated by the fact that one of the Labour candidates to take charge of SOE was Hugh Dalton, Minister of Economic Warfare and a close colleague of the party leader, Clement Attlee. Dalton, an outstanding economist once described as 'tall and broad . . . [whose] head rose in a mighty bald dome',[25] was convinced that SOE would complement his Ministry very nicely, and that it could become a very effective tool in the war against Germany. He forcefully petitioned Attlee to oppose Churchill's plan to place SOE under Swinton. After much disagreement, and against Churchill's wishes, Dalton eventually won the post of Minister for SOE.

However, Dalton's initial enthusiasm for SOE would turn to unease when he discovered exactly what the organisation's objectives were. Within a year of obtaining his brand-new Ministry, Dalton would fall from power with shocking speed, stripped of both SOE and Economic Warfare, and relegated to a minor role in the conduct of the war at the Board of Trade.

Some indications that things were not going to pan out for Dalton at SOE became apparent almost immediately. Even as he attained his glittering new ministerial post, he found that he had effectively become step-parent to twins, one of which he understood and wanted, and another with which he never really came to grips, and which would in the end prove to be his undoing. SO2's remit for sabotage and resistance was a form of warfare that was clear-cut and easily understood. Yet Dalton had scant experience of a dark-side organisation like SO1, led by men he had little in common with. He also had difficulty comprehending how far they were capable of going in their pursuit of undermining the enemy by political warfare. Thus, while SO2's cloak-and-dagger activities proceeded at a satisfactory pace, Dalton increasingly found his time taken up by SO1, based out at Woburn Abbey.

Friction soon developed between the professorial Dalton and Rex Leeper, the fifty-two-year-old Foreign Office civil servant leading SO1. Leeper had not been best pleased to find himself subordinated to Dalton. During the First World War, he had served in the Intelligence Department of the Foreign Office, where he had a special responsibility for Russia. After the Bolshevik revolution and the murder of the Tsar, Winston Churchill, then Secretary of State for War, sent British troops to Murmansk to aid the anti-Bolshevik forces.

What is not widely known is that Churchill, with the assistance of Rex Leeper, a British diplomat named Robert Bruce Lockhart, a Russian émigré named Georgi Rosenblum (better known under his alias as master-spy Sidney Reilly) and a British Intelligence agent named George Hill, also plotted unsuccessfully to bring about the downfall of Lenin and Bolshevism. This was a secret project that operated in Russia for months, and much money was spent trying to co-ordinate anti-Bolshevik forces to move against Lenin and his followers. On 31 August 1918 there was an assassination attempt on Lenin, and in the mayhem that ensued the anti-Bolshevik plot collapsed, Reilly vanished, Hill escaped, and Bruce Lockhart was arrested and detained. Bruce Lockhart was subsequently released in exchange for Maxim Litvinov, the unofficial Bolshevik Ambassador in London, but only after considerable pressure from the British government, conducted through the mediation of SIS's resident agent in Moscow – a certain thirty-eight-year-old Samuel Hoare.

After his sensational if unsuccessful wartime involvement in plots to bring Bolshevism crashing down, Rex Leeper returned to the Foreign Office, where he remained during the inter-war years, eventually taking over the Political Intelligence Department (PID) at the Foreign Office in the late 1930s. However, he did not break off his association with Churchill.

Throughout the 1930s Leeper was a frequent visitor to Churchill's home in Kent, Chartwell, keeping the great man advised on some of Britain's most sensitive foreign affairs matters, particularly those related to the great new threat to European democracy – German Nazism. Leeper also became very close to the Permanent Under-Secretary at the Foreign Office and later Chief Diplomatic Adviser to the Foreign Secretary Sir Robert Vansittart, another of Churchill's allies, and the three men joined forces in a secret, unofficial triumvirate to oppose German expansionism.

Following the Rhineland crisis of 1936, when Hitler, completely flouting the Treaty of Versailles, remilitarised the Rhineland, Leeper and Churchill devised a plan to use Churchill's standing to bring together those in Britain opposed to Nazism, under the unsubtle slogan 'Nazi Germany is the enemy of civilisation'. Among those present at the very first luncheon given by the new organisation, the Anti-Nazi League, was Hugh Dalton.[26]

Rex Leeper was therefore an insider. He had been involved in Churchill's anti-Bolshevik machinations in 1918, had kept him briefed about foreign affairs developments during the great man's wilderness years, and was an unofficial co-founder of the Anti-Nazi League. He was firmly entrenched amongst the small group of those who had early realised that Nazism would one day present a threat to European democracy. With the coming of war Leeper's PID became attached to Department EH, soon to be redesignated as SO1.[27] It was not long before Leeper and Churchill's old friends Robert Bruce Lockhart and George Hill also found themselves involved with SO1, along with a plethora of lesser-known men who were also experienced in the art of propaganda, subterfuge, and political and psychological warfare.

Despite his connection with SO1, Rex Leeper was not a belligerent hawk focused solely on the destruction of Germany. He could be as panicky about Britain's chances of survival as anyone else. In June 1940, a little over a week after Dunkirk, Bruce Lockhart noted that Leeper had been 'in a state of nervous tension; unable to work, alarmed, defeatist in the sense that he thought the end had come'.[28]

The calamitous events of May and June 1940 came as a great shock to many in the British government, the Foreign Office and the military, not to mention the civilian population. For most of the last hundred years Britain had assumed an air of dominance in the world, and those running the nation and the Empire believed her position to be unassailable. Britain still possessed the world's greatest empire, even if it was beginning to crumble a little at the edges. However, what had occurred with the fall of France was far more than the rout of the British Expeditionary Force: it caused the devastating realisation that a mere twenty miles of water stood between survival and defeat. The illusion of Britain's invincibility vanished like a candle puffed out by the hot, dry wind of war.

Because the malaise of Britain's pre-war government under Chamberlain could not be shrugged off in an instant, among Churchill's first tasks as Prime Minister had been to use the force of his personality – in the House of Commons, in Cabinet, with the High Command, and over the radio to the nation – to instil a degree of confidence that not only would Britain survive, but that she would win.

Rex Leeper, like many other people in Britain, had gone through a very personal process of psychological trauma, and had become very despondent. Now, through the medium of SO1 and with Churchill's inspirational words etched onto his soul, Leeper's confidence returned, and he became determined to use every means at his disposal to hit back at Germany. His letter to Hugh Gaitskell concerning the possibility of exploiting Hitler's peaceable attempts would lead to an SO1 operation that would undermine Hitler, Hess and Albrecht Haushofer's plans. It would also, eventually, bring Leeper into conflict with his new boss, Hugh Dalton.

SO1's primary role was the promulgation of black propaganda and misinformation to Germany. At the simplest, and least effective, level this could involve the dropping of leaflets over enemy and occupied territory. A more subtle and powerful tool was SO1's access to the multitude of free radio stations created by the BBC to broadcast to Germany and the occupied countries. However, while Goebbels' propaganda broadcasts to Britain were fairly crude, SO1 took the decision from the very start that, in the main, the news and information it broadcast to Germany and the occupied territories would be accurate. Avoiding the sort of outrageously false claims endemic of German broadcasts would engender confidence that the BBC broadcasts were objective. But on the back of this genuine service, SO1 slipped in what it called 'whispers', elements of black propaganda which suggested that all was not well in Germany, and in so doing created a feeling that incompetence and even lunacy existed in the Nazi hierarchy.

SO1 also undertook other, much more important work relating to its brief to carry out 'political warfare', a new tool in the conduct of war.

During the late spring of 1941 one of the key protagonists at SO1, Leonard St Clair Ingrams, a former Barings Bank executive, and 'star operative on the British side of the secret war of wits',[29] presented a report to a meeting of SO1's hierarchy. What he said revealed much about the behind-the-scenes econome-political investigations SO1 conducted. According to the minutes of the meeting:

> Mr. Ingrams gave the Committee a brief outline of Yugoslavia's economic resources, saying that her chief importance was because of the lead, copper and chrome which under German control would almost entirely cover Germany's outstanding requirements . . . With regards to the Axis oil supply, Mr. Ingrams said that Russia had sent no oil to Germany during March and that the little oil going from Albania to Italy would no doubt be stopped when fighting should break out in Northern Albania.[30]

With the help of economic data such as this, SO1 was able to cause very considerable political problems for the Axis. The scope of SO1's operations is evident in a 'most secret' report from November 1941, titled 'Central Plan of Political Warfare, Winter

1941–42'. In it, the top men of SO1 laid down their objectives over the next six months as:

1 To break down the morale of the [Axis] troops in North Africa.
2 To hamper their reinforcement.
3 To create such uncertainty and unrest in Italy that the Germans must occupy the country in force.
4 To bring French North Africa back into the war against Germany.
5 To turn out the Vichy government and force the total German occupation of France.
6 To get Finland out of the war in such a way that she becomes a liability to Germany.
7 To cause Germany to occupy the Balkans in force and to create so much resistance that she is unable to attack Turkey.
8 To cause Japan to break away from the Axis and to tread warily in the Pacific.
9 To disaffect Spain to a point where she would be a serious distraction to Germany.[31]

This was political warfare on a grand scale, and it had the potential to cause vast damage to Germany's ability to wage war. It also played a considerable role in Britain's war effort, far exceeding SO1's public remit of propagating black propaganda.

Among the staff at Woburn was a small and very select band whose task was to develop ingenious spanners to throw into the German government machinery that would unhinge German strategy and create political situations that would hinder Germany's ability to defeat Britain.

Thus, just as SOE was really two organisations, so too was SO1. The outward, acknowledged work of the organisation was to disseminate propaganda. The inner, hidden side of SO1, under the leadership of Rex Leeper, became a home for Britain's most highly motivated political warfare experts, from which they could conduct a secret political war against the German government.

These men were not chosen at random. They were in the main

either trusted friends, or came by personal recommendation. Nearly all of them had a talent for intelligence work, political intrigue and the art of manipulation – and nearly all also had past associations with Winston Churchill. They had shared his fears about the dangers posed by Nazi Germany in the 1930s, they had shared his determination in Britain's darkest hour, and they undoubtedly believed it legitimate to use whatever means necessary to win – including engaging the German leadership in bogus peace negotiations.

The exact origin of the Hitler/Hess deception is today shrouded in mystery. A major reason for this is that not only was SOE disbanded at the end of the war, but almost immediately there was a 'mysterious' fire that completely destroyed over 80 per cent of its records. The remaining documents give just a hint about what took place.

Very often in intelligence an operation originates following a trawl or a flag-waving exercise, to see who responds. Subsequent analysis of the response determines the direction of the project.

The invaluable clue left by Rex Leeper's letter to Hugh Gaitskell in mid-August 1940 suggests that the germ of the idea originated then. But Leeper and SO1 were unlikely to have had a specific objective in mind at that time. They undoubtedly knew of Hitler's desire for a peaceable accord with Britain, and would have received a brief concerning his many attempts to reach such an accord since the summer of 1939. They were also undoubtedly aware that he was likely to go to extraordinary lengths to achieve peace – even to the extent of offering to withdraw German forces from many of the occupied west European countries. They also, after the Weissauer approach, knew that Hitler was attempting to negotiate with the British whilst excluding his own government advisers and Foreign Office, an unheard-of act in modern twentieth-century politics. It was more akin to the era of Bismarck – and Hitler was definitely not a Bismarck, even if he liked to think otherwise.

The SO1 executive, in conjunction with certain top men within the Foreign Office such as Sir Robert Vansittart, Sir Alexander

Cadogan, Ivone Kirkpatrick and Assistant Under-Secretary William Strang – with all of whom Leeper had worked closely for many years – probably all made a significant contribution to the debate on how to use Hitler's desire for peace to the best effect. It is not possible sixty years after the event, with so few documents surviving, to say with certainty how or when this debate proceeded, or indeed what were the primary objectives at that time.

But, almost certainly, it was decided to satisfy Hitler's wish for peaceable negotiation. Given Britain's desperate situation, it may even have been secretly concluded that opening a covert line of communication to the German government would leave open the back door to an armistice if all else failed – a fallback position if Britain were faced with certain defeat. Most likely, however, it was decided that engaging in secret talks with Hitler would weaken his resolve to see Britain defeated. After all, the Foreign Office and government knew full well that Hitler's real objectives lay far away to the east, in the Ukraine and Caucasus. Not only was the Karl Haushofer plan for the Greater Germany and Reich outlined in *Mein Kampf*, but Hitler had even told Freddy Winterbotham, a leading member of SIS, that this was his intention way back in 1934.

There was however a major problem. SO1 and the Foreign Office were astute enough to realise that if the British government or Foreign Office were suddenly to make peace overtures, Hitler would become suspicious, for he was aware of Winston Churchill's mettle. Churchill was not a man to balk and sue for peace, especially now that Britain seemed to be just holding her own, safe for the immediate future behind the English Channel, and inflicting heavy loses upon the Luftwaffe in the Battle of Britain.

It must therefore have been concluded that if this line was to be pursued, it would have to be done with extreme subtlety. Hitler would have to be offered something he was likely to accept, while at the same time many doors would have to be left open to the British negotiators, from long-term stalling tactics through to outright denial. Hitler would also have to be most carefully ensnared. It would be no good the British Ambassador in Stockholm suddenly making a peace pitch to the German Ambassador. Not only would that be referred back to the wrong people – the German Foreign Ministry, complete with the arrogant Ribbentrop – but the Nazi leadership might smell a rat, or even worse go public, ruining Churchill's hopes of winning American support.

It was at this point that a curious coincidence occurred. The participation of Karl and Albrecht Haushofer in Hitler's foreign policy must have been known of by British Intelligence and the Foreign Office – and if the Foreign Office knew it, then so did Rex Leeper. Given the fact that in the 1920s and early thirties Patrick Roberts had introduced his friend Albrecht Haushofer to all his diplomatic contacts, as well as to many of Britain's up-and-coming young men, it is entirely possible that among those he introduced him to was his first cousin Walter Roberts, who had gone on to carve out a significant career for himself in the City of London, before becoming SO1's Establishment and Finance Officer.

It is therefore highly likely, given SO1's subsequent control over the Hitler/Hess deception operation, that in mid-August 1940 (i.e. after Leeper's letter to Gaitskell, but before Hess's meeting with Karl Haushofer on the last weekend of the month) Walter Roberts visited his aunt Violet Roberts in Oxford, and asked her to write to her old friend Professor Karl Haushofer. He may indeed have taken with him the draft of a passage concerning the horrors of war and her wish for European peace, cleverly concocted by the experts at SO1 to have just the right effect upon the Haushofers, which she was to include in her letter to the Professor.

This was the chain of events that had led to Karl Haushofer receiving – most unusually in time of war – a letter from his dear old English friend Violet Roberts, which he was to mention to Hess.

There was one more element that was unusual about SO1's secret project. Generally speaking, all intelligence operations are given code names, chosen in such a manner that they do not relate in any way to the project being undertaken. Thus in the war years SOE's operations received titles such as 'Agrippa', 'Balthazar',

'Platypus' or 'Foxley', none of which gave the slightest clue to what they represented.

But this operation was different. It touched on areas so controversial that it is doubtful if it was *ever* given an official title, for officially it did not exist. After all, operations like Foxley – a scheme to assassinate Hitler – are one thing. But to manipulate another nation's genuine peace moves, to engage in diplomatic negotiations in order to gain the upper military hand, is quite another. Peace negotiations are sacrosanct. You do not enter into them with the objective of causing another nation's downfall – at least, not if there's a risk of getting caught. This was particularly so given Britain's situation in 1940–41. What would have happened if the peace discussions became public? The British government could have found itself railroaded not only by American or dominion pressure, but also by a large segment of its own people, into a peace that left Hitler master of Europe. If such negotiations became public, it had the potential to split the nation and government right down the middle.

Thus the Hitler/Hess affair, it would appear, took place strictly *in camera*. It was unofficial, unnamed, and its objectives were never consigned to paper. It was planned and implemented by a very select band of men without the knowledge even of their own colleagues, and thus was almost certainly never given an official title.

Yet how do you refer to something with no name? In the coming months it undoubtedly became the practice to loosely refer to the project under a pseudonym. By a strange quirk of fate, the very parameters of the operation suggested a name: all four of those most closely involved in the negotiations on the German side – Hitler, Hess and the two Haushofers – had a surname that began with the letter 'H', as would some of the main British protagonists. The name by which Leeper's project would be referred to may have first occurred by accident, yet it was quickly adopted as the operational title: the 'Messrs HHHH operation'.[32]

The end objective of Messrs HHHH was probably formulated quite quickly. What Britain needed if it was to survive was Allies

– and the bigger the better. On Saturday, 10 May 1941 a meeting took place at SO1 HQ, Woburn, attended by the key protagonists of the operation. In attendance were the Foreign Secretary, Anthony Eden, the Minister for SOE and MEW, Hugh Dalton, Rex Leeper and eighteen others. It was the last time minutes would be kept for such a meeting. The object of SO1's endeavours in 1941 was to 'encourage the Germans to attack Russia by misleading Hitler and by hinting that the large sections both in Britain and the United States who preferred to see the overthrow of the Russian rather than the German regime might be prepared to force through a compromise peace between Britain and Germany and combine to destroy the common enemy, Communism'.[33]

This simple but devastating statement of intent is one of the very few records remaining in the SO1 papers that details what was secretly taking place. It is also worthy of note that the meeting took place on the very day Rudolf Hess arrived in Britain.

Within just a few weeks of the Haushofers' becoming embroiled in Hitler's latest peaceable attempt, a new Mr H was to appear on the scene. After sitting in dusty Madrid through the long, hot Spanish summer of 1940, Sir Samuel Hoare, Ambassador Extra-ordinary, was ready to add a new range of secret activities to his already busy schedule. Success would mean Britain's survival and eventual victory over Germany. Failure might well result in the German leadership gaining an understanding of Britain's true intentions; and that would mean war without end until Britain fell. For fall she would, unless the war could be widened to give Britain a desperately-needed ally.

CHAPTER 4

Negotiation

During the Nuremberg war crimes trials, the events of 1940–41 would return to haunt the protagonists of the Messrs HHHH operation, for documents had begun to surface in Germany that had not been tracked down by British Intelligence during the final German collapse in 1945. This led to considerable concern that the defendants – particularly Hess and perhaps Alfred Rosenberg, who as head of the Aussenpolitisches Amt and a close confederate of Hitler and Hess had been privy to much – might produce evidence in their defence which would suggest that the peaceable discussions of 1940–41 had been for real. Secondly, Whitehall was extremely worried that the unweeded German evidence, much of which lay in the hands of the Americans, might implicate prominent Britons. Worse yet, it might reveal potentially sensitive details behind the events leading to Hess's arrival in Scotland in 1941. This would almost certainly result in certain Britons being called to testify, and necessarily having to reveal the truth in order to defend themselves against mistaken charges of disloyalty, perhaps even of treason.

Such evidence did indeed soon appear, sending a flurry of concern sweeping through the British Foreign Office. However, it appeared from an unexpected quarter: it was a British file.

Keeping a very close eye on proceedings at Nuremberg was a certain Mr Con O'Neill from the Foreign Office. O'Neill was no mere Foreign Office minion; he was a former member of the recently disbanded SOE. He was also known to have been present at the Woburn meeting on 10 May 1941 which had specifically discussed the plot to make Hitler feel confident enough to turn his military attention eastward. O'Neill was therefore one of that very select band who knew what had really taken place. He was thus the ideal man to have on the spot to head off any problems before they became too damaging.

Such a problem occurred in the second week of January 1946, when O'Neill discovered that the prosecution in Hess's case was about to introduce evidence concerning 'the Duke of Hamilton's first interview with Hess on the 11th May 1941'. As O'Neill commented back to London with some urgency:

> Unfortunately, in this report the Duke refers to the fact that he had received a letter from Haushofer dated 23 September 1940. This, if it becomes known, will appear to confirm in a measure the contents of the Haushofer documents about [the] peace feelers. [It is] suggested that the British Prosecutor be authorised to say something on the following lines:-
>
> 'When the Duke of Hamilton received this letter from Haushofer dated the 23rd September 1940, he handed it forthwith to the authorities and, in view of the publicity which has recently been received by another document by Haushofer, perhaps I might be permitted to say ... (here insert any demente that we may care to make).'[1]

This statement is intriguing, for without exception the matter of Albrecht Haushofer's letter to the Duke of Hamilton has been dealt with ever since the war by a claim that the correspondence was intercepted by the 'British Censorship Headquarters' on 2 November 1940. However, it would subsequently be claimed that the Duke of Hamilton was not even aware of the letter's existence until February 1941, when he was invited to the Air Ministry and questioned about the Haushofer matter.

But that dilemma lay five years in the future. In the autumn of 1940, Albrecht Haushofer was thoroughly engrossed with Rudolf Hess in deciding the text of this very letter to the Duke of Hamilton.

Following Albrecht's meeting with Hess on Sunday, 8 September, at which the decision had been taken to write to Hamilton in an attempt to open a line of communication to the British hierarchy, the actual content of this letter had been the subject of considerable debate throughout the remainder of that month.

On 19 September, Albrecht wrote to his father enclosing 'the draft of a letter to D[ouglo (the Duke of Hamilton's nickname)], which I will keep to myself and not show anyone else'. Nazi Germany was a dangerous place, and Albrecht knew that keeping copies of the correspondence safely hidden away might well protect him in the future. At the same time, he wrote to Hess concerning the technical complexities of this new peace initiative via Violet Roberts to Hamilton:

> I have . . . been thinking of the technical route by which this message from me must travel before it can reach the Duke of H[amilton]. With your help, delivery to Lisbon can of course be assured without difficulty . . . In view of my close personal relations and intimate acquaintance with Douglas H[amilton] I can write a few lines to him (which should be enclosed with the letter to Mrs R. without any indication of place and without a full name – an A. would suffice for the signature) in such a way that *he alone* will recognise that behind my wish to see him in Lisbon there is something more serious than a personal whim.[2]

However, Albrecht was not about to raise false hopes for this avenue to peace. It was after all his idea, and he was mindful that because failure in the Reich was a risky if not punishable offence, it was advisable to qualify one's suggestions to start with. This was particularly relevant in Albrecht's case, for by mid-September he knew that Hess was acting on the Führer's behalf in this most sensitive of matters. He therefore went on to declare to Hess:

> I have already tried to explain to you not long ago that, for the reasons I gave, the possibilities of successful efforts at a settlement between the Führer and the British upper classes seem to me – to

my extreme regret – infinitesimally small. Nevertheless I should not want to close this letter without pointing out once more that I still think there would be a somewhat greater chance of success in going through Ambassador Lothian in Washington or Sir Samuel Hoare in Madrid rather than through my friend H[amilton].

Albrecht closed the letter by asking: 'Would you send me a line or give me a telephone call with some final instructions? . . . With cordial greetings and best wishes for your health, yours, etc. A[lbrecht].'[3]

Within a few days, Albrecht's letter to the Duke of Hamilton was on its way to the Iberian Peninsula, couriered by a German agent of the SD aboard a Junkers 52 of the Transport Flight. Its destination was PO Box 506, Lisbon.

The letter read:

My Dear Douglo,
Even if this letter has only a slight chance of reaching you – there is a chance and I want to make use of it.

First of all to give you a sign of unaltered and unalterable personal attachment. I do hope you have been spared in all this ordeal, and I hope the same is true of your brothers. I heard of your father's deliverance from long suffering;* and I heard that your brother-in-law Northumberland lost his life near Dunkirk.† I need hardly tell you how I feel about that . . .

Now there is one thing more. If you remember some of my last communications before the war started you will realise that there is a certain significance in the fact that I am, at present, able to ask you whether there is the slightest chance of our meeting and having a talk somewhere on the outskirts of Europe, perhaps in Portugal.

---

* Lord Clydesdale's father died in early 1940 after a long illness, leading to his son inheriting the title of Duke of Hamilton.
† The Duke of Northumberland, a serving member of the British Expeditionary Force, had been killed during the evacuation from Dunkirk in June 1940.

There are some things I could tell you, that might make it worth while for you to try a short trip to Lisbon – if you could make your authorities understand so much that they would give you leave. As to myself – I could reach Lisbon any time (without any kind of difficulty) within a few days after receiving news from you. If there is an answer to this letter, please address it to . . .'[4]

It has never been officially admitted whether there was a reply to Albrecht Haushofer's letter, and too many wartime documents have been captured, destroyed or withheld, in both Britain and Germany, for it to be possible to explore this question satisfactorily. However, there is another, rather surprising, source that reveals a great deal about what took place next.

On Saturday, 24 October 1942, Lavrenti Beria, head of the Soviet Union's security force the NKVD, forerunner of the KGB, wrote a letter to Stalin in which he asserted that not only Albrecht Haushofer had written to the Duke of Hamilton, but Rudolf Hess had as well.

In the months following the Deputy-Führer's bizarre arrival on British soil, the extremely suspicious Russians began their own secret in-depth investigation into the affair. During this investigation an extremely eminent source, Frantisek Moravetz, the Chief of the Czech Military Intelligence Service, informed the NKVD resident in London: 'All Hess's letters to Hamilton did not reach him but were intercepted by the Intelligence service where the answers to Hess in the name of Hamilton were manufactured.'[5] This was bad enough, but Russian alarm was compounded when they managed to obtain similar evidence from French Intelligence too.

In the summer of 1941, the French too were highly perturbed by Hess's arrival in Scotland in such strange circumstance. Concerned that the British and German governments might be up to something they should know about, they too had conducted their own discreet investigation. In a report written for the French General Staff, titled 'ANGLETERRE AFFAIRE HESS, number 398/B', dated 5 September 1941, the Russians were shocked to read:

A youthful Rudolf Hess serving as a fighter pilot at Charleroi on the Western Front in 1918.

Hess (top, far left) as a young political activist and fervent supporter of the new right-wing force sweeping Germany, caught on camera in October 1922 in a group photograph with other members of the SA.

The early days. Hess, Hitler and Julius Streicher at the Nazi Party's 1927 Nuremberg rally.

Left Martha and Karl Haushofer in the 1930s, when Professor Haushofer was at the height of his powers, and a much-sought expert on ethnicity and geopolitics. *Right* Albrecht Haushofer and his brother Heinz at the end of the First World War, a time of great upheaval in Germany. It was also at this time that Rudolf Hess first entered the Haushofer family home, soon to bring with him word of the radical new political force sweeping Germany – National Socialism.

Rudolf Hess (second from right) in the early 1930s with, on the left of the picture, his mentor, the Nazi Party's guru of geopolitics, Professor Karl Haushofer. With the coming to power of the Nazis in 1933, Haushofer's influence rose dramatically; his was the unseen hand behind much of Germany's foreign policy to come.

Hess, in his plane, discusses his latest flying adventure with his wife Ilse and colleagues. He had just won the 1934 Zugspitz flying race. Publicity such as this, together with his clean-living reputation, went a long way towards making Hess the acceptable face of Nazism.

Hess contemplates a discussion between Goebbels, head of the Reichsbank Hjalmar Schacht, and Dr Robert Ley, while Hitler enjoys a quiet nap in the background, aboard a Baltic cruise in the late 1930s.

Left Rudolf Hess, the Reich's Deputy-Führer with a special interest in foreign affairs, greets the Russian Foreign Minister, Vyacheslav Molotov, during a visit to Berlin. *Right* Albrecht Haushofer in the early 1930s, at the time when his old friend, and Germany's new Deputy-Führer, first began to consult him on European foreign affairs and diplomacy.

Hess seated next to his Führer amidst the ruling Nazi elite. In reality, Hess saw himself as much more of a behind-the-scenes political mover; he was regarded by others as 'the conscience of the party' and 'a safe pair of hands'.

A very rare photograph of Hitler attended by his confidential adviser on foreign affairs and Britain, Albrecht Haushofer (standing in the background, left), taken shortly before a banquet given at the Reich Chancellery on the evening of 26 March 1935 for the British Foreign Secretary, Sir John Simon, and the Lord Privy Seal, Anthony Eden.

Albrecht Haushofer delivers a lecture on European geography. His was the expertise that his close friend Rudolf Hess would call upon in the Nazi leadership's efforts to find a peace accord with Britain.

Albrecht Haushofer with his niece and nephews in the countryside south of Munich.

Amongst the select band of men at the British Foreign Office sufficiently trusted to participate in SO1's deception operation were Sir Robert Vansittart and Sir Alexander Cadogan. The two had worked closely together throughout the turmoils of the 1930s, and are seen here in Downing Street during the Czech crisis of 1937.

Anthony Eden (left) leaving the Foreign Office in 1937, accompanied by Sir Robert Vansittart. As Permanent Under-Secretary at the FO, Vansittart was a leading personality in British foreign policy in the 1930s, and one of the few with a keen understanding of the dangers posed by an expansionist Germany led by Hitler.

Winston Churchill and Sir Samuel Hoare in 1937. Publicly the two men were often bitter political rivals, but in private they enjoyed a cordial relationship that resulted in Churchill placing a great deal of trust in Hoare, posting him to Spain as Ambassador Extraordinaire.

They [British Intelligence], wishing to make up for the Best and Stevens affair [i.e. the Venlo Incident], had succeeded through an exchange of correspondence between imaginary Scottish conspirators (directed in the name of Lord Hamilton) and German agents ... the exchanges assumed the form of a serious conspiracy whose participants asked for and arranged for the arrival [in Scotland] of an important German representative to galvanise the conspirators. It was a source of great amazement to all concerned that this person turned out to be Rudolf Hess.[6]

The two reports were not entirely accurate. Moravetz somehow managed to transpose Hess's name for that of Haushofer as the writer of the letters, although it may be that he was trying to impart that the originator of the communications *behind* Haushofer had been Hess. The answer to this may never be known, but the revelations were close enough to the truth to cause Britain's allies – the Czechs, French and Russians – to regard the British government and Intelligence services with some suspicion.

However, it may be significant that the head of the Czech Bureau in London, and therefore the British government's liaison to the Czech government in exile, was Robert Bruce Lockhart, working for Rex Leeper's SO1 out at Woburn Abbey. He had also, incidentally, been a close friend of Frantisek Moravetz since the early 1930s.

While Hess and the Haushofers had been busy drafting and dispatching their letter to the Duke of Hamilton, Britain's Ambassador to Spain, Sir Samuel Hoare, had not been idle. He too was about to make his presence felt on the peace stage, causing the German protagonists in the affair considerable satisfaction. Hoare's involvement confirmed to Albrecht Haushofer much of what he had told Hess at the beginning of September, and it would send the German line of peaceable intent in a new and extremely complex direction.

On 25 September the German Ambassador in Madrid, Eberhard von Stohrer, transmitted a memorandum to Berlin concerning a conversation he had had that morning with the Spanish Minister of the Interior, Ramón Serrano Suñer. The diminutive Suñer was an extremely strange man, who Sam Hoare disliked intensely – he once described him as 'deliberately ill-mannered, spitefully feminine, small-minded, fanatical, impetuous, and not yet forty with snow-white hair'. However, Suñer was also very important and well-connected, his place within Spain's government secured by virtue of his being Generalissimo Franco's brother-in-law.

Suñer had been a key personality in the German government's machinations of the previous June and July, when they had attempted to persuade the Duke and Duchess of Windsor to reject the pressure exerted on them by the British government to abandon Europe for the duration of the war in favour of Bermuda. That plot had failed, along with the Duke of Windsor's own efforts to maintain an even-handed stance between the two warring parties. However, Suñer was extremely anti-British, primarily because of the ever-contentious issue of Gibraltar, and he never missed an opportunity to aid the German cause by passing on titbits of information that came his way. Thus, on the morning of Wednesday, 25 September 1940, Suñer showed the German Ambassador a letter he had received from his brother-in-law, the Generalissimo. The same day an excited Stohrer reported back to Berlin:

> In a private letter that arrived today with a special courier . . . Franco has informed his brother-in-law that . . . a Spanish Minister (not the Foreign Minister) . . . recently spoke with the English Ambassador, Sir Samuel Hoare, and told him that England had lost the war and was only making her situation worse by resisting further. The English Ambassador replied that he judged the situation similarly . . .
>
> The Spanish Minister of Interior [Suñer] considers both English statements to indicate visible weakness on the part of England and possibly even the beginning of an inclination toward peace.[7]

Any such report was bound to be eagerly lapped up by the top Nazis. It was just the sort of intelligence that might indicate a weakening of resolve by certain British political factions to drag the war on to a bitter and protracted end. Taken in conjunction with a report from the German Ambassador in Lisbon, Hoyningen-Huene, who had heard that there was growing political opposition to Churchill, this information might prove to be the chink in fortress Britain's defences.

British opposition to continuing the war did not constitute a serious movement yet, although Hoyningen-Huene commented that it was interesting that 'the most united [in opposing the war are] among the Conservatives themselves'. Expanding upon this, he noted that the seriousness of the situation was revealed by the fact that the British government were putting provisions in place to spirit the Cabinet across the Atlantic in case of impending defeat, where, it was suggested, Churchill would assume the role of adviser to President Roosevelt. This was in addition to the fact that 'preparations are [already] far advanced for the transfer of the Royal Family to Canada'.[8]

Despite the devastating nature of such information, its value to the German government was not so much that it was indicative of a British belief in impending defeat, but rather that the thought had occurred to Britain's leaders at all, and that measures were being put in place in case Britain's resistance reached a point of total collapse.

A little over a week later the Nazi leadership were further heartened to receive another report from Hoyningen-Huene which if anything was even more encouraging, stating optimistically that 'the organisation of London [is] completely destroyed by the air raids, looting, sabotage, and social tension'. However, the most important information Huene's political analysis and intelligence revealed was that: 'Anxious capitalists fear internal disorders. Growth of opposition against [the] Cabinet is plain. Churchill [and] Halifax are blamed for sacrificing England to destruction instead of seeking a compromise with Germany, for which it is still not too late.'[9]

From the German leadership's point of view it appeared that, with sufficient pressure, political opposition in Britain to a compromise peace might collapse, and some diplomatic progress might be made. The main problem, however, was that Churchill was an extremely strong leader who would have no truck with dissent, and would not stand by whilst those about him undermined his resolve to continue the war to its conclusion. Churchill was not a vacillating Neville Chamberlain, pushed in various directions by his advisers. He absolutely believed in leading from the front, and deep down he knew that if Britain could hold out long enough, sooner or later America would inevitably be sucked into the conflict, and then it would just be a matter of time until the Allies were victorious.

During those desperately gloomy days following the fall of France, a tense exchange had occurred between Churchill and Lord Halifax during a Cabinet meeting. Halifax had the temerity to suggest that perhaps Britain would after all have to negotiate with the German government. There seemed to be little choice. France's collapse had shocked Britain into the realisation that Hitler had forged the German war machine into a very formidable tool indeed. Churchill declared before the entire Cabinet that Halifax's mere mention of peace talks was tantamount to high treason. In the embarrassed silence that followed, an indignant Halifax had slipped a note to Churchill stating: 'You are really very unjust to my imprudent ideas. They might be silly, or courting danger but are not high treason. I dislike always quarrelling with you! but most of all on misunderstood grounds.'

Full of contrition, Churchill responded: 'Dear Edward, I had a spasm of fear. It was a deadly thought in this present atmosphere of frustration. You did not foresee this. Forgive me. W.'[10]

Churchill had certainly misunderstood the Foreign Secretary's motives, for as Halifax was later to annotate on that scrap of Downing Street headed notepaper: 'Exchange of notes with Winston C. after I had suggested one way to gain time was to *delude* the Germans by Peace Talks!'[11] (Author's italics.) The key word here is 'delude', for despite his pedigree as an appeaser under Chamberlain, Halifax was no longer under any illusion about the very considerable dangers presented by a victorious German army at loose on a continent aflame with war. However, he was enough of a professional politician not to allow gut instinct to rule his head. There were after all many advantages to playing the diplomatic game against Germany, even if it would only be a short-term measure.

Time was of the essence, and the whole Cabinet realised this, most of all Churchill. The most dangerous time for Britain was during the middle two quarters of every year – April to September, the so-called 'fighting seasons' – and she had only just managed to survive the fighting season of 1940. It was odds-on that Britain would not survive 1941 unless some extraordinary change in fortunes occurred.

By the autumn of 1940, Britain was like a severely knocked-about boxer, hanging on for the bell, supported only by the ropes. What she needed was either a second front to split the Axis war effort, or a powerful ally – neither of which she had any immediate prospect of attaining. Despite this, a small number of individuals within the inner circle of the War Cabinet and SO1 had some ideas on how they were going to resolve their problems. The letter from Violet Roberts to Professor Karl Haushofer was the opening gambit in a deadly game which they had to win in order to survive.

In themselves, the contents of Albrecht Haushofer's letter to the Duke of Hamilton were fairly mundane, mentioning his regret and sorrow at the coming of war. However, Haushofer's comments specifically drew attention to his ability to travel for a meeting, and this clearly indicated to SO1 that their labours were bearing fruit.

It is certain that SO1 used the Haushofers as a medium to get to the German leadership, but to begin with they had little means of knowing whether the proffered bait had been taken. They knew, after the Nazi peaceable attempts of 1939 and 1940, that there was an earnest desire by the German leadership to end the war in the west. However, there was no guarantee that either of the Haushofers were still in favour with the Nazi regime, or that they remained of sufficient importance to have access to Hitler. The letter from Albrecht to the Duke of Hamilton, therefore, revealed a great deal. It made clear that the Haushofers *had* retained their importance, that they had kept their friendship with Hess, and through Hess they had access to Hitler.

The first sign that SO1's plot was beginning to make headway occurred in Spain just a few weeks later, when an approach was made to Sir Samuel Hoare from a most unexpected quarter. It was, however, one that was so eminent that it demonstrated the very real intent of the German leadership to cut a deal with the British. Hoare was visited by the Papal Nuncio in Madrid, who informed him that 'he had been requested to communicate the following peace offer on behalf of the German government representative the Ambassador met last July at the home of Beigbeder (APA [Aussenpolitisches Amt] representative Haushofer), when the last round of peace offers were made'.[12]

Juan Beigbeder y Atienza had been the Spanish Foreign Minister until October 1940, but it is known that Sam Hoare continued to visit him socially even after his official capacity had ended. Furthermore, the reference to the fact that Hoare had met the Aussenpolitisches Amt representative the previous July indicates that the British Ambassador already had a track record in the negotiation process – July 1940 was the time when the Duke of Windsor had been making his private pitch for peace. Indeed, this meeting may have been the reason Albrecht Haushofer proposed to Hess on 8 September that they might use Hoare. This is not to suggest that Sam Hoare was disloyal. He would to write secretly to Anthony Eden within days of Hess's flight to Britain in May 1941: 'I have just written Winston a short personal note in view of the fact that he took so much interest last year in agreeing to our secret plans . . . I am enclosing a curious and very secret note that has just been passed to me by Beigbeder. The suggestions in it bear a remarkable resemblance to what I imagine Hess has been saying in England.'[13]

Thus Sir Samuel Hoare would be a key protagonist in any peace negotiations. He was a man the German leadership suspected of divided loyalties, as they believed was indicated by his banishment by Churchill. They believed he was keen for peace, and perhaps sympathetic to the German cause, given his record of appeasement and promulgation of the Hoare–Laval pact. Yet it is now known that Hoare was unquestionably loyal, otherwise Churchill would not have placed him in a position of such importance. The Germans, for all their expert analysis, failed to discern the important fact that Sir Samuel Hoare was actually Churchill's man through and through.

Sam Hoare was not adrift in neutral Spain all on his own. His was an important mission, and he needed assistance. Not the sort of assistance that could be rendered by a low-echelon diplomat; rather he needed a man who knew something of high deceit and subterfuge, a man capable of playing his cards close to his chest. Thus Hoare was attended during his meeting with the Papal Nuncio by his Naval Attaché, Captain Gareth Alan Hillgarth, who took copious notes on all that the Pope's Ambassador said, and subsequently typed up the report on the meeting personally.

Captain Gareth Alan Hillgarth is a fascinating personality, and his support for Hoare was very important indeed. Apart from being Naval Attaché at the British Embassy in Madrid, the bushy-eyebrowed, fiercely patriotic forty-year-old Hillgarth was the top SOE man in the Iberian Peninsula, and in the months to come he would participate not only in special secret work for SO1 and Sam Hoare, but also in activities for SO2 under the code name of agent 'YN'.[14]

Hillgarth had experience of carrying out extremely important intelligence work. He also had another important quality that made him a natural to assist Hoare's more covert activities.

In 1936, Hillgarth, serving as acting Vice-Consul in Majorca, met and later became firm friends with Winston Churchill. With the coming of war, this friendship and trust grew considerably, and Churchill entrusted Hillgarth with some extremely delicate covert operations involving millions of pounds paid to leading members of Franco's military regime to ensure that the Germans did not gain the upper hand in the Iberian Peninsula. Hillgarth's work undoubtedly helped prevent Franco from taking the decision to join the Axis. His importance is suggested by the fact that on his infrequent trips back to Britain he was one of the very few diplomatic corps attachés who were invited to stay at Chequers with the Prime Minister.[15]

Hillgarth's contribution to Sam Hoare's deception work was substantial, and his role in other covert activities so significant that Churchill once commented to Hoare, 'I find Hillgarth a great prop.'[16] After the war Hillgarth continued to be important to Churchill. He remained in touch with his old intelligence contacts, and sent Churchill regular reports on defence and intelligence affairs based on information he picked up in Whitehall. When Hillgarth died in 1978 his obituary described him as Churchill's protégé and favourite intelligence officer, and quoted Sam Hoare's encomium to him as 'the embodiment of drive' who gave Britain vital contacts in wartime Spain.[17]

Hillgarth was *in situ* at the Madrid Embassy and, being close to Churchill, he was trusted. It was to be a characteristic of this operation that everyone concerned with it was connected by close friendship. It was too important a matter to risk trusting 'outsiders'.

Thursday, 14 November 1940, when Sir Samuel Hoare met with the Papal Nuncio to discuss the sensitive subject of peace, was a bright and balmy autumn day in Madrid. The meeting undoubtedly took place behind closed doors in absolute confidentiality, either at Beigbeder's home or, more likely, at Hoare's private residence, rather than the Embassy.

The Papal Nuncio informed the British Ambassador of 'the German government's sincere wish to end the hostilities'. He went on say something which would have caused Hoare to prick up his ears – that he had been requested to hand over 'the following details for transmission to a party who would be willing to act upon them'.

This was important, for the Nuncio specifically did not mention the British government. His turn of phrase was undoubtedly designed to imply that the German leadership was prepared to negotiate with a party other than the British government, if that was what was required to attain peace.

This was something new. All previous peaceable attempts had been specifically directed towards the British government, but this one was being openly proffered to a different party. This suggested that Hitler had finally given up any notion of negotiating with Churchill or the incumbent government, and was now prepared to deal with an independent faction. Sam Hoare would immediately have realised that this was extremely important, for there is no point in negotiating peace with a party not in power, unless you believe that party will be in power when the time comes to enact the treaty under discussion.

Captain Hillgarth recorded that the Papal Nuncio went on to detail the German peace terms he had been asked to pass on as follows:

(1) A confidential meeting as soon as possible in Switzerland between the representatives who are prepared to negotiate, to arrange a more formal conference at a later date.
(2) Once the conference details have been agreed, then a meeting to take place between the parties to discuss Poland, guarantees, non-aggression pacts, disarmament, colonies, frontiers, the transfer of populations, and an end to hostilities.

The views of the German government on the subjects detailed in (2) were as follows:-

[1] The negotiating parties to meet on neutral territory under the stewardship of a neutral state, such as Switzerland or the United States of America.
[2] Norway, Denmark, Holland, Belgium, and France would be independent free states, able to choose their own constitution and government; but opposition to Germany must be excluded and assurances of non-retaliation given. Germany would withdraw her military forces, would not claim military concessions in these countries, and is prepared to negotiate a form of reparation for damage inflicted during conquest.
[3] All aggressive weapons to be destroyed and then armed forces

reduced to correspond with the economic and strategic requirements of each country.

[4] Germany requests a return of her former colonies but would advance no other territorial claims. South-West Africa might not be claimed. Germany might consider the payment of an indemnity for improvements effected in the colonies since 1918, and the purchase of property from present owners who might desire to leave.

[5] The political independence and national identity of 'a Polish State' to be restored, but the territory occupied by the Soviet Union is to be excluded from discussions. Czechoslovakia would not be prevented from developing her national character, but is to remain under the protection of the Reich.

[6] Greater European economic solidarity should be pursued, and the solution of important economic questions solved by negotiation and national European agreement.[18]

Finally, the Nuncio ended his pitch for peace by telling Sam Hoare something that revealed a curious change in Hitler's stance. He explained that the 'APA representative', that is Albrecht Haushofer, had told him that 'Hitler's desire for peace was based on the principle that he wished there to be "no victor or vanquished" stigma applied to any of the negotiating parties', and that if an amicable peace agreement were achieved, it would 'have to be validated by a plebiscite in all countries affected by an agreement'.[19]

The nature of what was on offer must have left SO1 gasping at the concessions Hitler was prepared to make to attain peace with Britain. This was not even a deal that had been worked out through hard negotiation. This whole plethora of remarkable concessions was just Hitler's opening gambit, the laying of his cards on the table in order to tempt a political faction in Britain to negotiate with him.

From Churchill's point of view, nothing could have been more dangerous. Everyone was now used to Hitler's bully-boy tactics, the threats of dire military consequences if he did not get what he wanted. Such a set of concessions was a remarkable development, which had the potential to bring Britain's war effort to a shuddering halt if it ever became public. That could not be allowed to happen. Hillgarth's report back to London concluded that the Nuncio had informed Hoare 'that a negotiated conclusion to the European conflict would have the full support of his Holiness the Pope, and that he had been informed that the Vatican would be willing to participate if further mediation were required'.[20]

What had begun as a subtle trawl – a flag-waving exercise – by a few men at SO1 had suddenly become an extremely deadly game indeed. It was one thing to tentatively suggest that Britain might be able to exploit Hitler's desire for peace, but the last thing anyone had expected was that the German Führer would respond by making an offer so good that it left the majority of Britain's official war aims hollow. What would happen if the governments in exile of Norway, Holland, Belgium and France were to discover that Hitler was offering to withdraw German forces from their countries and, what was more, intimating that he was prepared to pay for the damage that had occurred during the invasion? It was an extremely difficult and dangerous call for Churchill.

If Hitler had been careful about preserving absolute secrecy in Germany concerning Dr Weissauer's initiative, for fear of appearing weak before his own people, then this new initiative saw him putting his head firmly in the lion's mouth. It must have been very tempting for SO1 and Britain's top politicians at the centre of this intrigue to firmly close the lion's jaws, using this peace offer to destroy Hitler's credibility in Germany. How could Hitler justify the war to the German people if they ever discovered that he himself was secretly negotiating to give virtually everything away?

However, the Hitler–Hess–Haushofer peace offer was also a double-edged sword for the British. SO1 and Churchill could not use it for propaganda purposes for fear that sizeable sections of the Allied governments – and of the British government too – might demand that the terms be seriously considered, and perhaps even accepted.

Although Hitler's peace offer through the auspices of Dr Weissauer had been put before the dominions' governments for consideration (albeit with Churchill's recommendation that it be rejected), there is absolutely no record of the Hitler–Hess–Haushofer – the Messrs H – peace initiative ever being put before anybody. It was just too dangerous to tell anyone about.

This situation existed because Churchill had a major problem. At the time of the Papal Nuncio's visit to Samuel Hoare in November 1940, there were clear signs that Britain was losing the war, and some members of the government were beginning to question the sanity of continuing to fight. Churchill knew that if he did but once flinch, did but once intimate that perhaps there might be a way to negotiate an amicable conclusion to the conflict with Germany, it would be the end. There would be no hope of persuading the frightened men of Westminster to declare war again if Hitler's offers proved illusory.

Churchill knew from his intelligence briefings that there was no sign of the German war machine slowing down; indeed, the German government was making a sizeable effort to consolidate much of Europe under German politico-economic dominance. What would happen if Britain concluded a peace, then within a few months found herself facing a threat from Germany once again? It was too great a risk to take.

Churchill knew that Britain only needed to hang on, not to flinch either politically or militarily, until Hitler's instinct to attack Russia came to the fore. Britain needed to keep her nerve until the United States was dragged into the war, and then the Allies would ultimately win. Churchill knew he did not need to take the terrible risk of peace now, when the prospect of overall victory beckoned tantalisingly at some time in the not so distant future.

In the autumn of 1940 the British government's concern was not just that Britain's forces were being almost constantly defeated by the Axis in every military campaign they fought, but that Germany was obtaining substantial economic resources – machine parts, oil, petrol and food – from the Soviet Union. If it had been the case that Russia merely presented a lurking, but neutral, menace in the east, the turning of Germany on Russia would have been an unsavoury act, advantageous to Britain only in that Russia would become a bottomless pit into which Hitler would have to pour men, materiel and resources. However, Russia was not merely sitting on the sidelines of the conflict. She was providing considerable aid to the German war machine, and this legitimised her as a target. In February 1940, Germany had signed an economic treaty with the Soviet Union in which the Russians agreed to provide resources to the Reich in exchange for hard cash. These resources were so large that in the autumn of 1940 Karl Schnurre, head of Division W6 of the Economic Policy Department of the German Foreign Ministry, reported to Ribbentrop that:

> The supplies from the Russians have heretofore been a very substantial prop to the German war economy. Since the new economic treaties went into effect [earlier this year], Russia has supplied over 300 million Reichsmarks' worth of raw materials, roughly 100 million Reichsmarks of which was in grain ... Our sole economic connection with Iran, Afghanistan, Manchukuo, China, Japan and, beyond that, with South America, is the route across Russia, which is being used to an increasing extent for German raw material imports (soybeans from Manchukuo).[21]

The resources being provided by the Soviet Union gave the Germans an advantage that the British, and particularly Hugh Dalton (who as Minister of Economic Warfare was charged with the responsibility of cutting Germany off from all sources of supply), were determined to end at all costs. SO1's decision to delude Hitler by peace talks, to 'encourage the Germans to attack Russia by misleading Hitler ... that large sections in Britain [who] preferred to see the overthrow of the Russian rather than the German regime might be prepared to force through a compromise peace between Britain and Germany',[22] undoubtedly took this into consideration. It was too good an opportunity to miss. It would not only give Britain the desperately-needed second front, sucking the German war machine dry of men and materiel, it would also cut off a valuable source of supply to the Reich, while at the same time closing its access to trade from the east via Russia's rail networks. A double, if not triple, blow against Germany.

A little over a month after Sam Hoare's visit from the Papal Nuncio, an extraordinary situation began to develop, and Hoare's role in this whole affair began to be more clearly defined. On 17 December 1940, Captain Hillgarth dispatched a ciphered 'SECRET' telegram to London that read: 'Further to my meeting with Gen[eral] Vigon this morning I can confirm that a safe arrangement for the carriage of my Minister over dangerous territory has been concluded. Gen. Vigon was most helpful and confirmed that both the arrangements for the 20th and return on 21st have been cleared with the relevant parties, and so there should be no problems.'[23]

General Juan Vigon was chief of the Spanish Supreme General Staff, and head of the Spanish air force. Despite being an important member of Franco's government, he saw himself as a moderate, and attempted on several occasions to further the cause of peace, being politely but firmly rebuffed by the British.

Within weeks of his meeting with Hillgarth, General Vigon would make his own peaceable attempt between Britain and Germany. The secret British Foreign Office file of the time reads: 'General Vigon has held the view that the war will be a stalemate for a long time ... [and] it may be he who prompted General Franco to raise the question of a possible peace with Sir S. Hoare recently ...'[24] The Foreign Office civil servant who made this comment, a Mr W.S. Williams, added optimistically: 'If ... we are to bring Spain in on our side we should lose no opportunity of rubbing in to the Spaniards, what many still do not realise, that Germany alone is responsible for the war's continuance.'[25]

Despite his attempt to show diplomatic expertise, Mr Williams was evidently not that worldly, nor did he understand the complexities of what was taking place, for his superior, Frank Roberts (working under Assistant Under-Secretary William Strang), stingingly retorted: 'I am not sure that anything is to be gained by this. After all the Germans would be ready to end the war to-morrow on their own terms, which would probably look not unacceptable to Spain & Portugal. *It is we who are for excellent reasons, responsible for the continuation of the war* [author's italics]. I think our propaganda to Spain had better *not* concentrate on this theme.'[26]

Vigon, of course, was unaware of this subterfuge behind the closed doors of Whitehall. His meeting with Hillgarth on Tuesday, 17 December had been intended to further the likelihood of peace, although it is almost certain he was not told the true reason for the 'carriage' of Hoare 'over dangerous territory'.

The phrases used in Hillgarth's telegram were very unusual, and reveal much about the situation existing in the Foreign Office at that time. One need only read some of the other communications emanating from British embassies around the world to realise that diplomats were rarely reticent about saying exactly what they meant, particularly when their comments back to London were protected by complex Foreign Office ciphers. Hillgarth's covert language must mean that his telegram was only meant to be understood by a select few men in Whitehall; men who already knew exactly what was taking place.

The reference in Hillgarth's telegram to 'dangerous territory' is the strangest phrase of all, for Hoare, in Spain, was already in neutral territory. He could not have been travelling *to* occupied territory, because Hillgarth specifically states '*over* dangerous territory'. General Vigon's position as head of the Spanish air force suggests that Hillgarth arranged Spanish air transport for Hoare – hence the use of the word 'over'. There were few places Hoare could have travelled to from Spain 'over dangerous territory' to reach more neutral territory in 1940, other than Switzerland, which would mean he was about to fly over occupied France.

Furthermore, Hillgarth was very specific about the dates. Hoare was to fly out on the twentieth – a Friday – and back again on the twenty-first – Saturday. That was a very short stay for which to have flown so far, indicating that Hoare's mission was both important and extremely secret, for it was being conducted on a weekend, at a time when the likelihood of official Embassy business would be slim, and the chances of his travels being discovered slimmer still.

The biggest question this raises is, who did Hoare fly in secret to Switzerland to meet?

In October 1940 Ernst Bohle, head of the Auslandsorganisation and a close friend of Albrecht Haushofer's, was invited to Rudolf Hess's apartment in Berlin. The Deputy-Führer greeted Bohle cordially, then ushered him quickly through to his study. After making sure that the door was firmly shut, Hess informed Bohle that he wanted to discuss a 'very secret assignment' which no one, either in Hess's family – this specifically meant Hess's brother Alfred, who was Bohle's assistant – or on his staff, was to be informed about. 'I chose you,' Hess confided, 'because you speak English, know the British, and consider our war with Britain as much a mistake as I do.'[27] He explained that he was currently working on a secret project to end this war, and asked Bohle if he was willing to help.

When Bohle was interrogated by Allied Intelligence at the end of the war, he recalled: 'when I immediately agreed, Hess told me that above all others, my chief, Foreign Minister von Ribbentrop, must not hear even a breath of this intention as he would sabotage it at once'.[28] Hess, Bohle continued, then explained that he wanted to write to the Duke of Hamilton, who he understood had great influence in Britain, to suggest a private meeting in Switzerland. 'He handed me the draft of the first part of the letter, and asked me to translate it, right away, in an office next door.'[29] Over the next three or four months, Bohle asserted, Hess called him in to translate further drafts of the letter, the work of Hess's political mentor and his friend, Karl and Albrecht Haushofer.[30] Fired up with enthusiasm for this important project, Bohle asked the Deputy-Führer, 'If your plans come to pass, please suggest to the Führer that I accompany you.'[31]

Under interrogation in 1945, Bohle maintained that he personally had done all the translation work for Hess, which lasted from October 1940 to January or February 1941. He would also testify that:

> It was suggested by Professor Haushofer ... that I would meet
> [someone] in a neutral country, possibly Switzerland ... It was my
> firm opinion at the time, which I cannot prove today, that Hitler
> knew all about this because it seemed impossible to me that Hess
> would do anything of such importance without asking Hitler ...
> It was [also] my opinion that only three people in Germany knew
> anything about it, Hitler, Hess, and myself. I had orders to speak
> to nobody, not even to his [Hess's] own brother, who was in my
> own office, not even to his [Hess's] secretary.[32]

What is curious about this testimony is that Bohle asserted he had
worked translating papers for Hess for several months. This seems
odd, firstly because once the text of Hess's letter had been finalised,
its translation into English would not have taken long, and secondly because not only could Hess speak English with reasonable
fluency, but his close friend and co-conspirator in the initiative,
Albrecht Haushofer, was perfectly fluent.

Perhaps the explanation is that in Germany, just as in Britain,
there were those who knew exactly what was taking place, and
those who did not. Bohle's evidence seems to suggest that he was
one of those who were not taken into complete confidence. This
raises another interesting point. If Ernst Bohle was not in the inner
circle of those at the centre of the Messrs HHHH peace initiative,
perhaps he translated *other* important documents; documents that
did indeed relate to Switzerland. He may, when questioned by
Allied Intelligence five years later, and knowing the story of the
Deputy-Führer who had suddenly flown off to Britain, have
assumed that Hess was carrying with him the papers he himself
had translated, when the reality of the situation could have been
quite different.

This does not reveal who Hoare flew to Switzerland to meet,
but it is a starting point; and there is other evidence which comes
from an interesting source.

It is known that Captain Hillgarth arranged a flight for Sam
Hoare on Friday, 20 December, and a return flight on the following
day, but on the German side there is clear evidence of another

flight as well. The astonishing fact is that Rudolf Hess did not just jump aboard his plane on Saturday, 10 May 1941 and fly to Britain. He made several other flights throughout the autumn of 1940 and the spring of 1941 – but no one knows where he flew to.

Helmut Kaden, the chief test pilot at Messerschmitt's headquarters in Augsburg, personally responsible for the Deputy-Führer's private Messerschmitt 110E, registration VJ-OQ, was later to recall that Hess had made three prior attempts to fly to Britain. According to Kaden, Hess made his first attempt on Saturday, 21 December 1940,

> when he took off in clear weather but returned after just over three hours, to make apologies to the staff. He had dropped his signal pistol, the equivalent to the RAF's Verey pistol ... [which] had lodged underneath his seat, out of reach, and jammed the rudder controls. It was freed by the jolt when the Messerschmitt landed, and recovered by Hess before we reached the plane, but it prevented him continuing on that occasion.[33]

Taken at face value, this statement appears to indicate that in December 1940 Rudolf Hess was ready to fly to Britain to seek out the Duke of Hamilton. However, for several reasons that cannot be true. Hess could on occasion be prone to over-enthusiasm, but he was nevertheless an intelligent man and an astute politician. In the late spring of 1941 he had gone to considerable efforts to ensure the most propitious circumstances for his flight, checking the weather conditions and ordering several improvements to his plane. One of the key things that Hess maintained went wrong on the night of 10 May 1941 was that his plans became unstuck when he found himself plunged into darkness, and this affected his flight. In December, night would have fallen in Scotland before Hess was halfway to Britain, and it would have been a courageous or a foolhardy man indeed who braved the dark North Sea in winter.

A second reason why Kaden has to be incorrect is that information was an extremely dangerous commodity in Nazi Germany. After Hess's flight on 10 May 1941, everyone who had had personal, political or professional dealings with him was rounded up by the Reich's internal security and questioned. All of them, including Helmut Kaden, expressed shock and surprise on discovering Hess's destination. Hitler, Hess and Albrecht Haushofer were engaged in extremely sensitive peace negotiations with an enemy power, secret even from the other leading Nazis. Hitler and Hess did not draw Foreign Minister Ribbentrop into their confidence, and Ernst Bohle was only given information on a need-to-know basis – even being instructed not to tell Hess's own brother what was taking place. No one knew.

Rudolf Hess would certainly not have told Helmut Kaden or any other person at Messerschmitt, particularly in December 1940, about the real purposes of his mysterious flights. They were mere minions, and Germany's Deputy-Führer would not have felt it necessary to inform them about his plans in any but the vaguest of terms. Thus Kaden's opinion that Britain was Hess's objective on Saturday, 21 December 1940 must have been an assumption based on his subsequent knowledge of Hess's destination.

Finally, Kaden stated that Hess returned because his Verey pistol became stuck under his seat, jamming his rudder controls. This is also very unlikely to be true, particularly since the item miraculously became unstuck before anyone else saw it. However, Kaden's testimony is valuable, for it tells us several key things. It gives us the date of Hess's December flight, and it reveals how long he was away from Augsburg.

It was part of Hess's role as Deputy-Führer of the Reich to travel about, and he did far more than merely sit at his desk from 1939 to 1941. There were several instances when he flew as far afield as the Baltic in the north and the Iberian Peninsula in the south. He thought little of travelling a long way for a brief meeting, for such is the nature of politics.

If the details of Hess's flight on Saturday, 21 December 1940 are examined and set against the technical specifications of an Me-110E, a very interesting possibility becomes apparent.

The Me-110E was an extremely powerful all-weather capability fighter-bomber. With its twin Daimler Benz DB-601N engines, each producing 1395 horsepower, it was a high-quality machine capable of a top speed of over 360 miles per hour. Let us assume that Hess flew sensibly at the plane's upper cruising speed of 310 miles per hour. From Augsburg to Zürich is 150 miles, or a flying time of twenty-nine minutes at 310 miles per hour. With the return flight, that gives an overall travelling time of about an hour. According to Kaden, Hess was away from Augsburg for 'just over three hours'. This means that he could have been in Switzerland for nearly two hours, during which he could have met Sam Hoare, who had travelled at considerable effort to arrive in Switzerland that same day, Saturday, 21 December 1940.

So long after the event, it may never be discovered exactly where Germany's Deputy-Führer met Britain's Ambassador Extraordinary to discuss peace. It is unlikely that their secret meeting was conducted close to Zürich airport, as the risk of discovery by Intelligence or the press would have been considerable. It may, however, be significant that Hess had two aunts living nearby. Frau Emma Rothacker lived in Zürich itself, whilst Frau Helene Hess lived quietly in the countryside near the city. In all likelihood Aunt Helene's house was the more secure, particularly since she was already known to Albrecht Haushofer, who was, without a doubt, also present in Switzerland that day, as almost certainly was Captain Hillgarth. Significantly for an operation that would come to be known as 'Messrs HHHH', the men involved on this occasion were Hess, Hoare, Haushofer and Hillgarth.

The exact details of what was debated at that two-hour meeting on Saturday, 21 December 1940 will probably never be known, except that the terms of a possible peaceable agreement, as imparted to Hoare by the Papal Nuncio, were undoubtedly paramount. It would have been necessary for Hoare and Hess to discuss how such a deal could be implemented, for it would become increasingly clear over the next few months that the German leadership did not believe they were negotiating with the British government, but rather with a powerful faction, headed by Lord Halifax and Hoare, who were poised to usurp power constitutionally from Churchill and his supporters. In May 1940, Lord Halifax had almost become

Britain's Prime Minister instead of Churchill. However, Halifax's credibility as a war leader had been critically damaged by his support of Chamberlain's appeasement. He had been charged with being one of the 'guilty men', and the mud had stuck. From May until December 1940 he had been a man under siege, consistently sniped at by the press as one of those responsible for Britain's predicament.

Perhaps the most important question that can be asked about this meeting is how we can be sure that Sir Samuel Hoare did indeed travel all the way from Madrid to Switzerland for a highly secret meeting. After all, the Hillgarth/Vigon evidence is rather tenuous. The answer is that Hoare did not merely travel for one meeting. The whole exercise would be repeated within just a few weeks – only that time the situation would become considerably more complicated when Britain's Ambassador in Berne, David Kelly, found out.

On Wednesday, 18 December 1940, two days before Hess almost certainly flew to Switzerland, Hitler issued a new military directive that would change the whole nature of the war. Having previously sworn that he would never again commit Germany to the stupidity of a two-front war, Hitler now ordered that Germany's armed forces should prepare 'to crush the Soviet Union in a quick campaign ... even before the conclusion of the war against England'. This was the infamous Directive No. 21, Hitler's order to prepare for Operation Barbarossa. The preparations, Hitler stated, 'requiring more time to get under way are to be started now – if this has not yet been done – and are to be completed by May 15, 1941'[34] – only five months away.

Despite Russia's substantial contribution to Germany's war effort, Hitler was becoming increasingly uncomfortable about the opportunistic noises emanating from Moscow. At the same time he was aware that a successful pre-emptive strike against Russia would secure all the Ukrainian wheat and Caucasian oil Germany could ever need.

To all appearances, the Russo–German entente seemed to be

proceeding very nicely, particularly on the economic front; yet behind the scenes Germany was beginning to take an increasingly belligerent stance, indicative of its belief that the Reich was attaining the economo-politico-military upper hand. However, much of this was a façade created by the Nazis to hide the reality that Germany's economic joints were beginning to creak alarmingly under the strains of maintaining a prolonged command economy. Add to this the fact that the Reich's Economics Ministry was predicting famine in occupied Europe for the winter of 1941, and Germany's situation had the potential to become untenable very quickly.

In Britain meanwhile, events had taken an unexpected turn. On 12 December, Britain's Ambassador to the United States, Lord Lothian (an old friend of Albrecht Haushofer's), suddenly died, leaving a diplomatic vacuum in Washington at a critical time in Anglo–American relations. This was a key position in Britain's war effort, and an unsuitable appointment could have had disastrous repercussions. In the event Lord Lothian's death presented an opportunity for Churchill to kill several birds with one stone. His first and primary objective was to foster ever closer relations between London and Washington; yet he might also have the opportunity to remove a political rival, whilst at the same time furthering the impression of a divided British political hierarchy in the eyes of the German leadership.

Thus Churchill decided to relieve Lord Halifax of his position as Foreign Secretary, and post him to Washington as Britain's new Ambassador. This appeared to be a resounding slap in the face for someone of Halifax's political stature, and it has long been believed that he was yet another of those banished because of his support for appeasement and a compromise peace. Yet this is a fallacy. The impression that Halifax was banished to the United States was very useful to SO1. In fact the last thing Winston Churchill would have done during Britain's darkest hour would have been to send a powerful political rival to the very place where he had the potential to cause the most harm. Such a person, as Albrecht Haushofer had joked in 1939, would in reality have found himself appointed as Consul to 'Paramaribo' in deepest South America, or banished to somewhere such as the Bahamas, where he would be isolated and in no position to pursue policies at odds with the British government's line.

While it was true that Halifax had supported Chamberlain's policies of appeasing the dictators of Europe, and had been Churchill's main challenger for the premiership in May 1940, he had also provided an effective counterbalance to the Prime Minister's more radical ideas. This did not necessarily mean they were political enemies. Undoubtedly Churchill had his own reasons for wanting to oust Halifax from the Foreign Office and replace him with his loyal stalwart Anthony Eden. However, Churchill was a pragmatic leader, and would not have dismissed his Foreign Secretary and sent him to Washington for merely personal motives.

A number of people had been proposed for the Washington post, including Sir Robert Vansittart, Lord Cranborne, Sir Dudley Pound, Oliver Lyttelton and Sir Ronald Lindsay. Indeed Lady Astor and Lady Diana Cooper even canvassed for their own husbands to have the posting,[35] so desirable was the appointment as Ambassador to Washington.

Despite this, by the time Churchill and Eden settled down to watch a private screening of *Gone with the Wind* at the Prime Minister's country retreat, Ditchley Park in Oxfordshire, on the evening of Sunday, 22 December, it would seem that the identity of the new Ambassador had already been decided upon. Churchill would first offer the appointment to David Lloyd George, knowing that the elderly former Prime Minister would turn it down. This he duly did, pleading ill health, and Lord Halifax, publicly expressing dismay at his sudden demotion and banishment, decamped for Washington in the first few days of 1941.

Although a loyal supporter of Churchill, the new Foreign Secretary, Anthony Eden, was no mere yes-man. He had attained his first political post at the Foreign Office under Austin Chamberlain in the early 1930s, and had quickly gained a reputation as an expert in foreign affairs.[36] His career thereafter had been meteoric, and in 1935 he became Britain's youngest Foreign Secretary since 1807.

However, his career had suddenly stalled in 1938, when he resigned from Neville Chamberlain's Cabinet over Chamberlain's acceptance of Mussolini's conquest of Abyssinia. Thereafter he became a natural member of Churchill's camp, and it was through Churchill that Eden became Secretary of War in May 1940. No one had any doubt that he owed his return to the helm of the Foreign Office to his patron Winston Churchill.

The German leadership believed that this new development offered them much hope. It matched exactly what they perceived to be the political situation in London, as they had come to understand it through the expert advice of Albrecht Haushofer. As they interpreted events, Lord Halifax, a man receptive to peace, had been banished to Washington by a Churchill fearful of a political challenge. This undoubtedly reassured Hitler, Hess and Haushofer that Halifax, who had almost become Prime Minister in May 1940, would be more amenable than ever to a compromise peace.

In the first few weeks of a particularly bitter and cold January 1941, British Military Intelligence was commissioned to assess for Churchill the likelihood of a German attack on Russia. Their assessment was most enlightening, not only for its conclusions, but for what it revealed about the British politico-military state of mind at that time. It was a great fear of the British government that the fighting season of 1941 would see Germany consolidate her strategic and military superiority with a push eastwards into the Middle East via Turkey and North Africa. If Britain lost her Middle Eastern oilfields, her war effort would come to a shuddering halt, and Germany would almost immediately emerge victorious. Thus Britain's entire hope of surviving the fighting season of 1941 lay in ensuring that Germany attacked Russia, and did not aim for the Middle East.

The 'SECRET' report, headed 'Military Indications of German Intentions towards Russia', began by stating: 'There have been a number of suggestions recently that Germany may be intending to attack Russia. We have examined all the available evidence to see whether there are any *military* indications that such a move is contemplated.' The report examined Germany's military dispositions in Norway, Finland, Poland and east Prussia, Slovakia and Romania, before going on to look for more subtle signs of German intentions. However, it gloomily continued: 'There have been no reports of improvements to communications between Roumania and Russia. The improvements to roads in Roumania indicate that the Germans are preparing for a S.E. rather than a N.E. move.' It concluded: 'To sum up. The *military* evidence available does not at the present support the view that Germany intends to attack Russia. The most significant factor against this view is the low proportion of divisions of the field army in Poland. German troop dispositions and other military preparations in the neighbourhood of the Russian frontiers cannot at the moment be described as anything but normal.'[37]

The outlook was sombre, for if Hitler was not preparing for a campaign against Russia, it was reasoned that his primary objective for the fighting season of 1941 would be to knock Britain out of the war, almost certainly through the strategy of taking the Middle East. It appeared that Hitler required further persuasion that Britain was not going to be Germany's primary opponent for much longer. SO1's activities took on a new importance.

In the early hours of Sunday, 19 January 1941, a ciphered telegram was received at the Foreign Office that immediately set alarm bells ringing in Woburn Abbey, Whitehall and Downing Street. The telegram had originated from Britain's Ambassador in Berne, David Kelly, who earlier that day had made a disconcerting discovery about events taking place on his 'patch':

SECRET
Information has come to my attention that the Ambassador to Spain Sir Samuel Hoare was in Berne today. How can this be. Please advise. I need not inform you of the delicate situation here particularly with respect to the Swedish courier Blonde [sic] whom I do not wish to compromise.[38]

This brief telegram, which gives the impression that David Kelly was flustered and annoyed at being kept in the dark, is important not only for what it reveals about Sam Hoare's movements (yet again he was in Switzerland for a covert Saturday meeting), but because it further demonstrates that there were different strata of trust within the British government, Foreign Office and Intelligence Services. Kelly, despite his position as British Ambassador in Switzerland, and the fact that he was of an eminence to be conducting his own secret missions, was not sufficiently trusted to be told of Hoare's mission. This must have come as a devastating realisation to him when, within seventy-two hours, he received a stinging ciphered reply that in effect told him to mind his own business and keep his mouth shut:

> The Foreign Secretary acknowledges receipt of your information.
>
> To confirm or deny presence of the Ambassador to Spain might compromise his future work. You may be assured that if matters relate to Anglo Swiss relations you will be informed.
>
> Please refrain from enquiry if such an instance comes to your attention again.[39]

This firm rejection of his query must have left Kelly wondering what was taking place, for he was no diplomatic nonentity sitting serenely in Berne. He too had been engaged in deep covert diplomacy aimed at concluding the conflict, and had secretly met not only Himmler and Ribbentrop's private emissary Prince Hohenlohe, but also Baron Bonde, an eminent Swedish diplomat stationed in Switzerland who was acting as a confidential intermediary to Göring. The crucial difference was that the SO1 line was targeted directly at Adolf Hitler himself.

It is at this point that an important point should be noted. The real attempts at an Anglo–German understanding, like all the others of 1940–41, were rejected out of hand. As Churchill communicated to Eden later that January: 'Our attitude to all such inquiries or suggestions should be absolute silence'[40] – i.e. real diplomatic peace initiatives should be ignored, because they could undermine the war effort and the government's resolve to see Nazism defeated once and for all. The effort being undertaken by Sam Hoare on the other hand, as the instrument of SO1's Messrs HHHH operation, was fulfilling an entirely different function. It was not real. Its objective was deception and the undermining of Adolf Hitler through the medium of political warfare. What Hoare was doing was so sensitive that it had the potential, if it came to light, to cause catastrophic disaster. Not only would Hitler discover he was being duped, but he would finally understand that there was no prospect of peace with Britain, and would thus turn his military attention towards the Middle East and its oil, rather than towards Russia.

Throughout the winter of 1940–41, Rudolf Hess had been test-flying his Messerschmitt 110 around Germany, from airfields as far apart as Kiel and the Thuringian forests in the north, to the Alps in the south. Furthermore, he was requesting unusual technical improvements to his aircraft that were designed to enable a lone pilot to more easily handle a plane designed for three people. Among these requests were: 'Is it possible to install an automatic pilot in the cockpit?' and 'Can the wireless set mounted in the rear for use by the observer/wireless operator ... be moved to the pilot's cockpit?'[41]

On the morning of Saturday, 18 January 1941, Germany's Deputy-Führer was preparing to fly again. While he was waiting for his plane to be prepared he handed his adjutant, Lieutenant Pintsch, two sealed letters. One was addressed to Adolf Hitler, the other to Pintsch himself. Hess instructed Pintsch that if he did not return in four hours, he was to open his letter, and take the other to Hitler personally.[42] Helmut Kaden, evidently believing that this was Hess's second unsuccessful attempt to fly to Scotland, recalled: 'Hess ... [again] returned after about three and a half hours. On this occasion, he reported that there was something wrong with the Anflugnavigation approach system, a form of radio compass which had been installed in the machine ... Josef Blumel, the Chief Radio Operator at the Messerschmitt works, explained' that Hess had not tuned the equipment to the correct wavelength.[43]

Pitsch's evidence, however, makes it clear that Hess had had no intention of flying to Scotland on 18 January 1941, for he had made it clear that he intended to return within four hours. As before, it would have been perfectly possible for Hess to fly the 150 miles from Augsburg to Zürich in about thirty minutes, have had a two-hour meeting, then flown home again.

Wartime Switzerland – an alpine island of peace amidst a European sea of conflict – was not only bursting at the seams with refugees, but was a place where enemies encountered each other in neutral territory. It was therefore a hotbed of intrigue, subterfuge and, most importantly of all, surveillance. Thus Sam Hoare's presence there on 18 January was undoubtedly noted by someone from the British Embassy, who promptly reported it to David Kelly, who in turn queried the situation with the Foreign Office.

Back in London, meanwhile, other intelligence was flowing across the desks of Whitehall, and it was making grim reading. At the end of January, the War Office had been requested to prepare another paper for the Directors of Military Operations and the Prime Minister. This was to be both an assessment of the current military situation and an attempt to predict the direction of the war during the fighting season of 1941. The assessment began by declaring: 'Germany is the main enemy and has the initiative. Her army is stronger than is necessary for actual operations – excluding a war against USSR which is unlikely for the present – and she still has great numerical superiority in the air, though relatively less than she had in 1940.'[44]

It then noted that 'from the economic point of view Germany's situation is less favourable; she may suffer from shortage of oil in 1941 and her difficulties in the transportation and distribution of goods and foodstuffs must increase ... [It was therefore essential to forecast] Germany's probable strategy so as to plan countermeasures and organise our available resources to check, and if possible defeat her in action.' The paper went on to assess German military strength, and the possible courses of action available to her in 1941. One section, headed 'General Axis Strategy in the Mediterranean', concluded: 'There are many indications that Germany may be contemplating action through Spain, France, Italy or the Balkans, extending possibly into French North Africa, and even against Egypt via Libya or Turkey.'

This last point would have been read with concern by Churchill, for as the report stated, if Germany could 'persuade Greece to make peace with Italy . . . she would probably demand the occupation of Salonika – which Greece, under threats, could not refuse'. The report went on that it was most likely that Germany would continue with her objective of heading towards the Middle East, attacking Turkey and then Egypt:

> It is probable that Germany might defeat the Turks in Thrace and reach the Straits [of the Dardanelles] in not more than six weeks after the occupation of Salonika – say by the middle of May . . . [and] it might be possible for a German force to establish itself south of the Taurus by the end of July – this depending on the degree of Turkish resistance – it is estimated that eight divisions (increasing to twelve after two months) could be maintained through Anatolia for an advance via Syria on Egypt.

Finally, the report concluded:

It seems that Germany has sufficient land forces for:-
(a) The occupation of the whole of France.
(b) The occupation of Spain and Portugal, and an attack on Gibraltar.
(c) Action against French Morocco.
(d) Occupation of the Balkans and Greece.
It is unlikely that she could, at the same time, undertake operations through Anatolia against Turkey, Libya or Tunisia. The campaigns in Anatolia and Libya would be difficult operations employing considerable air forces, and would not immediately influence the result she aims at, the decisive defeat of Great Britain. But any of

the operations (b) to (d) above would directly threaten our hold on the Mediterranean.

It is now known that Germany did not have a strategic plan for the invasion of Anatolia in the fighting season of 1941, even if this could have led to an invasion of the Middle East; but Britain's analysts at the War Office did not know that, and the results of such a move would have been disastrous. It must therefore have been regarded as imperative that the Messrs HHHH operation should successfully undermine the German leadership's plans for the fighting season of 1941. Inciting Hitler to open a second front by declaring war on Russia had the potential to cause Nazi Germany's downfall, whereas an all-out German offensive against British forces, whether in North Africa or the Middle East, would see Britain fall to certain defeat.

With the benefit of hindsight, the War Office's strategic analysis of early February 1941 was incorrect, for a push towards the Middle East was very low on Hitler's list of priorities. That he was already planning a completely different eastern campaign of conquest for the fighting season of 1941 is perhaps the clearest indication that the Messrs HHHH operation was beginning to have a discernible effect. Hitler's decision to turn German forces on Russia – thus making a new and potentially lethal enemy – does not make sense unless there was some other set of factors at play.

Hitler was not so trusting as to declare war on Russia solely because he thought he had an inside track to peace with Britain. Despite Sir Samuel Hoare's eminence, he was in reality only a high-echelon middle-man, and the German leadership needed verification that he was acting on behalf of more influential figures. It was this seeking of verification that gave London the first sign that Hitler and his close associates had hungrily grabbed the bait proffered by SO1's operation.

On Saturday, 8 February 1941, Lord Halifax, newly installed as Britain's Ambassador in Washington, sent a confidential message to his replacement at the Foreign Office, Anthony Eden. Halifax revealed that an intermediary acting on behalf of the German Ambassador had attempted to make contact with him directly. This new development was potentially a serious complication, for it indicated yet again the instability of the top Nazi leadership. They would not play by the rules – albeit rules dictated by London – and negotiate solely through Sam Hoare. Instead they had made an attempt to open a direct line of communication to the man they *thought* they were ultimately dealing with, Lord Halifax – when in reality the only people they were negotiating with were the members of the inner circle at SO1 Woburn.

Lord Halifax had recoiled in horror at the thought of Nazis attempting to contact him directly. To him it was a sign of deep deceit – and deceivers can be unpredictable. All concerned, not least Halifax, would have been aware that if the Americans found out about the secret peace negotiations, and mistakenly believed they were genuine, it would deal a potentially mortal blow to the Anglo–American relationship. Any revelations now about a possible generous peace offer from Germany could be catastrophic for Britain's efforts to obtain American aid, and might also undo all Churchill's hopes of eventually dragging the United States into the war on Britain's side.

Just a year before, Churchill had greatly feared that Germany might leak information about Chamberlain's negotiations connected with the Venlo Incident. Now he was facing a similar dilemma. What if the Germans turned the Messrs HHHH operation on him? It could cause the worst of all disasters. American political pressure might even be exerted on the British government to accept Germany's peace offer. There was, after all, very little in the Hitler–Hess–Haushofer proposals that would not have appeared acceptable in early 1941.

Despite these immense dangers, the German attempt to open a line directly to Lord Halifax did have one encouraging feature: it indicated that Hitler, together with Hess and Haushofer, had swallowed the fiction about a potentially powerful British peace faction, which would appear to have been led by Lord Halifax and

Sam Hoare. The main concern now was to ensure that they remained deceived, which meant they would have to be kept away from Halifax. The extent of his involvement was mainly to represent a potential leader, and he is unlikely to have had much knowledge about what SO1 and Hoare were negotiating, ostensibly on his behalf.

Within a few days of receiving Halifax's telegram, Sir Alexander Cadogan, the Permanent Under-Secretary at the Foreign Office, replied to it in a 'MOST SECRET' telegram. After opening with a cordial 'Dear Edward,' Cadogan immediately became very serious:

Further to your telegram to the Foreign Secretary of 8th February regarding the approach by an emissary of [German Ambassador] Dieckhoff concerning the H matter, I have been instructed to pass on the following guidance.

All matters regarding H must be managed under the strictest diplomatic protocols, as we instructed Sam [Hoare] to inform the emissary last November. As we all agreed, the emissary was ordered not to contact you directly, so as to confuse their assessment of the situation, and to prevent your compromise should there be a mistake. We do not believe the opposition would intentionally leak as it will end their whole operation, and we certainly would not as we are not supposed to know – but mistakes do happen.

Both Winston and Anthony [Eden] agree that if any further approach is made, feign anger and walk away. For our part we have informed Sam to tell the emissary that any further attempt to influence you will result in an immediate end to negotiations.

Tellingly, Cadogan concluded the telegram by stating:

I need hardly emphasise how dangerous a failure during the coming sensitive stage could be. Please destroy this telegram after digesting the content.

Yours ever AC[45]

Cadogan's telegram is an extremely interesting document, for it reveals many things – some obvious, others less so – with very important implications indeed. Primarily, it refers to the 'H' matter, confirming Sam Hoare's involvement since the previous November when he had met the Papal Nuncio, and the fact that he had instructed the Germans that no direct contact to Halifax was to be made. Of greater importance, however, is the statement that 'We [i.e. Churchill and Eden, who are mentioned, and possibly SO1 too] do not believe the opposition [the Germans] would intentionally leak as it will end their whole operation, and we certainly would not as we are not supposed to know'.

This last is the most important statement of all. It is the smoking gun which indicates that all this subterfuge – the pretence of negotiations with a non-existent peace faction within Britain – was being conducted with the full knowledge of Churchill, through the secret political warfare organisation operating out of Woburn Abbey. The statement cannot be misconstrued to mean anything else, particularly in light of the later comment: 'Both Winston and Anthony agree that if any further approach is made, feign anger and walk away.' This is telling not only because it reveals who was being consulted, but because of the use of the phrase to *feign* anger – i.e. not even Halifax's indignation at being contacted by the Nazis was to be genuine.

Throughout the six months that the Messrs HHHH operation had been in existence a key participant, as head of SOE, had been Hugh Dalton. His relationship with Rex Leeper had not much eased during the autumn and winter of 1940, and there continued to be friction between them. With Halifax's departure for Washington, Dalton had lost an unlikely but valuable ally. At first the Conservative Lord Halifax had not been inclined to look favourably upon the socialist Dalton – indeed, as late as the summer of 1940 he had referred to him as a 'naturally offensive creature'.[46] However, over the months that followed the two men began to recognise each other's abilities, and had developed a good working relationship.[47]

Now Dalton found Anthony Eden – much more of a devotee

of the Churchillian style of conducting war than Halifax could ever be – in Halifax's place at the Foreign Office. Dalton rapidly found himself an isolated figure amongst Churchill and his old cronies, including Leeper, Hoare, Ingrams, Eden and Bruce Lockhart. As the Messrs HHHH operation picked up momentum, Dalton's conscience begin to trouble him with increasing frequency, particularly when he realised that its ultimate objective was the turning of Germany on Russia.

On 28 February 1941, Dalton wrote an urgent note directly to Anthony Eden to voice his fears, saying: 'I have been in deep contemplation ever since the matter we discussed yesterday with the P[rime] M[inister], and feel I must put my concerns to you before we take any further action.'[48] He went on: 'Leeper's assessment on Saturday was pretty close to the mark, and his conclusions that despite being unable, probably, to win in Europe, we could win a world war has, of course, been bandied about for the last month or two.'

As Dalton voices his fears about what is planned, it becomes clear that serious discussions were taking place behind closed doors concerning Britain's long-term war strategy. He reveals that it had secretly been concluded that a lone Britain could not win a European war. If, however, the conflict could be expanded into a world war, bringing in other nations – particularly the United States – Germany would undoubtedly lose in the end. Dalton commented: 'what Winston now proposes is a truly terrible thing, and I am not sure my conscience will allow me to participate'.

Dalton was not a weak man opposed to war, and his recoiling from action must have taken his colleagues by surprise. He must have realised the terrible consequences of a German push into the east – and it should be remembered that Hitler's invasion of Russia would indeed be marked by tens of millions of deaths. He continued: 'I have always maintained that in this war body-line bowling of the Hun is justified, and the Messrs HHHH Operation, once we took it over, was intended to fulfil that function, but I do not believe we can be morally justified to use it to cause the suggested end result. I feel we must have another meeting to discuss where we are going to take this matter.' Dalton concluded his letter to Eden by using the old political trick of attempting to bring an adversary on side by asking for his counsel and advice: 'I would appreciate your opinion.'

If Hugh Dalton believed that Anthony Eden would support him against the use of Messrs HHHH to achieve what he saw as a dreadful end, he was mistaken. Furthermore, he made two fatal blunders. Firstly, he overestimated his own importance as Minister of both Economic Warfare and SOE. Secondly, at the same time as writing to Eden, Dalton also sent a letter to Churchill voicing his concerns over the direction the Messrs HHHH operation was taking. What Churchill regarded as his weakening of resolve would prove to be Dalton's political undoing for the remainder of the war.

That same weekend Robert Vansittart, who had undoubtedly been to see Churchill, wrote a brief note to Rex Leeper:

> Dear Rex,
> I thought I should send you this short note concerning the H[ugh] D[alton] matter. I have rarely seen Winston so annoyed as when he received HD's letter yesterday. It has thrown the whole matter in turmoil, but I believe we can keep HD on side long enough to conclude the matter at hand.
> I would appreciate first hand news of any problems with HD, as I believe BB has been given the go ahead to reduce him once the operation has reached its conclusion.[49]

'BB' was Churchill's loyal stalwart Brendan Bracken, described by some as his 'faithful chela', whose political career rose and fell with that of his mentor. A brash, red-haired Irishman of humble origins, Bracken had been a prominent journalist and MP during the inter-war period, and by early 1941 had become Churchill's Political Private secretary.[50] His loyalty and friendship would be rewarded in 1941 when, having 'reduced' Dalton and banished him to the Board of Trade, Churchill made Bracken Minister of Information. Thus he in effect inherited SO1, which was soon to be renamed the Political Warfare Executive, or PWE, and placed under the Ministry of Information.

In later years Dalton would call Bracken a 'most malevolent influence upon Mr Churchill', and a 'force of evil'.[51] In the early spring of 1941, however, Dalton had little idea of the forces beginning to range against him, or that soon he would become expendable. No one, not even a senior government Minister, would be allowed to jeopardise this most crucial of operations, upon which Britain's very survival might depend.

However, Bracken himself would also occasionally prove problematic in later years. During a visit to New York in 1943 he created an uncomfortable stir when he blithely made it public that 'Hess had been firmly convinced that certain circles in Britain would topple the Churchill government and join forces in crushing the Soviet Union'.[52] That was a little too close for comfort, and earned him sharp a rebuke from Churchill on his return to Britain.

CHAPTER 5

A Tense Spring

Throughout the spring of 1941 Churchill's concern about the possibility of a German push through the Balkans towards Britain's source of oil in the Middle East steadily increased. The beginning of 1941's fighting season was almost upon him, and Churchill knew that the next few months would be crucial in determining whether Britain was going to survive, or go under.

In the late autumn of 1940 Italian troops had marched from occupied Albania into north-west Greece. At first all seemed to go well for the Italians, but soon they hit an impasse as the fiercely independent Greek troops first fought them to a standstill, then began to push them back beyond the Albanian–Greek frontier. It was all very embarrassing for Hitler's ally Mussolini.

Now, in the spring of 1941, a new development arose, which in part originated from Churchill's fear that Germany might also attack Greece, and then force its way through Thrace to the Dardanelles.[1] It was a region that haunted Churchill, but his disastrous Dardanelles campaign of 1915 would pale into insignificance if this really was the direction of Hitler's intent in 1941 – for beyond the Dardanelles lay Turkey, Anatolia and the gateway to the Middle East. No matter how good the strategic planning in London, the military efforts in North Africa or the sacrifices made by the Merchant Navy facing German U-boats in the Atlantic, it would all be for nothing if Hitler's troops could take the Middle East's oil reserves.

Churchill would later recall that the early spring of 1941 was 'the moment ... when the irrevocable decision [had to] be taken whether or not to send the Army of the Nile to Greece. This grave step was required not only to help Greece in her peril and torment, but to form against the impending German attack [on the] Balkan Front ... We did not then know that he [Hitler] was already deeply set upon his gigantic invasion of Russia.'[2] Mindful of the need to protect Britain's Middle Eastern flank, at the end of February Anthony Eden travelled out to the eastern Mediterranean to negotiate an arrangement with the Greek government for British military support. It was a strategy that would prove disastrous, and would almost cause complete catastrophe.

During the late autumn and winter of 1940, British forces in North Africa had at long last managed to turn back the Axis tide of conquest, pushing the enemy westward away from Egypt and the Suez Canal. After heavy fighting and loss of life, the British North African Army had even managed to take Sidi Barani in Libya, and allowed themselves to dream that they might actually win the campaign.

Now Churchill began to make his plans known of removing a considerable chunk of the North African Army to Greece, with the objective not only of defending the east Mediterranean flank and the route to the Middle East, but of giving Hitler another front to worry about. On 4 March the C-in-C Mediterranean, Admiral Sir Andrew Cunningham, based in Alexandria, counselled caution against such a move, enumerating the very considerable risks involved in removing such a substantial segment of the British Army and Air Force from Egypt and North Africa for deployment in Greece. His warnings were not heeded.

On 1 March German forces had poured across the Romanian frontier into Bulgaria, and the tensions in the region rose inexorably. On 6 March Churchill telegrammed to Eden in Cairo:

> Situation has indeed changed for worse ... Failure of [Greek General] Papagos to act as agreed with you on Feb. 22, obvious difficulty of his extricating his army from contact in Albania ... together with other adverse factors ... make it difficult for Cabinet to believe

that we now have any power to avert fate of Greece unless Turkey and/or Yugoslavia come in, which seems most improbable. We have done our best to promote Balkan combination against Germany.

Loss of Greece and Balkans by no means a major catastrophe for us, provided Turkey remains honest neutral . . . We are advised from many quarters that our ignominious ejection from Greece would do us more harm in Spain and Vichy than the fact of submission of Balkans, which with our scanty forces alone we have never been expected to prevent . . .[3]

After the war Churchill received considerable criticism for the Greek campaign, and comments were made that had he not drawn much-needed men and materiel from North Africa, the desert war would have ended much sooner, and the costly toing and froing across Libya from 1941 to 1942 might never have occurred. However, as his telegraphically communicated fears of a German push through Greece made clear, Churchill had very considerable worries in the spring of 1941. Britain simply did not possess sufficient armed forces to cover all eventualities, and in the months ahead this situation would grow steadily worse.

By the end of March the Balkans had become a hotbed of turmoil. There would be revolution in Yugoslavia, and in early April Germany, boasting an overwhelming military presence, invaded both Yugoslavia and Greece. It did indeed seem that the fighting season of 1941 would see the Balkans fall to German conquest, opening up the eastern Mediterranean and raising the prospect of a Middle Eastern campaign.

Despite this, there was still a multiplicity of confusing signals emanating from the German government. The Nazi leadership's carrot-and-stick style of warfare persisted, with unremitting war and devastation threatened on the one hand, with tentative offers of peace on the other. In this perplexing and bizarre situation Sam Hoare, skilled in the arts of politics and diplomacy, was in his element. On the same day that Churchill telegrammed Anthony Eden in Cairo, Hoare was also preparing a communication. It appeared that someone else in Germany was trying to cut a peace deal; what was more, he seemed to know that Britain's Ambassador to Spain, Sir Samuel Hoare, was the key man to approach.

This new protagonist had a track record in peaceable approaches. A Sudeten German aristocrat, Prince Max zu Hohenlohe had in the months preceding his approach to Sam Hoare been busily engaged in an attempt at peace mediation with David Kelly, the British Ambassador in Berne, on behalf of Himmler and Ribbentrop. Now, however, he appeared to be speaking with the authority of someone considerably more eminent, there being covert signals of a connection to Hitler through Hermann Göring.

An intrigued Hoare agreed to a secret meeting with Hohenlohe at the Madrid flat of his old friend Brigadier Torr. On this occasion, as the reports made clear, Hoare was wearing his official hat as the representative of the British government in Spain, and not his unofficial one as SO1 go-between to a fictitious political faction led by Lord Halifax. This stance was taken because it was known that Hohenlohe was not connected to the Hess–Haushofer line of communication.

In view of the delicacy of the situation, Hoare communicated what had taken place directly to Sir Alexander Cadogan, Permanent Under-Secretary at the Foreign Office, in a 'Personal & Secret' note accompanied by a closely-typed two-page report. Hoare wrote:

> I had not, of course, seen [Hohenlohe] since the months just before the war when we met from time to time socially in London. He appeared to be ill at ease at the beginning of the talk. This made the Military Attaché and myself take the view that he had come to Madrid with some kind of special mission from Göring. This impression has been subsequently increased by the fact that . . . after I left . . . he told the Military Attaché that he had recently been staying with Göring.[4]

Hoare went on to reveal that after Hohenlohe had begun with 'a few platitudes about his properties in Europe and our mutual friends in London', the conversation had quickly 'moved into more serious questions'. Hohenlohe had stated that 'it was a calamity that the war was continuing, Hitler had been ready to make peace last July [1940] after his great success [at the fall of France]'. Hohenlohe had then asked 'Why were we not ready to make peace now after our great [North] African successes?'

Over the next hour Hohenlohe tried to impress upon Hoare the futility of continued conflict, declaring that as 'Germany could never be defeated, and as the English believe they could never be defeated, the only result of the continuance of the war would be the devastation of Europe, the end of European civilisation and the Communism or Americanisation of the world'. Hoare reported Hohenlohe as claiming that 'Hitler . . . never wanted to fight Great Britain, and if peace were made now we [the British government] should find him very reasonable.'

At this point Hoare interrupted, asking the German Prince what he meant by Hitler's 'reasonableness'.

'Hitler,' Hohenlohe replied, 'wanted Eastern Europe and China. As to Western Europe and the rest of the world, he wanted little or nothing.'

Hoare commented to Cadogan that at this point 'I said to him . . . no one in England believed Hitler's word,' to which Hohenlohe retorted that if Britain 'would not make peace with Hitler we should never be able to make peace at all'.

'Supposing that Göring took his [Hitler's] place tomorrow,' Hohenlohe conjectured. 'Göring's rivals would make him even more intransigent than Hitler. Hitler was the only man who counted in Germany and if Hitler declared for peace, he would carry the country with him. With Göring or anyone else it would be different.' At this point Hohenlohe became very critical about Ribbentrop, who he said 'had lost influence with Hitler, presumably from having told him that England would never fight'.

Towards the end of the conversation Hohenlohe commented on the Russian situation that 'Sooner or later, and in his view the sooner the better, Germany would have to absorb the Ukraine and Russian oilfields. He expressed the greatest contempt for the Russian army and implied that they would get what they wanted without having to fight for it.' This was very important information, more than justifying Hoare's secret meeting with Prince Hohenlohe. For months Hoare had been battling with an intransigent Hugh Dalton, who as Minister of Economic Warfare had been pressing hard for a naval blockade of Spain. It was a well-kept secret that throughout the war, supposedly neutral Spain acted as a very effective conduit for iron, mercury, rubber, oil and a plethora of other essential supplies which were shipped via the Canary Islands to Spain, before going on to aid the Reich.

Sam Hoare knew that a neutral Spain, albeit supplying Germany, was infinitely more valuable to Britain in its present state than it would be under a blockade, which might well push it into the Axis fold, setting up a potential chain reaction. An Axis-allied Spain would almost certainly see Gibraltar fall to German control. With that, Britain's access to the Mediterranean would end, leading to British defeat in North Africa, and the loss of Egypt and the Middle East.

Now Samuel Hoare had learned, direct from the horse's mouth, that Hitler was greedily eyeing the Ukraine and the Caucasus. This was another small but highly significant pointer that German economic need, tied to the Nazis' political ideology of *Lebensraum*, and almost certainly helped along by SO1's deception campaign, was slowly but inexorably steering the German Führer in the desired direction.

Shortly after this important statement, Hoare and Hohenlohe's meeting concluded, but Hoare later heard from Brigadier Torr that after he had left, Hohenlohe had remained behind, becoming more relaxed now that he was not speaking officially to the Ambassador. Hoare reported that to Torr the Prince 'lowered the German claims in Europe, saying that of course he had to put them very high to me'.

The fact that Prince Hohenlohe was allowed to travel to Spain indicates that his peace approach was semi-official. It was, as Albrecht Haushofer would say, 'significant' that he could travel to a neutral state. It was known that Hohenlohe had been busy during the winter of 1940 attempting to mediate though the British Ambassador in Berne, David Kelly, on behalf of Himmler and

Ribbentrop. Despite this, he was now trying to open another line of communication to the British government.

SO1's main criteria was to stall, but as Hitler's peaceable offer had been a good deal to start with, it would not be long before the Germans demanded some sign of intent from the fictitious Halifax faction. This, allied to Britain's precarious strategic position, was making it a tense spring for all concerned with Messrs HHHH.

There had been increasing problems in the Middle East since the beginning of the year when, unbeknownst to the British, the Grand Mufti of Jerusalem, Husayni al Haj Amin, had written personally to Hitler from Baghdad requesting German assistance in overthrowing the British in Iraq, declaring with a dramatic flourish: 'Excellency. England, that relentless and crafty enemy of true liberty of peoples, has never tired of forging chains to enslave and subjugate the Arab peoples . . .'[5]

In an attempt to further his aim of ousting the British, the Grand Mufti had then sent his private secretary to Berlin to request financial assistance and 'a subsidy in the form of credits for arms deliveries'. The emissary had assured Ernst Woermann, the Director of the Political Division of the Auswärtiges Amt, that 'apart from small contingents of the English Air Force there were no English troops on Iraq territory', and that his country would resume diplomatic relations with Germany 'if Iraq received the desired political declaration from us and if the question of supporting Iraq in case of war with England was clarified'.[6]

In the late spring of 1941 Winston Churchill received a clear-cut military assessment of the Middle Eastern situation that stated:

If the Germans should launch an attack on Syria or Iraq by air borne troops:-

(a) Syria: they might succeed in establishing a hold on a part of Syria and perhaps raise the country against the French, unless we can send military aid to General Dentz [the High

Commissioner and commander-in-chief for the Vichy government in Syria].

(b) Iraq: i)they could support the Iraqi Army at Mosul and Baghdad and ultimately threaten our position at Basra, unless we can provide additional Forces. ii) they could capture Ratbah and cut the oil pipe line.

It was however recorded in the draft handwritten notes that: 'All our information points to an attack on Crete as the first step, & this is believed to be imminent. On the other hand if the British situation in Iraq seriously deteriorates – it would be possible [for Germany] to launch an expedition from the Dodecanese directly to Iraq.'[7]

This was worrying enough in itself, but only weeks before Churchill had received a 'MOST SECRET' three-page appreciation on 'German Relations with the USSR', prepared by MI14,* which made grim reading. It reported that 'a suggestion made recently to the Soviet government by the British Ambassador that Great Britain was indifferent to the integrity of the USSR and might be tempted to conclude a peace [with Germany] on the basis of a German withdrawal from occupied countries in return for a free hand in the East got a cold reception'. The trawled bait of implying that Britain might make peace with Germany in exchange for a German withdrawal from her western conquests had not been taken up. The report had pessimistically concluded:

In the light of the foregoing paragraphs, a German attack on the U.S.S.R. seems most unlikely in the immediate future. The question may be expected, however, to remain open, so that it can be used:-

(a) as a forceful warning to ensure the continuation by the U.S.S.R. of economic collaboration and to indicate that interference with Germany's plans will not be tolerated.

---

* A subdivision of MI3 which analysed intelligence and prepared assessments of possible German military intentions.

(b) to keep the British government and, in a lesser degree, the Turkish government guessing as to Germany's future intentions.[8]

The implications were clear, particularly to the select few in Whitehall who were familiar with the deception campaign being mounted against the German leadership by SO1. Germany, left to its own devices, was unlikely to move against Russia until, one way or another, Britain ceased to be perceived as a long-term threat. The Messrs HHHH operation had gone some way towards satisfying Hitler that this would soon be the case, that a political clique would soon, by constitutional means, manoeuvre Churchill out of the premiership and form a new government which had, prior to its legal coup, already negotiated the parameters under which an armistice could take place.

Sixty years after the event, we know that by the winter of 1940 Hitler was already planning Operation Barbarossa. What is not clear, however, is the extent to which his decision to attack Russia and create a second front was influenced by his belief that an Anglo–German peace was being negotiated. The paucity of British Intelligence documents from this period, particularly of those referring to SO1's political warfare initiatives, makes this difficult to ascertain. Yet it can be said with some certainty that even had Hitler already decided on the invasion of Russia by the winter of 1940–41, SO1's deception operation helped to bolster that decision.

However, we do know the importance which Churchill placed upon the setting of Germany against Russia. In a speech to the House of Commons in the spring of 1941, he declared: 'I beg His Majesty's government to get some brutal truths into their heads. Without an effective Eastern front, there can be no satisfactory defence of our interests in the West, and without Russia there can be no effective Eastern Front.'[9]

On Wednesday, 26 March 1941, just at the moment when the peace negotiations seemed to have run out of puff, and a German push towards the Middle East seemed certain, Samuel Hoare was unexpectedly notified that Albrecht Haushofer was back in Madrid, and requesting a meeting. Once again, as so many times before, Hoare found himself in the home of Colonel Juan Beigbeder y Atienza, which seems to have become a wartime Anglo–German place of special neutrality, an *in camera* environment where the two opposing parties could meet far from public scrutiny and the dangers of press attention. Hoare wrote back to London:

> Dear Alec [Cadogan]
> . . . I have now had a further meeting with Haushofer at the home of Beigbeder. I understand he is here at his superior's insistence . . .

However, Hoare noted, all was not well, for

> it was evident during our meeting that he and his kin are now becoming most agitated by the lack of progress.
> During the course of our conversation H[aushofer] asked why Edward [i.e. Lord Halifax] had not yet made any move, etc. I explained the complexities of the situation, which would make any action a long process. H understood completely, but responded that his superior has insisted on a meeting with a close representative of the man of influence on neutral territory.[10]

Haushofer's question as to why Halifax had made no move revealed that the German leadership was becoming impatient. They wanted an indication, even a small one, that Halifax was preparing to move against Churchill. This could have been a subtle public criticism of the Prime Minister in the neutral United States, or an indication of political disagreement in Britain. Hoare was forced to explain to Haushofer that because of the extreme sensitivity of the situation, any move by the Halifax faction would have to be conducted very carefully.

Hoare was well aware that Albrecht Haushofer, as an expert on Britain, understood that in British politics the majority of activity takes place behind closed doors, and that a public move by Halifax and his clique – for example the call for a vote of no confidence against Churchill – would only be made when they were absolutely sure of success.

However, although Haushofer understood the situation, he made it clear to Hoare that 'his superiors' – Hess and Hitler – did not. On the whole Nazi politicians were relatively unsophisticated, and found it difficult to fathom the subtleties of British politics. In their anxiety to discover how much support the Halifax faction really possessed, Haushofer's superiors fell back on their old instincts. They wanted a face-to-face discussion with a trusted emissary who could interpret the signs. Thus they were insisting on a meeting with a 'close representative of the man of influence'.

Hoare's curious phraseology indicates that he was carefully avoiding naming the 'man of influence'. Throughout the Messrs H – Hitler – Hess – Haushofer – Hoare – Halifax – discussions, SO1 had striven to present as convincing a façade as possible to the German leadership. For this reason it had been necessary to imply that Halifax had significant support.

Throughout his time as Ambassador in Madrid, Samuel Hoare demonstrated few qualms in his correspondence about casually naming his acquaintances 'Winston' Churchill, 'Anthony' Eden, 'Alec' Cadogan and 'Edward' Halifax, even under the constraints of the Messrs HHHH correspondence of 1940–41. The implication is that the 'man of influence' to whom he referred was superior to Halifax, and would remain so even once Halifax attained the premiership. Under the British constitution there is only one person of more influence than the Prime Minister, and that is the head of state. Hoare was therefore discreetly referring to a 'close representative' of King George VI.

Any successful ousting of Churchill in 1941 – a political *coup d'état*, for lack of a better description – would have to receive the support of the head of state. It must have been intimated to the Germans at some point during the course of the negotiations that Lord Halifax had the support of George VI, and that if Churchill lost a vote of confidence, the King would invite Halifax to form a new government. This is the only scenario that Haushofer – an expert on the British constitution – would have believed, and that would have led him to assure Hess and the Führer that the scheme could work. Lord Halifax would form a government and, after a decent interval, announce that the war was untenable and open armistice negotiations, having already secretly agreed terms that would see all the occupied west European states liberated from German control.

However, Sam Hoare's letter to London of 26 March 1941 indicated that there was a problem. After months of seemingly satisfactory negotiation on neutral territory, with the tacit understanding that an armistice would shortly be forthcoming, perhaps as soon as that summer, Haushofer had appeared with a demand from the German leadership for a high-level meeting. What had gone wrong?

It may be that the Germans, disappointed at the lack of progress, smelled a rat. Perhaps they had received a hint from a high-level source that all was not as it seemed. Or it may even be that as the deadline for Barbarossa approached an increasingly paranoid Hitler was becoming anxious to safely tie one source of danger down before embarking on another campaign. Beyond the fact that it is indicative of uncertainty, the reason for the sudden German demand may never be known.

An evidently concerned Hoare wrote to Cadogan: 'After I pointed out that this was out of the question, H[aushofer] informed me that it has already been arranged for their Head of AO [Auslandsorganisation] to journey anywhere for a confidential meeting, if it would resolve the impasse.'

This presented a very difficult situation. A meeting on neutral territory was unlikely to be permitted by SO1, for fear of losing control of the situation. However, Hoare concluded: 'There is undoubtedly an urgency on their part now, and their demands are unrealistic if not dangerous, but ... I am also convinced we shall have to facilitate some sort of meeting if the matter is not to fail.'

There were, as yet, no indications as to who the 'close representative of the man of influence' was going to be, and it may well be that Hoare himself did not know. Indeed, since the purpose of all SO1's subterfuge thus far had been to intimate that a fictitious peace faction within the British government was preparing to launch a *coup d'état*, it may be that they had not made any provision for such a German demand. That, however, was about to change.

So far SO1 had successfully managed to suck the German leadership into a fantasy world of peaceable intent by offering them just what they wanted to see: signs of dissent among leading figures in the British government who were prepared to negotiate their country out of the war. Furthermore, the Germans had been led to believe that these politicians were plotting to constitutionally usurp power from Churchill to attain their objectives. The men of Woburn Abbey had put too much effort into this high-risk operation to let it collapse for lack of a credible figurehead to serve up to the Nazis.

Meanwhile, a report was dispatched to Rome by the Italian Ambassador in Madrid, Francesco Lequio, which hinted that a little information was beginning to spill from SO1's nest of intrigue. Lequio reported that Samuel Hoare had recently stated to a German emissary that the British government was not secure, and that Churchill could 'no longer rely on a majority [in the House of Commons]'. Furthermore, Lequio stated that Hoare had declared that sooner or later he expected to be 'called back to London to take over the government with the precise task of concluding a compromise peace', and that Hoare had gone on to say that Anthony Eden would have to be removed as Foreign Secretary and replaced by R.A. 'Rab' Butler.[11]

On the surface, Lequio's report seems fairly damning evidence of Hoare's disloyalty to Churchill. But in the context of the Messrs HHHH operation, it can be seen in a very different light. What is less clear is to whom Hoare's comments were made. Lequio intimated that they were made to Hohenlohe, and it is certainly the case that his report was submitted more than a week prior to the Haushofer–Hoare meeting of 26 March. However, Hoare is unlikely to have made his comments during his 6 March meeting with Hohenlohe, since there is no evidence to indicate that

Brigadier Torr, who was present throughout, was involved in SO1's operation. This therefore suggests that another meeting must have taken place between 6 and 14 March 1941, of which there is no record.

There is, however, a clue in Sam Hoare's letter to Cadogan to the chain of events about to occur in late April and early May 1941. This is the demand, as imparted by Haushofer, that the intermediary the German leadership proposed to meet the 'representative of the man of influence' was the head of the Auslandsorganisation, Ernst Bohle.

Despite his senior position and his friendship with Hess, Bohle had not been drawn into the full confidence of the Hitler–Hess–Haushofer inner circle. Yet he was an important figure in Nazi foreign policy, and his Auslandsorganisation played a key role in furthering the Nazis' foreign aims, maintaining contact with ethnic Germans as far afield as Italy, Spain, the United States, Japan and Argentina. The fact that he had been entrusted with a great deal of Hess's translation work meant that he was close to the affair, although he did not know the full details. He could thus have been swiftly brought up to speed on the negotiations, should it prove necessary.

Bohle's position on the fringe of the peace affair became clearer in 1945, when he was questioned by Allied Intelligence. Under oath, he stated: 'It was suggested by Professor Haushofer, [the] well-known Munich professor, that I would meet [someone] in neutral territory, possibly Switzerland.' He caused a flurry of excitement when he went on: 'I didn't know he [Hess] was going to England; [I] thought he was going to Switzerland.'[12]

In the weeks which followed Sam Hoare's letter to Cadogan, Germany's military strategy in the Mediterranean took an ominous turn.

Britain's forces in North Africa had been tapped of much of their strength in order to support Greece against the expected Axis offensive in the Balkans. To Churchill's great discomfort it was now discovered that Hitler had dispatched substantial forces to

North Africa to stiffen the Italians. The Afrika Korps, under the brilliant leadership of Erwin Rommel, began pummelling the remaining British forces into a withdrawal back towards Egypt.

On the afternoon of 6 April 1941, an emergency conference was held at GCHQ Cairo. It was attended by Anthony Eden (still in Egypt after his negotiations with the Greek government), Generals Wavell and Dill, Air Marshal Longmore and Admiral Cunningham. The subject of their debate was whether the British Army should make a stand in the western desert or rapidly withdraw to the Nile delta. Unsurprisingly, the politicians said the army should make a stand; but the military men's opinion was that a tactical withdrawal two hundred miles back towards Egypt would enable a better defensive line to be created, supported by much shorter lines of communication. This was duly reported back to London. The following morning, an extremely concerned Churchill telegraphed General Wavell, saying: 'You should surely be able to hold Tobruk . . . at least until or unless the enemy brings up strong artillery forces. It seems difficult to believe that he can do this for some weeks. He would run a great risk in masking Tobruk and advancing upon Egypt.' In phraseology more characteristic of Hitler's panicked proclamations to his army trapped in Stalingrad just two years later, Churchill commented: 'Tobruk therefore seems to be a place to be held to the death without thought of retirement.'[13]

On receiving this sobering communication, Wavell immediately flew from Cairo to Tobruk to assess the situation for himself. It was to be a trip from which the Commander-in-Chief was lucky to return. After touring Tobruk and seeing for himself the inadequacy of its defences Wavell flew back to Egypt, but his plane developed engine trouble and crashed in the desert. As luck would have it no one was seriously injured, but it was a very subdued Wavell who – in the panic of the crash he had hastily burnt all his secret papers – limped back into Cairo in the early hours of the following morning to report: 'I do not feel we shall have long respite . . . Tobruk is not [a] good defensive position; [and the] long line of communication behind is hardly protected at all.'[14]

This was dire news for Churchill, who now saw the prospect of a successful two-pronged German push via the Balkans and North Africa descending on the Middle East to take both the Suez Canal and Britain's oil. He could perceive with devastating clarity the dangers ahead, and was forced to take a firm stand against the generals who were counselling a tactical withdrawal. He immediately drafted a telegram to Wavell that declared:

> From here it seems unthinkable that the fortress of Tobruk should be abandoned without offering the most prolonged resistance ... The enemy's line is long and should be vulnerable provided he is not given time to organise at leisure. So long as Tobruk is held and its garrison includes even a few armoured vehicles which can lick out his communications, nothing but a raid dare go past Tobruk. If you leave Tobruk and go 260 miles back to Mersa Matruh may you not find yourself faced with something like the same problem? We are convinced you should fight it out at Tobruk.[15]

Before he could dispatch this backbone-stiffening telegram Churchill was relieved to receive a message from Cairo that Wavell had, despite grave concern, decided 'to hold Tobruk ... and build up ... [the] defences in Mursa Mutruh area'. However, Wavell commented, 'My resources are very limited ... [and] it will be a race against time.' Breathing a huge sigh of relief, Churchill shelved his original telegram, instead sending a placatory: 'We all cordially endorse your decision to hold Tobruk, and will do all in our power to bring you aid.'[16]

History has not recorded Wavell's response, but he had no illusions that he and his troops were facing a desperate fight with their backs to the wall.

In London, Churchill's mood was no better. Not only was North Africa a desperate worry, but the Balkans were swiftly proving to be a catastrophe as well. The fall of western Europe had been devastating both psychologically and strategically, but it was a disaster against which island Britain could, with effort and resolve, hold out. If, however, Hitler's objective in 1941 was the Middle East, then the fall of the Balkans might herald an entirely more serious situation. The fall of Greece would, in just a few weeks, cause Churchill to wire President Roosevelt: '[Do] not underrate the gravity of the consequences which may follow from a Middle Eastern collapse. In this war every post is a winning-post, and how many more are we going to lose?'[17]

That same day Churchill would also dispatch an urgent telegram to Wavell, informing him:

A commitment in Iraq was inevitable. We had to establish a base at Basra [oil terminal], and control that port to safeguard Persian oil in case of need ... The security of Egypt remains paramount. But it is essential to do all in our power to save Habbaniya [Britain's RAF base in the Iraqi desert, providing air superiority in the region] and to control the [oil] pipe-line to the Mediterranean.[18]

The insecurity of Britain's position in the spring of 1941 should not be underestimated, for the events taking place had the potential to see Britain quickly fall to defeat. The situation was also causing Churchill deep political concern, and his premiership could have been at risk had Britain suffered another major reverse. In March MP Harold Nicolson, working under Duff Cooper at the Ministry of Information, noted the rumblings of disquiet, and commented that while the country might be able to withstand Hitler's worst, the people were becoming so exhausted by the war that it might soon become difficult for the government to reject a reasonable German peace offer. If things became very bad, he wrote, there might even be a move 'to attribute the whole disaster to the "war mongers", and to replace Churchill by Sam Hoare or some appeaser'.[19]

Such comments, restricted to the confidentiality of a diary, were bad enough, but they were indicative of the underlying political mood. Churchill would have been fully aware of this, as such noises were being made even in the corridors of power. The previous autumn David Lloyd George had circulated a memorandum to friends and supporters in which he expressed the view that Britain's only chance of victory was 'if Hitler was stupid enough to attack Russia'. His conclusion was that 'terms must therefore be sought in order to avoid a wasting war'.[20] By mid-spring 1941 Lloyd George's line had hardened, and he was openly expressing his dissatisfaction with Churchill's leadership.[21] Churchill, for his part, repaid the compliment by comparing the aged politician to the leader of Vichy France, the 'illustrious and venerable Marshal Pétain'.[22]

If the long, hot summer of 1940 is recognised as Britain's time of greatest danger, then the spring of 1941 was the time of Winston Churchill's worst political peril. As Prime Minister since May 1940, Churchill had almost single-handedly held Britain together in the post-Dunkirk period, through the Battle of Britain and the dangerous winter of 1940. Yet now, at the time when Britain's fate seemed to hang in the balance, the voices of dissent in Westminster and Whitehall were growing ever stronger.

On 16 April, with the military situation in Greece deteriorating by the hour, Churchill reluctantly sent secret orders to Admiral Cunningham to set plans in motion for an emergency evacuation from Greece. It was, as Churchill later commented, a 'grim prospect [that] now gaped upon us all'.[23]

Oliver Harvey, close friend and confidant of Anthony Eden, and soon to become the Foreign Secretary's Principal Private Secretary, encapsulated the political mood in his diary, noting there was 'much criticism of Winston, I hear, in City circles, for bad judgement'. The next day he augmented this, commenting that there was rising condemnation of Churchill, led by 'the remnants of the Chamberlainites', who were using Britain's military failures as a 'dishonest cloak of defeatism – at the end of that road lies L[loyd] G[eorge], who, abetted by that ass [Basil] Liddell Hart, would readily be a Pétain to us, with the support of the Press Barons and City Magnates'.[24] At the same time, Harold Nicolson was writing in his diary, 'as in last July, I wake up with terror in the dawn'.[25]

Despite the dire politico-military situation, Churchill himself did not surrender to despair. Regardless of all the signs of impending disaster in North Africa, the Balkans and possibly the Middle East as well, by mid-April 1941 the Prime Minister was at long last beginning to receive heartening intelligence reports which indicated that Hitler might be about to level his sights on Russia.

On 16 April Churchill had received a secret intelligence submission from MI14 entitled 'World Assessment'. It contained a report on the Russian situation that declared: 'For some considerable time there have been persistent rumours that Germany intends to attack Russia, mainly in order to secure the Ukraine as a rich source of food supplies.' This was tempered with the comment: 'For the present, however, it seems most likely that Germany is intending merely to warn Russia against any interference with her Balkan plans.' Despite these mixed signals, the report ended on an optimistic note: 'Nevertheless, Germany almost certainly, eventually intends sooner or later to seize the Ukraine.'[26]

In addition to these Military Intelligence appraisals, Churchill had received many important 'ULTRA' decrypts from Britain's top-secret code-breaking establishment, Station X, based at Bletchley Park. During the early part of the war Germany's Enigma codes had seemed unbreakable. The information gleaned from this source was still minimal in April 1941, but the code-breakers were able to detect a pattern which bore a strong resemblance to that which had occurred prior to the German attack on the west in 1940. The names of high-level officers – von Bock, Kluge, Guderian, Kleist and others – were beginning to be associated with a major military build-up in the east. It was not associated with the Balkan campaign, which left only Russia. Another range of signals decrypted at Bletchley Park was associated with the Luftwaffe and the Reichsbahn (the railroads), and indicated that Germany was constructing aerodromes alongside railway lines in occupied Poland, and that spurs were being put in place to connect these aerodromes to Germany's rail network. The military analysts concluded that the ground was being prepared for a large-scale eastern campaign.

In April 1941 the number of signals being intercepted was not great, suggesting that a campaign was not yet imminent; but the signs were that the German leadership was gearing up for a major campaign that summer. The question was whether Hitler would choose to attack the Middle East first, as a way of knocking Britain out of the war, and postpone the invasion of Russia till a later date. On this complicated politico-military balancing act Britain's survival depended. The success or failure of SO1's deception campaign could make all the difference.

Many such important matters occurred during that eventful April of 1941, including on the sixteenth the proposal by Anthony Eden (newly returned from Egypt) to the Russian Ambassador in London, Ivan Maiski, of an Anglo–Soviet pact. This came to nothing, as Stalin saw it as just another ploy by the West to embroil him in a war with Germany.[27]

Russian Intelligence was just as good as that of the west – indeed was superior in several key respects – so Stalin was almost certainly already aware of the German military build-up in the east. However, having negotiated with the German government in the past, Stalin misread all the signs.

The Nazis always liked to negotiate from strength, even in trade and economic matters. Thus the Russians mistakenly concluded that the German build-up in the east was a ruse to strengthen the Reich's hand in a fresh round of trade negotiations, and so gain almost the entire Ukrainian wheat harvest, greater access to Russian mineral resources and industrial output, and more Caucasian oil. The Russians failed to understand that Hitler was, by 1941, of a mind to obtain what he wanted permanently, and by force.

There is one last key element that enabled Churchill to realise that there was a genuine German intent towards invasion of the Ukraine and southern Russia. It is likely that at some point during the previous five months of peace negotiations, either Haushofer or Hess informed Samuel Hoare that they were sincere in their wish for peace with Britain because Germany intended to pursue her *Lebensraum* priorities in the east. That was after all what Prince Hohenlohe had openly declared to Hoare at their meeting in Madrid in early March, and it could well have been imparted with greater authority by Haushofer or Hess as well, as the urgency of obtaining the British peace faction's agreement for an armistice increased.

That the tension was rising on both sides was clear – on the British side because SO1 wanted to see some return for their efforts; and on the German side because the leadership wanted a clear indication that the conflict with Britain would soon end, thus allowing the Nazis' primary objective of eastward expansion into Russia. The German leadership's need for success in the peace negotiations began to cause precipitate and unpredictable actions in which Rudolf Hess would take a lead, attempting to force the timid Britons into an agreement that would see an end to the war in the west.

CHAPTER 6

Someone is Expected

On Saturday, 19 April 1941, Rudolf Hess was again preparing to fly his Me-110E from the Messerschmitt company's airstrip in Augsburg. Chief test pilot Helmut Kaden would later recall that 'Hess's last attempt to fly to Britain occurred on 19 April.'[1] However, this trip would not be like the others, and Hess's presence at the Augsburg airstrip this day would raise more questions than it answered.

A week previously, Hess had met his old friend Albrecht Haushofer, who had briefed him on the details of his latest discussions with Sam Hoare in Madrid. It is possible that Haushofer also gave the Deputy-Führer his own assessment of the likelihood of the peace negotiations', and the Hoare–Halifax *coup d'état*'s, success. There would have been little reason to send Haushofer all the way to Madrid simply to pass a message to Hoare unless he was also there to glean as much as he could about the progress of this most important of missions.

On the afternoon of Friday, 18 April, the Messerschmitt works had received a telephone call from the Deputy-Führer's office instructing them to prepare his plane once again. It was to be ready and waiting for him the following morning.

Thus on the morning of Saturday, 19 April, Hess's Me-110E was taken from its hangar, the pre-flight checks were completed, the fuel tanks filled, and the twin Daimler-Benz engines run up to temperature. Hess soon arrived with his usual entourage, changed into his flying gear, boarded his plane and taxied it to the edge of the runway. However, he did not take off, but sat on the runway for nearly twenty minutes, risking serious damage to the plane's powerful engines, which were not designed for prolonged ground-based tickover. He was eventually forced to shut them down for fear of overheating them. Yet he remained in his plane,[2] waiting for something – no one knew what – exchanging an occasional pleasantry with the ground crew, who knew better than to ask the Reich's Deputy-Führer what he was doing.

Eventually, after a further fifteen minutes, a telephone call from Berlin came through to Messerschmitt's runway office, and 'a car was sent out to bring him [Hess] back to the office to take the call. Within a few minutes Hess strode out from the building, saying: "That's it, it's off for today!" '[3] To everyone's surprise, the Deputy-Führer promptly changed out of his flying kit, clambered into his car, and he and his entire entourage left again. It was all very strange, to say the least.

It has been suggested that this was yet another failed attempt by Rudolf Hess to fly to Britain; but again, that was not actually the case.

It is now known, from Albrecht Haushofer's confidential conversation with Sam Hoare, that by the late spring of 1941 the German negotiators were insisting that a British VIP – the representative of the 'man of influence' – travel to some neutral spot for a meeting with the head of the Auslandsorganisation. Yet neither the Germans nor, more importantly, the British were ready for such a meeting. If previous events are examined in relation to the situation on 19 April, a pattern emerges which gives an indication of what caused Hess to abandon his flight.

All the evidence indicates that Sam Hoare had made several trips to Switzerland for covert meetings with Hess. It is known that Albrecht Haushofer was also meeting Hoare, not only in Switzerland but in Madrid too. All the previous occasions on which Hoare and Captain Hillgarth, as well as Haushofer and Hess, had travelled to Switzerland were weekends. They also tended to be near the middle of the month – there may have been a political or technical reason for this. Yet on this occasion, Saturday, 19 April, Sam Hoare was not in Switzerland, but was involved in a series of meetings connected to the security of Gibraltar, which was of course critically important to Britain's continued access to the Mediterranean.

Britain's Governor of Gibraltar, General Mason-MacFarlane, had been to London in March and early April to meet the Chiefs of Staff, following which he planned to return to Gibraltar via Lisbon. On hearing this news, Hoare had immediately wired the Foreign Office in London that he urgently needed to meet Mason-MacFarlane, and would travel to Lisbon with his three service attachés, to catch Mason-MacFarlane during his brief stopover. Cadogan immediately wired back: 'Is not a visit by yourself and your three service chiefs to Lisbon a rather spectacular step and likely to provoke undesirable speculation?'[4] Hoare, on reflection, cancelled his trip; but he did not entirely give up on the idea.

In the second week of April, Hoare suddenly departed Madrid without consulting London. He headed south, fetching up on Mason-MacFarlane's doorstep in Gibraltar. It was a course of action that created much annoyance in the Foreign Office, causing Assistant Under-Secretary Roger Makins to comment angrily: 'The Ambassador went to Gibraltar in spite of categorical instructions that he was not to do so. He did not inform us of his movements, nor has he given any explanation why it was necessary for him to spend a week in Gibraltar. As we feared, he has laid himself open both to speculation and attack.'[5]

The reason for Sir Samuel Hoare's sudden urgent need to meet Mason-MacFarlane has never been revealed. It may have been in connection with the delicate situation in Madrid, but that is unlikely, as far more sensitive diplomatic matters were routinely communicated by ciphered telegram, nor would it have been necessary for Hoare to remain in Gibraltar for nearly a week. If, however, Hoare's need to meet Mason-MacFarlane was connected to the Governor's trip to London, where he had privately met Churchill, it makes a great deal more sense – particularly if Hoare was becoming nervous at the demands now being made by the German leadership. Mason-MacFarlane may even have been bearing an off-the-record communiqué from Churchill for Sir Samuel Hoare's ears alone. Whatever the reason for Hoare's trip to Gibraltar, the result was that he had only just returned to Madrid by the weekend of 19–20 April. He was not, therefore, free to fly at short notice to Switzerland.

The question remains: if Hoare was not in Switzerland, and Hess was not ready to fly to Britain, why was the Deputy-Führer sitting in his aircraft at Augsburg on the morning of Saturday, 19 April? Could it be that he had demanded a meeting, and was awaiting telephone confirmation from Berlin that Hoare had arrived at the designated place in Switzerland? Did Hess urgently require to see Hoare in order to press forcefully for the desired meeting with a 'close representative of the man of influence'? It may be that the political warfare experts at Woburn Abbey had decided that the next stage in their psychological campaign was to back off for a while – to stall.

How would the German leadership react to being impeded in this way? Would, for instance, Hoare be covertly summoned to Beigbeder's house for another meeting with Albrecht Haushofer? Or were matters now becoming so critical that the German leadership might do something unexpected? Whatever possibilities had occurred to the astute minds at Woburn Abbey and in Whitehall, it is unlikely that they were prepared for what was to happen next.

Within seventy-two hours, on Tuesday, 22 April, a civil servant at the Foreign Office drafted an urgent memo to his superior querying an alarming rumour that had just reached the corridors of Whitehall, and that had caused many eyebrows to be raised. At the War Office, a certain Major Bright of Military Intelligence wrote to the Foreign Office to ask if they would 'secure Sir S. Hoare's comments on the reported visit of Hess to Madrid'.

The civil servant at the Foreign Office immediately checked with his superior at the Central Department, Frank Roberts, working under Assistant Under-Secretary William Strang, asking whether it was possible to telegraph Hoare.

'I see no objection,' Roberts, replied, 'although Sir S. Hoare will presumably report automatically.'[6]

Within three hours, at 9.30 p.m., a ciphered telegram marked

'IMPORTANT' was flying through the ether to the British Embassy in Madrid. It stated: 'The press carry reports from Vichy that Hess has flown to Madrid with a personal letter from Hitler to Franco. There are also rumours from Vichy of a German demand for the right of passage through Spain to Gibraltar. Have you any confirmation?'[7]

One of the facts known about the late spring of 1941 is that while Germany was very keen to persuade Franco to throw in his lot with the Axis, there were minimal German forces available at this time for a campaign in yet another corner of Europe. Hitler may well have lusted after Gibraltar, but that was a far cry from the considerable effort it would have taken to realise his ambition of taking it. There had been German hopes in January and February that action might be taken to invade Gibraltar with the objective of closing the Mediterranean to Britain, but as Hitler stated to the Spanish Ambassador in Berlin when they met on 28 April, such action had not been possible.[8]

The spring of 1941 saw Germany already heavily committed in North Africa and the Balkans, and preparing to amass vast military dispositions in the east – in Prussia, Poland, Hungary and Romania – to attack Russia. Gibraltar was an irritating complication that would have to wait. It was also undoubtedly the case that if Hitler believed he was on the verge of attaining peace with Britain by the summer of 1941, taking Gibraltar would have been unnecessary anyway.

Within a few days of the Foreign Office's enquiry regarding Hess, Sam Hoare dispatched a reply, steeped in the art of diplomatic double-speak, which non-committally declared: 'If Hess has come here his arrival has been kept remarkably secret and his presence in town is not even rumoured yet.'[9]

The following day Frank Roberts minuted: 'The scare of last weekend has turned out to be at least premature.' To which Roger Makins responded, 'Yes. It is the first of many scares of the same kind.'[10]

To be fair, there are no papers open to public scrutiny that indicate Hoare met Hess during his mysterious visit to Spain.

However, as there are many Madrid Embassy files from the spring of 1941 classed 'Unavailable', all significantly closed until the year 2017, it is currently impossible to determine whether such a meeting took place or not. But Hess is unlikely to have flown to Spain as a mere messenger-boy for Hitler carrying a demand to Franco. If Hess really travelled to Madrid – and there is a plethora of evidence to suggest he did – he would have had his own very important reasons for doing so.

There is an interesting footnote to this matter. In 1959 Heinrich Stahmers, an old friend of Albrecht Haushofer's who was based in Germany's Madrid Embassy during the war, revealed that he had been Albrecht's go-between to Sam Hoare. He claimed that a meeting in Spain had been proposed in the spring of 1941 between Hoare and Lord Halifax on one side, and Hess and Haushofer on the other. Although such a meeting could not have taken place for the good reason that Halifax was in Washington throughout this period, Stahmer's testimony is important inasmuch as it indicates what the German leadership believed at the time. It may therefore indicate that a Hoare–Hess meeting did indeed take place.

Three days after Sam Hoare's message to London concerning Hess's presence in Madrid, William Strang wrote a confidential memorandum to Sir Alexander Cadogan, Anthony Eden's second-in-command at the Foreign Office.

Strang was a forty-eight-year-old career diplomat, and a member of the trusted inner circle involved in the Messrs HHHH operation. In the years to come, his abilities would see him rise to become Political Adviser to the Commander-in-Chief of British Forces in post-war Germany, attain the post of Permanent Under-Secretary at the Foreign Office in 1949, and end his career with a baronetcy as Lord Strang. He was one of the bright lights of the Foreign Office, a high flyer who had become head of the Central Department in 1937. He was also incidentally an old and close friend of both Rex Leeper and Robert Bruce Lockhart, as well as most of the men who had banded together in the 1930s to form the anti-appeasement faction headed by Churchill. In 1939 Strang had been a leading member of the delegation dispatched to Moscow by the Foreign Office during the final calamitous months before the outbreak of war, when it had been hoped Russia might be persuaded to stand with Britain and France against German expansionism.

Unfortunately, the unwise men running the Foreign Office during the terrible rush to war made two devastating errors. Firstly, Strang was subordinated to an inept old warhorse named Admiral the Hon. Sir Reginald Plunkett-Ernle-Erle Drax (which the Russians stood no chance of pronouncing), a man completely out of touch with the political dangers facing Europe. Secondly, Whitehall dispatched its delegation to Moscow completely unaware that Ribbentrop had got there first, and had for months been busily negotiating the Russo–German non-aggression pact with the Soviet Foreign Minister Molotov. The result was the total failure of the British mission. It was a painful if educative experience, and if anything it hardened Strang's resolve to see Britain victorious, whatever the price. By the spring of 1941 Strang was recognised as a determined and effective personality within the Foreign Office, and was one of those entrusted with leading Britain back from the brink of disaster.

Strang had been involved in the Messrs HHHH operation almost from its inception, and his expertise was put to good use following Sam Hoare's report that the German leadership, through Albrecht Haushofer, had demanded that Ernst Bohle be granted access to a major British politico-constitutional VIP. Sir Alexander Cadogan duly charged Strang with bringing this important and complicated strand of the operation together.

On Monday, 28 April 1941, Strang wrote to Cadogan: 'Further to our discussion concerning the H matter last week . . . I attended a meeting with HRH the Duke of Kent last Friday. After I explained a little of the situation he seemed most willing to assist in this most delicate affair.'[11] However, as Strang noted, Prince George, Duke of Kent – the younger brother of the King – had immediately realised the extreme sensitivity and potential political hazards of the task he had been asked to perform, and the jeopardy

Churchill, accompanied by Brendan Bracken (centre), welcomes President Roosevelt's emissary Harry Hopkins to London in January 1941. On the night of 10 May 1941, all three would be together at Ditchley Park.

Left Ernst Bohle, head of the Auslandsorganisation, with Churchill in pre-war London. Had a peace been possible between Britain and Germany, Bohle would almost certainly have become Nazi Germany's first post-war Ambassador to Britain. *Right* Ernst Bohle at the height of his power in the 1930s.

Lord Halifax (left) and Anthony Eden during the desperately dangerous weeks in May 1940 when the British Expeditionary Force was defeated on continental Europe, and was soon to be ejected from Dunkirk. In a little over six months Halifax too would be ejected from his position as Foreign Secretary. His successor would be Eden.

Hugh Dalton, pictured in 1948 as Chancellor of the Exchequer, restored to the centre of political power after the defeat of Churchill in the 1945 general election. In 1940 and 1941 he had been a powerful member of the government as Minister of Economic Warfare and the first Minister of SOE, until he was broken and sidelined after the conclusion of the Hess affair.

Woburn Abbey, deep in the Bedfordshire countryside, was the wartime headquarters of SOE. It was from here that SO1, under the leadership of 'Rex' Leeper, became a home for Britain's political warfare and black propaganda experts.

Rudolf Hess boards his personal Me-110, registration VJ-OQ, for a test flight in the months preceding his flight to Britain. Hess was an expert pilot, and his skill at the controls of this fighter-bomber was considerable.

The powerful and fast Messerschmitt-110. The latest in German aviation technology at the start of the Second World War, and the aircraft Hess chose as the one that would best suit his needs.

The Duke of Hamilton (left), together with his younger brother, serenading the young Princesses Margaret and Elizabeth during the first weeks of the war, in a photograph which illustrates his prominence and connections.

The Duke of Hamilton as a high-ranking RAF officer in London in the early part of the war.

The Duke of Kent (left) with RAF officers early in the war.

The Duke of Kent views bomb damage in London in January 1941. As King George VI's younger brother, the Duke held an important position in the late 1930s and early 1940s, and was considered by many to be the most astute of the Windsor brothers.

The wartime aircraft hangars, maintenance facilities and offices (known as 'the Kennels') at Dungavel House. Clearly much more than a mere grassy airstrip and a few sheds, as has always previously been implied.

Left RAF recovery personnel pose with the wreckage of Hess's Messerschmitt-110. *Right* Near the end. A haggard and weary Albrecht Haushofer in 1944. The anti-Hitler July bomb plot would cost him his freedom, and ultimately his life.

A rare photograph of 'Rex' Leeper (seated), pictured in 1946, now Sir Reginald and Ambassador to Argentina, far from the austerity and rationing of post-war Britain.

Rudolf Hess, newly returned to Germany from incarceration in Britain, is questioned by US Army Colonel John Amen at the beginning of the Nuremberg International Military Tribunal process in autumn 1945. Note that Hess still possesses the flying boots he wore for his fateful flight to Britain in May 1941.

A gaunt and tired-looking Hess sits in the dock at Nuremberg in October 1946 between his former partners in government Hermann Göring and Joachim von Ribbentrop. He had already been a prisoner for five years, and would remain one for the rest of his days.

he would place himself in if he did not obtain corroboration of Strang's request from a higher authority.

The Duke of Kent did not know William Strang, and he was not prepared to risk taking part in some devious British Intelligence/ Foreign Office plot only to discover subsequently that his participation could be used against him. It was, after all, still fresh in everyone's memory that his eldest brother Edward, now Duke of Windsor, had dabbled in politics, and look what had happened to him – he was currently banished to the Bahamas. Rather than suffer a similar humiliation, the Duke of Kent demanded confirmation of political support, and a prominent witness. As Strang wrote to Cadogan: 'before placing himself at our disposal he [Kent] has requested that either you or the Foreign Secretary clarify one or two details of his task. Also, he wishes his acquaintance, [the Duke of] Buccleugh [sic], to be present, as he [Buccleuch] has met the visiting gentleman concerned, whilst he has not.' Strang recognised that Kent's request for clarification by a top authority was a polite way of saying he was not about to put himself in jeopardy without an official endorsement that he really *was* undertaking a mission for Anthony Eden – and by implication for Churchill.

Strang's letter to Cadogan is interesting on several levels, not least for revealing that the Duke of Kent was considerably more astute than history subsequently judged him. He was perfectly aware of the risks of becoming involved in a British Intelligence operation. Many a political career had been destroyed through well-meaning, though naïve, involvement.

Prince George, Duke of Kent, was no novice in the world of political subterfuge and international affairs. The youngest and most politically astute of King George V's sons, he had covertly met with officials of the Nazi Party during the 1930s, first on behalf of his father, and then for his eldest brother during his brief reign as Edward VIII. In January 1935 Kent had gone to Munich to secretly meet a representative of the Aussenpolitisches Amt, who reported back to Berlin that the Duke had 'declared Britain was reconciled to Hitler's determination to rearm Germany', and 'was deeply interested, too, to know what made Hitler tick, and

Hess, Göring, and Goebbels as well'.[12] The fact that this meeting took place does not indicate that the Duke of Kent had Nazi sympathies; rather that he was acting as a confidential adviser to his father, King George V.

Several months later, Reichsleiter Alfred Rosenberg, head of the Aussenpolitsches Amt, submitted a report to Hitler, informing him that: 'At the end of last year we were notified that the King of England had pronounced himself dissatisfied with the official press reports.'[13] This indicated that George V was finding it difficult to obtain accurate information on the powerful, radical and possibly dangerous new government in Germany. Rosenberg went on: 'The Duke of Kent's visit to Munich had only worsened the English King's opinion regarding official news reporting, and ... [thus] we received the request from London to explain National Socialism down to the last detail to the Duke of Kent for the purpose of informing the King of England.' As a consequence of this request, Rosenberg dispatched a confidential agent to London, where he had a discreet three-hour conversation with the Duke of Kent, who then reported to the King. The confidential agent acting for Rosenberg's APA was Baron 'Bill' de Ropp, the old friend of Captain Freddy Winterbotham, head of Britain's Air Intelligence Group.

It has long been suspected that de Ropp was a double-agent. In fact he was a double-double-agent: a British agent pretending to the Germans that he really worked for them, while in actuality he was Winterbotham's man through and through. It may therefore be deduced that de Ropp was a very guileful man indeed.

The Duke of Kent's participation in this event, as both go-between and confidential adviser to the King, would not be forgotten by British Intelligence or the Germans; nor indeed would de Ropp's involvement.

Kent's role as a politico-diplomatic adviser did not end with the death of George V. His elder brothers Edward VIII (for ten months) and George VI were also occasionally reliant on him for the same purpose. This was not lost on the British government, nor indeed on Hitler, Hess and Haushofer. Both parties were fully aware of the important, if extremely discreet, role the youngest of the Windsor brothers played.

With the coming of war, the Duke of Kent had continued to be discreetly called upon to perform delicate politico-diplomatic missions for the British monarch and government. In June 1940 he had journeyed to Lisbon by flying boat as part of the British delegation to Portugal's three-hundredth-anniversary celebrations. That, at least, had been the public reason for the visit. Behind the scenes, Kent played a significant role in the British government's negotiations with the Portuguese dictator Antonio Salazar to persuade him to keep Portugal neutral in the war that was sweeping across Europe.[14]

The important role that Kent had played in the past indicated to SO1 and the Foreign Office – and Strang and Cadogan in particular – that he was capable of understanding the complexities of a subtle political situation, and that if well briefed and supported he would more than fulfil Albrecht Haushofer's requirement of a 'close representative' of King George VI to meet an official of the AO.

There was really no one else. George V's third son Prince Henry, Duke of Gloucester, was widely recognised as a fellow of simple tastes, and an even simpler intellect. The Duke of Windsor – who in any case had little remaining influence in Britain – was sitting in the Bahamas, intentionally placed far from the dangers of war and of political intrigue. The Duke of Kent, on the other hand, had a good track record for mediation and in acting as the monarch's representative. He would eminently satisfy the demands of the German leadership, who were perhaps becoming suspicious at the length of time it was taking Hoare and Halifax to act.

There were, however, two problems with the latest developments, and they would later return to haunt the Foreign Office and SO1 protagonists.

The first was Haushofer's request that the meeting with the Auslandsorganisation official should take place on neutral territory. This the British swiftly rejected as too hazardous. What would happen if the Germans, playing for very high stakes indeed, became suspicious enough to attempt the kidnapping of the unfortunate eminent person, with the intention of interrogating him for information? The Venlo Incident was still a fresh and raw memory to British Intelligence, as was the Duke of Windsor's ill-conceived sojourn in Spain and Portugal less than twelve months before. The Nazis had a history of unreliability, and the only way an intermediary's security could be guaranteed would be for the meeting to take place in territory controlled by Britain.

The second problem was a little more delicate. After hearing William Strang out, the Duke of Kent had requested that he be accompanied by his old friend the Duke of Buccleuch. The difficulty was that the Foreign Office had dealt with Buccleuch in the past. Outwardly he was an eminent aristocrat, related to the highest in the land. However, scrape a little of his gilt off, and the men of Whitehall were perturbed by what showed through.

The Duke of Buccleuch had, since the mid-1930s, held the post of Lord Steward of the Royal Household, an important position that not only made him one of the King's advisers, but carried with it an automatic appointment as Privy Councillor, placing him close to the heart of constitutional government. As George VI's intermediary to the House of Lords, all official communications from the House of Lords to the monarch passed through Buccleuch. Yet his bonds to the royal family went further than that. His daughter Alice was married to the Duke of Gloucester, and Buccleuch was therefore connected right into the heart of Buckingham Palace, where he retained an office and staff.

However, there was one aspect of the Duke of Buccleuch's character that had made him unpopular with Winston Churchill and the anti-appeasement clique in the latter 1930s, and had cost him his post as Lord Steward of the Royal Household as soon as Churchill became Prime Minister in May 1940. During the thirties he had adopted an increasingly pro-German stance. He, like many others, became enamoured of the strength of the Nazis and their clear-cut objective to restore Germany to prominence in Europe, and their potential to become a bastion against the Bolshevik menace lurking in the east. Buccleuch had been horrified by the devastating conflict that swept across Europe in 1939, and unwisely stated publicly that the war would 'play into the hands of Soviet Russia, [the] Jews and Americans'.[15] He was nothing if not tenacious, and despite the unpopularity of his views he had stuck to his guns even after many months of war. His pro-German and anti-war stance not unnaturally resulted in his being placed under surveillance by MI5.

There were, however, many facets to the Duke of Buccleuch's personality, and though he was known to favour cutting a deal with the Nazis to end the war, his stance was not based simply on his personal right-wing beliefs. The Duke belonged to a select band of top Britons who espoused 'imperial isolationism'.[16] He therefore had agendas on several levels, and his inclination to appease Nazism accorded with his conviction that it would aid the overall well-being of Britain and her empire. This did not make him any less dangerous in the eyes of many in the British government.

On 15 February 1941, the Duke of Buccleuch had laboriously handwritten a six-page letter to 'Rab' Butler (at that time an Under-Secretary at the Foreign Office) querying the situation with regard to a peace proposal that had recently emanated from a German diplomat named Ulrich von Hassell (yet another acquaintance of Albrecht Haushofer) and a Briton at loose in continental Europe, Lonsdale Bryans. Bryans had been causing considerable embarrassment to the Foreign Office, busily making all sorts of peace overtures in Europe's neutral states for months, and falsely purporting to represent Lord Halifax. The Foreign Office, intimating that Bryans was a nuisance who might well require psychiatric help, had instructed the Embassy in Lisbon to pressure him into returning to Britain.

The Duke of Buccleuch's letter to Butler had caused concern at the Foreign Office. Although ostensibly querying a peace proposal emanating from von Hassell through the auspices of the dubious Mr Bryans, it was evident that Buccleuch had something else on his mind. In a memorandum written the following day, Butler commented to Cadogan that 'the Duke's native shrewdness on certain matters comes out [in] the red [marked] portion'.[17]

What Butler was referring to was the fact that despite Buccleuch being a strong proponent of a peaceable accord if one could be found, he had nevertheless divined for himself that there were greater politico-international affairs afoot than Britain holding its own against Germany militarily, for he had written: 'Latest reports if correct indicate a much larger objective south and east via Bulgaria [i.e. Greece, Anatolia and thence the Middle East]. Can Moscow be expected to disclose any less favourable attitude to Berlin if and while USA are helping us to equalise with Germany?'[18]

Several days later Buccleuch sent another letter to Butler, again on the subject of peace, but on this occasion he was more open. He was subtly attempting to impart that despite past differences, and his 'closer associations than is customary with men of German nationality', he was still loyal to Britain. He meaningfully stated: 'I regret that, however much some of your colleagues may have considered me a nuisance, they should regard me with suspicion rather than as a friend and ally. Even now some find it desirable to have me watched, as far as I can see more with the intention of causing me trouble than of finding fault.'[19] It was clear that Buccleuch was looking for a way back into the circles of power, and was suggesting that he could make a valuable contribution to Britain's efforts to survive.

There was, however, a curious circumstance connected to Buccleuch's situation. When he had lost his post as Lord Steward of the Royal Household in 1940, the man who replaced him was none other than Winston Churchill's friend the Duke of Hamilton. This means that there was an important additional reason why Albrecht Haushofer had nominated Hamilton as the man he should contact to negotiate peace. Hamilton was chosen not only because of his friendship with both Haushofer and Churchill, but because of his position close to King George VI. This made him the ideal man to contact, as he would give Haushofer (and Hitler and Hess) a conduit directly into Buckingham Palace itself. There was thus an added constitutional aspect to the German decision to write via Violet Roberts to the Duke of Hamilton.

However, perhaps the most interesting information William

Strang imparted to Sir Alexander Cadogan was the Duke of Kent's reason for involving the Duke of Buccleuch, rather than some other eminent or trusted friend. Strang's attention had been aroused when Kent commented that Buccleuch had previously 'met the visiting gentleman concerned'[20] – the head of AO, Ernst Bohle.

Ernst Wilhelm Bohle had very curious origins for a man destined to lead one of the Nazi Party's top foreign affairs organisations. The thirty-eight-year-old head of Auslandsorganisation, with responsibility for the political well-being of ethnic Germans living overseas, had been born in Bradford, Yorkshire, in 1903. In early childhood his parents had emigrated to South Africa, where the young Ernst had gone to the South African College High School in Cape Town. In 1920 his father had paid for Ernst to attend the University of Cologne, where he studied economics and political science.[21] Bohle was therefore very much of the same generation as Albrecht Haushofer. He too had viewed the horrors of the Great War from the security of youth, being too young to be called up to fight. However, had he been a few years older, he would have found himself on the British side, not the German, for Ernst Bohle was, until 1937, a British citizen.

Having gained his doctorate in Commerce in 1923, Bohle's early career had been in the import and export business, based first in Rotterdam and then in Hamburg. In 1931 he had seen an advertisement in a newspaper for a post within the Nazi Party's new foreign policy office. He had applied, been accepted – and the rest, as they say, is history. Bohle thus had a common background with Hess. They were both *Auslanders* by birth, they had both begun their careers in commerce, and had both worked in the import trade in Hamburg. As a result the two got on very well together, often sharing jokes about past experiences that others in the Nazi Party were unable to understand. By 1932 Bohle was heading the small but increasingly important Auslandsorganisation, where he remained for the next ten years, nine of them under one superior – Rudolf Hess.

In 1937 Ernst Bohle's career within the Nazi Party had

blossomed. As a result of his expertise in the field of foreign relations, with agents from Finland to Shanghai, he was inducted into the German Foreign Ministry, becoming a 'Secretary of State in the Foreign Office' on 30 January 1937.[22] Later that year he visited London, with the objective of furthering a long-term Anglo–German peaceable accord. He was later to comment: 'I personally didn't believe in war, and I made that pretty public in my speech in London in 1937.'[23]

While Bohle was in London he entered into the social circuit, meeting and dining with Britain's high and mighty, no doubt dropping a confidential word here and there aimed at furthering the cause of Anglo–German peace and understanding, tempered of course with the occasional subtle reference to the virtues of National Socialism. This was, after all, the *raison d'être* for his visit.

Bohle made some interesting friends in Britain in 1937, one of whom invited him to stay for an extended weekend at his country home in Dumfriesshire. His name was the Duke of Buccleuch, and his home was Drumlanrig Castle – a mere twenty miles from Dungavel House, Rudolf Hess's destination on the night of 10 May 1941.

While this cannot be attributed to anything more than a curious coincidence, a certain level of synchronicity (as theorised by Jung) may well have taken place. When William Strang briefed the Duke of Kent on 25 April 1941, asking if he would participate in a meeting with Ernst Bohle, he may have intimated that the meeting was to take place at the Duke of Hamilton's home, Dungavel House, which possessed a very good airstrip. The Duke of Kent would have known that Buccleuch's country home was nearby, and this may have triggered his memory that Buccleuch knew Bohle – hence his request that Buccleuch accompany him.

Indeed, the synchronicity may have been twofold, as the German suggestion of Bohle as the emissary could have been triggered by something along the same lines. Hitler, Hess and Haushofer may well have believed that Bohle's origins would make him more acceptable as an emissary to the British. Hitler even suggested in private that Bohle might be Germany's next Ambassador to London, should peace result from an Anglo–German armistice.[24]

The desperate need for the Duke of Kent's participation in the proposed meeting left SO1 and Whitehall with no choice regarding the Duke of Buccleuch's involvement, and William Strang wrote to Cadogan on 28 April: 'I agreed in principle . . . as I felt he [Kent] might not . . . participate otherwise. Perhaps you could let me know when it will be convenient for you to meet with HRH [Kent], and I shall then make the necessary arrangements.'[25]

Within a very few days, a brief annotation was scrawled in the margin of Strang's letter which indicated who the protagonists behind the request to Kent really were: 'I agree.'[26] It was initialled 'RL' – Rex Leeper.

On the same day William Strang wrote his memorandum to Cadogan, setting in motion the chain of events that would culminate at Dungavel House in less than twelve days' time, Albrecht Haushofer was in Switzerland working towards the same objective. Like Strang, Haushofer believed he was helping to arrange a meeting between an eminent British personage and the head of the Auslands-organisation, Ernst Bohle. The fact that both sides would prove so devastatingly mistaken about who would actually arrive in Scotland is one of the strangest elements of this whole strange story.

On the bright and sunny morning of Monday, 28 April 1941, Albrecht Haushofer travelled to his appointment in Geneva with the Vice-President of the International Red Cross, Carl Burckhardt. The two were old acquaintances, and over the years their relationship had grown to encompass Rudolf Hess. The Deputy-Führer had been instrumental in recommending Burckhardt for the post of High Commissioner to the port of Danzig in 1937.[27] That appointment had paved the way for Burckhardt's entry into the senior management of the Red Cross. Unlike many who in post-war Europe would have no hope of an eminent career because of their connections with the Nazis, Carl Burckhardt's work for the International Red Cross would not go unrecognised, and he would one day become its President.

Burckhardt had been contacted earlier that spring by Ilse von Hassell, another old friend of Albrecht Haushofer's, who told him that Haushofer would shortly be coming to see him, 'ostensibly for Hess'. Burckhardt's position on the fringe of neutrality, as a leading official of the Red Cross, had already resulted in an approach from an agent of Heinrich Himmler, who had come to him to find out whether England would be prepared to make peace with Himmler instead of Hitler.[28] Thus, while the British had Sir Samuel Hoare sitting in neutral territory, in an ideal position to act as a conduit to the enemy, the Nazi leadership perceived Carl Burckhardt in the same light. But when Haushofer arrived in Geneva on 28 April, he found Burckhardt terrified that his role as an intermediary would be publicly exposed.[29]

In the late spring of 1941, Carl Burckhardt was in a dilemma. As a prominent man in neutral territory, connected to a worldwide-recognised body in the International Red Cross, he had found himself being increasingly petitioned by top Nazis pursuing agendas of their own. However, the petitions had not emanated only from the German side. In June 1940 Burckhardt had been contacted by Rab Butler, who wished to open a line of communication to Prince Max Hohenlohe (at that time a member of Himmler's circle) in the hope of making contacts with the German hierarchy in pursuit of peace.[30] It was understood by all concerned that Butler was closely associated with Lord Halifax – another strand which was later exploited by SO1 to make the German leadership believe that Halifax would act against Churchill.

To the Nazis, all the facts appeared to suggest that a political faction in Britain was poised to usurp power from Churchill constitutionally. The problem for the Germans lay in how to ignite the blue touchpaper of action, when the British seemed inclined to inactivity, protracted negotiation and ever more debate. It was a situation that could not persist.

The details of what Albrecht Haushofer and Burckhardt talked about on 28 April have never been fully disclosed. However, Haushofer subsequently reported that they had discussed the peace soundings, and that Burckhardt revealed that he had recently been contacted by 'a person well known and respected in London ... [who] had in a rather long conversation expressed the wish of important English circles for an examination of the possibilities for peace'.[31] Furthermore, Haushofer commented, Burckhardt had said that his impression was that the peaceable faction in Britain had only three main areas of interest: south-eastern Europe, an end to the occupation of the western European states, and the colonial question.

However, there was more to the Haushofer–Burckhardt discussion than Albrecht Haushofer reported. Shortly after the end of the war, in an interview with journalist Erica Mann, Karl Haushofer revealed that Burckhardt had agreed to Albrecht's request that he act as an intermediary between Rudolf Hess and Sam Hoare at a meeting proposed for the latter half of May 1941. That meeting, it was revealed, was to take place at an isolated spot – an abandoned tennis court – near Madrid.[32]

Besides arranging Carl Burckhardt's involvement, Albrecht Haushofer's trip to Switzerland was to have another important, if less easily recognised, consequence. It took him away from the centre of intrigue for a crucial few days, during which he missed vital clues that might have set alarm bells ringing in his brain – clues which indicated that the delicate negotiations were about to go disastrously wrong; and that the emissary to the British was *not* going to be Ernst Bohle.

The Haushofers continued to meet with Rudolf Hess, who, unbeknownst to them, was putting the last arrangements in place for what he believed would be the biggest political coup of his career, a coup that would see him establish his credentials as a prominent politician once and for all.

Hess's position within the Nazi hierarchy had been gradually weakening ever since the war had started, and the whispered jokes about him as an old worrier, and about his earnest work ethic, had not gone unnoticed. Now, however, he saw a chance to assure his political ascendancy. He had worked long and hard with Hitler to bring about a politico-diplomatic coup that would see Germany freed of the unwanted war with Britain. The Führer's image as a political miracle-worker would be restored, and at his right hand would be his loyal Deputy.

Many leading members of the Nazi Party had secretly been in despair at the prospect of total war with Britain, and Hitler's reputation as the infallible and all-seeing Führer had taken a major dent. The fall of France had rectified that somewhat, but it would mean nothing if it led to war without end against the British. Now, however, Hitler had the chance to pull off a dramatic coup in the style of his great days – Germany's economic restoration, the reoccupation of the Rhineland, the Austrian *Anschluss*, his political ascendancy over Europe's leaders during the Sudeten crisis. Hess must have believed that his part in this success would enable him to eclipse rivals like Ribbentrop, Himmler, Göring and Goebbels. Most important of all, Hitler would privately know exactly who had been largely responsible for delivering him his long-sought peace with Britain.

But Rudolf Hess was about to allow personal ambition to cloud his judgement. Hess had always been mightily impressed by Neville Chamberlain's waving the piece of paper which guaranteed 'peace in our time' on his return from Munich in 1938. The guarantee had of course turned out to be nothing of the sort, but Hess still regarded Chamberlain's performance as a wonderful public-relations coup. As Ernst Bohle would later say: 'That the Prime Minister . . . should come over, was absolutely unheard of.'[33]

Despite the likelihood that Hess's personal ambitions were the primary factor behind his taking Bohle's place on the mission to Scotland, the fact that Bohle himself was never told he was to fly to Britain suggests that Hitler and Hess had always secretly planned for Hess to meet the 'close representative' of Britain's head of state. There may also be another reason, apart from self-seeking opportunism, for Hess's decision to fly to Britain on 10 May 1941.

After all their years together, Hitler and Hess's association went beyond mere political alliance. Hess was one of the handful of people Hitler considered a friend. He was, as Churchill would later comment, one of the few men 'capable of understanding

Hitler's inner mind – his hatred of Soviet Russia, his lust to destroy Bolshevism, his admiration for Britain and earnest wish to be friends with the British Empire . . . no one knew Hitler better or saw him more often in his unguarded moments'.[34]

The two men had been plotting and scheming their way through the tortuous complexities of trying to negotiate a peace with Britain since the early autumn of 1940. All Hitler's previous attempts had failed abysmally. However, as the launch date for Barbarossa crept ever closer, his worries about committing Germany to a two-front war mounted. He thus not only needed peace with Britain, he needed it quickly. Yet apart from Sam Hoare's attendance at covert meetings in Spain and the occasional anti-Churchill stands being taken in the House of Commons, there was no sign of the Hoare–Halifax plot bearing fruit, or of Churchill's premiership being in any danger. Then, in the first week of May 1941, Hitler and Hess were given heart when Reuters suddenly began to report that Churchill was fighting for his political survival. His conduct of the war had been challenged in the House of Commons, and he was facing a vote of confidence.

It may well be, therefore, that in demanding a meeting with an eminent Briton Hitler was calling the British bluff. If this was the case, it is likely that the decision to send Hess in Bohle's stead was in part taken so that the Deputy-Führer of the German Reich could look deep into the eyes of the British emissaries and discern if all this plot and intrigue was for real, or was a terrible deception.

Hess must have realised that if it was a deception, he would be placing himself in great jeopardy. However, if everything went well, and he found that the Hoare–Halifax faction did indeed have constitutional support, the political rewards for him would be enormous. He may therefore have planned his trip to Britain blind to the possibilities of failure, focused solely on the prestige that would accrue to him as the man who brought peace.

Saturday, 10 May 1941, the date of the Deputy-Führer's mysterious arrival in Scotland, was the culmination of months of ever-increasing activity, beginning in the late summer of 1940 with the Haushofer–Violet Roberts correspondence. Now, in the first days of May 1941, the success of these negotiations depended on Rudolf Hess and Albrecht Haushofer's almost daily attention, right up to the moment the Deputy-Führer boarded his plane and departed for Britain.

A week prior to Hess's flight, the Deputy-Führer's schedule became increasingly complicated. He had already arranged that on that weekend (his last as a free man, although he didn't know it) he would fly to Berlin from his home in Munich to attend a special meeting of the Reichstag. However, he delayed his departure to have a private telephone conversation with Karl Haushofer, who had important news concerning his son Albrecht's latest efforts in Switzerland.

There was, Karl Haushofer reported, a complication. Albrecht had been in Zürich for twenty-four hours awaiting Sam Hoare,[35] but Hoare had yet to arrive. After mulling this over, Hess decided to leave for Berlin anyway, but he ordered his assistant, Günther Sorof, to remain in Munich with Karl Haushofer, and to report any information to him as soon as Albrecht had telephoned his father.

After many hours of waiting at the Professor's central Munich flat, a call eventually came through in the early evening. Albrecht's message was guarded and brief, yet also self-explanatory. Sorof promptly telephoned Hess in Berlin, and repeated it verbatim. 'On a scale of one to six,' he told the Deputy-Führer, 'things stand at around three or four and more needs doing.'[36]

At the Reich Chancellery, Hess's personal security officer, Detective Superintendent Franz Lutz, observed the Deputy-Führer's reaction with interest. On receiving the message, Hess immediately took it directly through to Hitler.[37]

The following day, Sunday, 4 May 1941, was to be a significant date in the National Socialist calendar. On that day Hitler would give his first major speech since the fall of France. For several weeks he had been composing this important oration. However, Franz Lutz noted that on receipt of Haushofer's message, Hitler immediately sat down with Hess, and together the two began drafting changes to the speech.

Once they had finally agreed the text, another strange incident occurred. Hess summoned Ernst Bohle, who had been waiting patiently all evening in the Chancellery's great gallery, and handed him Hitler's speech, ordering him first to carefully translate it into English, and then to have several copies typed up for him. Not in German, but in English.[38]

The next morning, with his altered speech in hand, Hitler stood before the glittering panoply of the Reich's political elite gathered together in the Kroll Opera House, substituting for the Reichstag's main chamber, and delivered one of his most powerful orations. However, as many of those seated before him noted with curiosity, the Führer's speech had a very similar theme to that he had given at the Reichstag in July 1940, repeatedly stressing the disasters of conflict, and how he had never wanted war with England. The present situation, he claimed, had come about largely as a result of Chamberlain's intransigence over the Polish situation, and the war was being continued only because of Churchill's absolute refusal to consider any form of negotiation that might lead to peace. Hitler went so far as to declare: 'All my endeavours to come to an understanding with Britain were wrecked by the determination of a small clique which, whether from motives of hate or for the sake of material gain, rejected every German proposal for an understanding due to their resolve, which they never concealed, to resort to war, whatever happened.'[39]

In distant Britain, Winston Churchill sat in his study at Chequers before a radio tuned to the German wavelength, and listened to Germany's Führer talking to the Reich. Amongst the words of peaceable intent – tempered of course with typical Hitlerite declarations about German might – Churchill heard himself characterised as 'a man who is as miserable a politician as soldier, and as wretched a soldier as politician[40] ... If ever any other politician had met such defeats, or if a soldier had met such catastrophes, he would not have kept his job six months.'[41]

Churchill was not dismayed by such rhetoric; he knew these were mere words spouted for public consumption. Despite Britain's desperate situation in May 1941, the Prime Minister was not pessimistic. Regardless of his many worries concerning Britain's strategic position, he had many a trick up his sleeve yet. An insight into his state of mind at this time can be gained from his conversation after a private lunch at Downing Street the previous week. Amongst Churchill's guests was the Swedish Ambassador, Bjorn Prytz. Through a neutral's eyes, the Swede had seen the death and destruction being visited nightly upon London, and he tentatively asked Churchill how Britain could continue against such an onslaught.

While others at the table fidgeted uncomfortably, Churchill had been completely unperturbed by this rather direct question. He had swirled his brandy in his glass for a few moments, a smile slowly spreading across his face. Then, looking Prytz in the eye, he surprised everyone by responding to his question in a manner more suited to a child's bedtime story.

'Once upon a time there were two frogs,' the Prime Minister began. 'Mr Optimist Frog and Mr Pessimist Frog. One evening the two frogs hippety-hopped across the meadow enchanted by the smell of fresh milk from a dairy. They hopped through the dairy window and plopped right into a pail of milk.'

Churchill, enjoying the attention his fable was attracting, paused to take a sip of his brandy and to apply a fresh match to his cigar. 'The pail's sides were too steep,' he continued. 'Mr Pessimist Frog soon gave up and sank to the bottom. But Mr Optimist Frog took courage and began thrashing around, hoping to get out somehow. He didn't known how, but he wasn't going to give up without a fight. He churned around all night, and by morning – oh joy! – he was floating on a pat of butter!'

As his small audience sat smiling silently, the Prime Minister drew heavily on his cigar and concluded: 'I'm Mr Optimist Frog!'[42]

Over the next week, Rudolf Hess's activities back in Germany began to increase in tempo. On the morning of Monday, 5 May, he again visited Hitler at the Reich Chancellery. Reclining in easy chairs in the privacy of the Führer's vast office, a room sixty feet long with walls of gleaming pink and grey marble, Hitler and Hess held an extremely confidential conversation that lasted four hours. It would be the last time the two men ever met.

Despite the subsequent impression that Hess was about to undertake a lunatic expedition against his Führer's wishes, the evidence indicates nothing could be further from the truth.

Another of Hess's assistants, his Adjutant Alfred Leitgen, who was in attendance outside the office, later recalled that of the snippets of Hitler's conversation he overheard, only the phrases 'Albrecht Haushofer' and 'Hamilton' were discernible. In conversation the Führer's voice was deep (his higher pitch when addressing large audiences was a trick he had learned to make his voice carry), and thus would have been hard to understand through a solid oak door. Hess's voice, on the other hand, was higher than Hitler's, and he had clearer diction. Leitgen asserted that at one point in the conversation he clearly heard Hess say '... no problems at all with the aeroplane'. A few minutes later he heard Hess saying '... have me simply declared insane'.[43] If this really is what Leitgen heard, it may indicate that Hitler asked Hess what he should do if anything went wrong with Hess's mission – if he was captured by the British and used for propaganda purposes, or if the secret of his flight leaked out. The Deputy-Führer gave the simplest answer, little realising that the phrase would become synonymous with him and his flight for the rest of his life.

At the end of their meeting, the Führer and his loyal Deputy emerged in good humour, and Hitler astonished those waiting outside by placing a paternal arm around Hess's shoulders. 'Hess,' he joked, 'you are and always were thoroughly pig-headed.'

This casual behaviour was very unusual for Hitler, who was never so informal in front of his staff. He normally reserved such intimacy for the Berghof and the privacy of his inner circle. It would, however, be understandable as a rare public expression of comradeship between two old friends embarking upon a great but perilous undertaking, for which they had great hopes.

Following his meeting with Hitler, Hess travelled back to Munich on Tuesday, 6 May, to continue making preparations for his mission. He met Albrecht Haushofer, newly returned from Zürich and staying at his parents' flat on Kolbergstrasse, but did not reveal to his old friend that he intended travelling to Britain in Bohle's place. No one really knows when this decision was taken. The why is a little clearer. It is certainly the case that Hitler by now wanted to see some progress in finalising the deal with the powerful British peace faction poised to oust Churchill, which was much more likely to succeed under Hess than Bohle, but still Albrecht remained completely unaware that Bohle had never even received a briefing about his supposed trip to meet a British VIP. The meeting was a tricky one for him, as its purpose was specifically for Albrecht to report on his talks the previous Saturday with Sam Hoare. Karl Haushofer would tell officers of American Intelligence in 1945: 'Albrecht was sent to Switzerland. There he met a British confidential agent – a Lord Templewood [i.e. Samuel Hoare] ... When my son returned, he was immediately called to Augsburg to see Hess. A few days later Hess flew to England.'[44]

Albrecht Haushofer and Sam Hoare's covert meeting in Switzerland on Saturday, 3 May is confirmed by Karl Haushofer, Günther Sorof and Franz Lutz's evidence. Indeed, on the night of his return to Germany his mother, Martha, had noted in her diary: 'Albrecht's conversations have been fruitful.'[45] This secret conversation was almost certainly to finalise the last details concerning the meeting of the German emissary and the 'close representative of the man of influence'.

The details of what Sam Hoare and Haushofer discussed on 3 May 1941 have never been revealed, but given SO1's involvement and Captain Hillgarth's role as a SOE's man in the Iberian Peninsula, it is almost certain that prior to his departure for Switzerland, Hoare had been briefed about the British arrangements for the German emissary's visit. That Hess would adopt a holding pattern over the North Sea for a full and precise hour on the evening of 10 May suggests that an arrival time had been specified, and there may have been other details to impart as well, such as a flight-plan and call-signs.

One other piece of the puzzle may also have been a subject of the Hoare–Haushofer discussion. During the Second World War, the Duke of Hamilton did not reside at Dungavel House, and part of the building was given over to provide offices for the International Red Cross. Carl Burckhardt's involvement in the Messrs HHHH affair may have been connected to this fact, which could explain documents captured by the Americans after the war which revealed that Albrecht Haushofer had 'used a prominent Swiss official of the International Red Cross as intermediary'.[46] The participants in the affair – both British and German – may well have agreed that the Red Cross's offices at Dungavel House would be considered neutral territory, and thus an appropriate venue for the meeting.[47]

Finally, it is known that on 10 May Rudolf Hess told his wife to expect him back on Monday, 12 May. This suggests that arrangements were made between Hoare and Haushofer for the German emissary to arrive at Dungavel House on the night of Saturday, 10 May, and to depart on the evening of Sunday, 11 May, arriving back at Augsburg in the early hours of Monday, 12 May.

One thing, however, is certain. The top men at SO1 and in Whitehall all believed, as did Karl and Albrecht Haushofer, that it was Ernst Bohle who would meet the Duke of Kent that weekend. Even at this late stage Rudolf Hess, focused on the coup that was to be the high point of his career, still kept his plans to take Bohle's place completely secret. Albrecht Haushofer remained unaware of the spectacular disaster his friend was about to cause.

Following his meeting with Albrecht, Hess had a busy schedule to complete on Tuesday, 6 May. That afternoon he was driven out to the Messerschmitt works at Augsburg, where for an hour he put his plane through its paces, diving and rolling, checking all its systems at altitude, practising all the skills necessary to ensure the success of his flight.

In a London described by Chips Channon as looking 'like a battered old war horse'[48] after constant heavy air raids, Winston Churchill too was very active in the days preceding SO1's extravaganza at Dungavel House. At the same time Churchill was treading warily through a minefield of political turmoil.

In recent weeks Britain's Prime Minister had received a fresh Intelligence assessment that gave him little cause for comfort. While the War Office was suggesting that Hitler might indeed be about to turn on Russia (this was supported by Enigma decrypts indicating 'major concentrations of German troops and air support converging ... on Oderberg, near Cracow'[49]), this latest paper, on 'Axis Strategy' threw an unwieldy spanner in the works, for it declared: 'It seems ... that a German invasion of Russia is out of the question until the result of the Battle for the Atlantic is more or less certain. I believe the present rumours of such an attack being imminent are propagated by Germany as a warning to Russia to keep clear of German activities in South-East Europe.'[50]

There were two points in this report which indicated how important a German campaign against Russia would be to Britain's survival. The first noted: 'If, on the other hand, Germany gets involved in Russia and increases her commitments as far as an occupation of Moscow, it would have a militarily weakening effect quite apart from the temporary loss of oil and raw material deliveries.'

More heartening by far was the second point, dealing with the situation in Iraq, which had in recent weeks undergone a chaotic *coup d'état* orchestrated by the anti-British Rashid Ali with the support of German money. Despite dire concerns about the stability of the region, it appeared that Britain's source of oil might remain safe:

> The recent coup has been successful in that it has produced a certain dispersion of our forces. But unless Germany can really raise Iraq and Persia against us she cannot menace our position in Abadeh [strategically important for maintaining the security of the oil pipeline] unless she can send her own troops there, and for this the co-operation of Turkey and/or Russia is necessary. Therefore Germany must for the moment regard Iraq as a sideshow.

On reading this appreciation, only the most ardent pessimist would not have heaved a sigh of relief. Yes, Britain had major problems with Arab nationalists in the region, but despite the heavy demands made on British military resources by the war in Europe, she still had sufficient forces in the Gulf to maintain the security of her vital sources of oil. Iraq, it seemed, was safe from German attack in 1941.

Despite this upturn in the Middle East, on the home front things were far from easy for Churchill. There were growing rumbles of discontent in Westminster at the conduct of the war, and Germany's spring air offensive was reaching a vicious climax. The statistics for air raids on Britain during the first five months of 1941 told a grim story. Week on week, month on month, they had been increasing in severity, and many in the British government were beginning to wonder how much more the nation could take.

The previous summer Hitler had changed the priorities of Germany's air offensive from a strategic campaign to psychological warfare, to coincide with the Weissauer initiative. It is possible that the new onslaught in the spring of 1941 may have been intended to weaken Britain's resolve to continue the war. Indeed, the severity of the raids was causing mounting discontent in the House of Commons by May 1941. Politicians of the stature of Lloyd George were asking where the war was leading, and what Britain's objectives were.

News of Churchill's political difficulties would have been welcomed by Haushofer, Hess and Hitler, who must have believed that the Halifax faction was making ground, if not actually poised to act. In reality, however, this was not the case.

The Blitz would reach its climax of death and destruction on the night of 10 May 1941, with the heaviest raid of the war on London. Then, from 11 May, it suddenly petered away to almost nothing. This was in part due to the Luftwaffe's new commitments to Barbarossa, but that campaign was still six weeks away. Many British politicians harboured the uncomfortable suspicion that there was a psychological motivation behind the fluctuations of the German air campaign.

With hindsight it is possible to discern that there was indeed a diabolical intelligence at work behind the scenes. Adolf Hitler, repeating his agenda of August 1940, was using a colossal carrot and stick in his conduct of the war with Britain. Death and destruction on one hand, offset against the prospect of peace, tranquillity and a negotiated armistice on the other.

Winston Churchill was later to record: 'Nearly three years were to pass before ... London had to deal with [such an] onslaught [again] ... In the twelve months from June 1940 to June 1941 our civilian casualties were 43,381 killed and 50,556 seriously injured, a total of 94,237.'[51] These were not military casualties, but civilians – men, women and a terrible number of children – killed in bed, hiding under tables or stairwells, or in air-raid shelters. It is very hard today to comprehend the horror of this period, or even the logistical nightmare of disposing of so many dead, and caring for so many injured.

Partially as a consequence of these losses, allied to Britain's grim strategic position, on Tuesday, 6 May, while Rudolf Hess was meeting Albrecht Haushofer in Augsburg, a great debate began in the House of Commons. It was a highly politicised deliberation that questioned both the strategic decisions recently taken and the government's whole war policy. For Churchill it was a precarious road to a vote of confidence in him and his administration. To lose the vote would mean the end of his premiership, and perhaps of Britain's participation in the war, for there were many politicians who by 1941 were advocating negotiation rather than continued conflict. The debate was, according to Chips Channon, 'acrimonious and rude'.[52] For once Churchill looked vulnerable and 'uncomfortable', and Channon 'despaired of England and of democracy all day'.

Anthony Eden made considerable efforts to fend off the government's critics, but when the debate continued the following day the venerable Lloyd George took up the reins of attack, venting his spleen against the government for a full hour: 'he was weak at times, at others sly and shrewd, and often vindictive as he attacked the government', wrote Channon, who was seated immediately behind the Prime Minister and Foreign Secretary. He later recalled that he had watched 'Anthony [Eden] chew his nails as he whispered to Winston who was obviously shaken, for he [Churchill] shook, twitched, and his hands were never still . . . [However] soon after 4 o'clock Winston rose, and never have I heard him in such brilliant form: he was pungent, amusing, cruel, hard-hitting and he lashed out at Lloyd George . . . with all his inimitable wit and venom. [Churchill] tore his opponents to shreds and captivated the House.'[53] When the division of the House was called, Churchill won by 447 votes to three. His power as an orator had, despite the swingeing criticism, resoundingly won the House over.

However, this victory was cold comfort, for as Channon noted, although it was 'a triumph on paper . . . in reality the government has been shaken and both Anthony and Winston know it'. The lack of resolve among Britain's MPs could be a dangerous taste of things to come, particularly if Churchill did not soon serve up some desperately needed military victories. Channon wrote ominously: 'these two days are the thunder before the real storm which I predict will break in July'.[54]

The House of Commons debate, together with the confidence vote in Churchill's leadership and his government, would have been noted in Germany, as would another political event that occurred in Britain at this time. Churchill, at this most crucial moment, suddenly decided upon a Cabinet reshuffle, one element of which in particular would have been perceived as important by Haushofer, Hess and Hitler. During the first days of May, Churchill took the decision to create a new post within his Cabinet, that of Minister of State without Portfolio. Into this position he shuffled a confederate of old, Lord Beaverbrook. It was a post the American press instantly dubbed Deputy Prime Minister, such was its importance.

Despite his credentials as a loyal Churchill stalwart, Lord Beaverbrook, nicknamed 'the Beaver', was a man any genuine peace faction in England would have to woo, for he was not only Fleet Street's most dynamic press baron, but a potent parliamentarian in his own right, and one credited with strong peaceable inclinations.

Beaverbrook had also been a close friend of Sam Hoare's since the 1920s, and had helped to promote Hoare's career, even once writing: 'I think he will be Prime Minister one day.'[55] Add to this complicated political brew the fact that Beaverbrook had also met Hitler and Hess, and had been a frequent visitor to Nazi Germany in the 1930s, and his potential importance becomes considerable.

On Friday, 9 May, Robert Bruce Lockhart, in London from Woburn Abbey for a meeting with Frank Roberts, had a rather curious conversation with the Foreign Office's Deputy Under-Secretary, Orme Sargent. Bruce Lockhart had known Sargent for many years, but was considerably taken aback when he pointedly asked him if he thought that 'the Beaver had been appointed Deputy P.M. in order for Winston to stand down and let [the] Beaver make a compromise peace'.[56]

Bruce Lockhart had been quick to respond that he thought this idea 'nonsense'. But if an eminent member of the Foreign Office like Orme Sargent could be so mistaken about the true political situation – about the security of Churchill's premiership – what were the signals being picked up in Berlin? Would it not be likely that Hitler, Hess and Haushofer – working to a large degree blind, reliant on foreign press reports, and subverted by a deep deception campaign orchestrated by SO1 – would come to the same conclusion? That they would believe that Churchill and his defiantly pro-war/anti-Nazi faction were vulnerable to a coup orchestrated by members of the British government led by the man who had almost become Prime Minister in Churchill's stead twelve months before – Lord Halifax?

Intriguingly, in the weeks and months ahead, Lord Beaverbrook would be one of the very few men in Britain granted access to Rudolf Hess.

Back in Germany events were now taking on their own momentum. Not all of these events were to Hitler's liking.

Several weeks before, the Führer had met with the OKW Chiefs of Staff to discuss Operation Barbarossa. His speech to the Reichstag on 4 May had, as well as raising the problems of continued conflict with Britain, also included a triumphant report on Germany's success in the Balkans: the Reich now controlled an unbroken swathe of Europe from the Atlantic to the Aegean.

No European power had achieved such dominance since ancient Rome, a fact that was not lost on Hitler, who saw the Third Reich as recreating that vast and stable empire. Indeed, within six weeks he would say over dinner one evening: 'The Roman Empire, under Germanic influence, would have developed in the direction of world-domination, and humanity would not have extinguished fifteen centuries of civilisation at a single stroke.'[57] In Hitler's mind, the twentieth century would see the restoration of European empire, and the Reich would one day surpass ancient Rome. In the meantime, the unforeseen necessity of conquering and occupying the Balkans to prevent Britain having easy access to the soft underbelly of Hitler's empire, Romania – and with it the Reich's primary source of oil in Bessarabia – had created a major problem.

In 'Directive 21: OPERATION BARBAROSSA', issued on 18 December 1940, Hitler had instructed that preparations for the invasion of Russia be completed by 15 May 1941;[58] only five days after Rudolf Hess's flight to Britain to seal his pact with the anti-Churchill forces waiting to pounce. However, having fought hard to take the Balkans from the Allies, Germany's military forces were now severely behind schedule in their preparations to attack Russia. Furthermore, they would need to be regrouped and reinforced, and that would take time. Yet Hitler knew he did not have time to spare. If Russia was to be conquered, an invasion had to begin within the next six weeks, so that the campaign was concluded before the Russian winter descended, blowing the OKW's strategic plans completely asunder.

At the end of the war, with Berlin lying in ruins about him and the Russians banging on the Reich Chancellery door, Hitler would comment bitterly, 'If we had attacked Russia from 15 May onwards ... we would have been in a position to conclude the eastern campaign before the onset of winter.'[59]

*　　*　　*

As a result of complications including the Hess initiative, the Balkans and, not least, the fact that the enormous Pripet Marshes of eastern Poland were still largely impassable after unusually heavy snow falls the previous winter, Hitler was forced to postpone the offensive against Russia until 22 June 1941. He was painfully aware that there absolutely could not be any more delays. If the campaign was not under way by the end of June, he would have to put it off to the late spring of 1942 – by which time Stalin would have brought the Red Army up to strength and created new defences along his western frontiers. The Reich *had* to move against Russia, for its Ukrainian wheat and Caucasian oil, in June 1941.

This made the events of the next few days all the more critical, and Hitler most of all must have been aware of the enormous consequences of failure. On Thursday, 8 May, two days before Rudolf Hess's flight, Hitler departed from Berlin and withdrew to the Berghof.

On the afternoon of Friday, 9 May, Alfred Rosenberg, the forty-eight-year-old head of the Aussenpolitisches Amt, was surprised to received a telephone call from Hess. The Deputy-Führer wanted a meeting with him to discuss certain urgent matters. The subject of their telephone conversation is not known, but as head of the Nazi Party's own foreign affairs office and a close confidant of Hitler's, Rosenberg had been party to the peaceable attempts of 1940. During the early 1930s he had been invited to Britain where he had been introduced to many eminent Britons, including Lord Hailsham and Lord Lloyd, Montagu Norman, the Governor of the Bank of England, and Sir Henry Deterding, one of Britain's wealthiest men and a prodigious businessman. After meeting the persuasive Rosenberg, Deterding would loan Hitler the enormous sum of £55 million.[60] The British press had reported:

> In light of the present European situation, this purely private talk
> between Hitler's Foreign Adviser (Rosenberg) and the dominant
> figure in European oil politics [Deterding] is of profound interest.
> It supports suggestions current in well-informed political circles

that the big oil interests had been closely in touch with the Nazi Party in Germany.[61]

Of deeper interest is the fact that Rosenberg's trip to Britain in the early 1930s had been sponsored and accompanied by two men working for British Intelligence, Freddy Winterbotham and his good friend Baron 'Bill' de Ropp. Both Rosenberg and de Ropp were expatriate Balts with strong ties to Estonia and Lithuania, and thus shared a strong desire to see their homeland rescued from Soviet Russian domination. One of them would be at Dungavel House on the night of 10 May – and it was not Rosenberg.

On that Friday afternoon Hess pressed Rosenberg to travel to Munich for an urgent meeting. Hess presumably had some important questions to ask which Rosenberg, with his experience of dealing with the British, was well-suited to answer. But Rosenberg, busy with his Aussenpolitisches Amt empire, was not keen. After a considerable amount of wrangling he was persuaded to travel to Munich the following morning, but only after Hess offered to lay on a special plane for him.[62]

As the sun began to set on the evening of Friday, 9 May 1941, many rather important people in Britain were becoming very busy indeed. There were going to be three different gatherings of men that weekend, and who went where reveals much.

The most important of these men was Winston Churchill himself, travelling out to Ditchley Park near Oxford, which had been loaned to him in 1940 by the MP Ronald Tree as the Prime Minister's wartime country residence in preference to Chequers, which was more vulnerable to Luftwaffe attack. Churchill was to spend the whole weekend there with a select band of confederates, amongst whom would be some who were knowledgeable about the Messrs HHHH operation: Brendan Bracken and Sir Archibald Sinclair, an old friend of Churchill's and currently the Secretary of State for Air. Churchill would also, interestingly, have a house guest that weekend – President Roosevelt's special envoy, Harry Hopkins.

Others who were key to the Messrs HHHH operation were also on the move that Friday evening, gravitating towards Ditchley Park, SO1 headquarters at Woburn Abbey, or Dungavel House. They all undoubtedly knew it was to be an extraordinary weekend ahead, but it was about to become more extraordinary than any of them could have expected.

Whilst all this was taking place in Britain, in Germany Rudolf Hess was spending a quiet evening at Harlaching with his wife Ilse and four-year-old son Wolf Rüdiger, nicknamed 'Buzz'. It would be the last such evening; his life as a free man, as Deputy-Führer of the German Reich, had less than twenty-four hours left to run.

CHAPTER 7

An Emissary Comes

Saturday, 10 May 1941 dawned bright and clear over western Europe. Two areas of high pressure sat over the North Sea and the Atlantic, and Britain, midway between them, enjoyed a warm spring morning.

Seated in the rear of his chauffeured Wolsley, Foreign Secretary Anthony Eden travelled north-west out of London along the A5 into the Bedfordshire countryside, his car crossing the Chiltern hills before descending towards Leighton Buzzard. Ahead lay a special meeting at SO1 HQ Woburn Abbey. Behind him, had he turned his head to look through the car's rear window, he would have seen a pall of grey-white smoke drifting lazily into the clear morning sky above London, the aftermath of the heaviest overnight blitz of the war. Eden would not be returning to London that evening, as he had after all previous meetings at Woburn Abbey. He would be staying the night, together with a select band of men awaiting news of SO1's best-kept secret, the arrival of Hitler's emissary to a representative of Britain's 'man of influence'.

The minutes of the meeting of SO1 held that Saturday lunchtime, dramatically overstamped with the words 'MOST SECRET' in inch-high letters, is a fascinating and revealing document. Its front-page list of those present numbers twenty-nine important members of SO1, the Foreign Office, the Ministry of Information and the Ministry of Economic Warfare, among them Hugh Dalton, Anthony Eden, Sir Robert Vansittart, Rex Leeper, Hugh Gaitskell, Robert Bruce Lockhart, Brigadier Brooks, Thomas Barman, Valentine Williams, Professor Seton-Watson, Leonard St Clair

Ingrams and Richard Crossman (the two men charged ten months before with the task of undermining a Hitler deemed 'ripe for exploitation'), and Con O'Neill.[1]

Just prior to the meeting, Bruce Lockhart and Eden had a brief private chat about the Czechoslovak government in exile, to whom Lockhart was liaison officer. Bruce Lockhart later recalled that Eden 'asked about [the Czech leader in exile Eduard] Beneš. I said – always buoyant – taken knocks better than anyone I know. Eden agreed and said: "He's had enough too." '[2] Bruce Lockhart undoubtedly kept his diary without a thought that it might one day be opened to public scrutiny, for he also noted: 'I went on to say I was sorry meeting postponed, coz [sic] I considered matter urgent lest Germans forestall. [Eden] told me he would have meeting earliest possible day next week.' This curious statement was, given the time and place, almost certainly connected to the Messrs HHHH operation in some way. Perhaps Bruce Lockhart felt the meeting should have occurred earlier in the week, thereby giving more time in case something untoward about the planning for the German emissary's arrival was discovered.

The participants took their seats around the large central table in one of Woburn Abbey's staterooms, converted into a conference room for the duration, and the meeting began with a briefing from Brigadier Brooks. He gave a brief review of Britain's current strategic situation, detailing the position in the Western Desert and Abyssinia, before going on to describe the precarious state of affairs in Malta, Crete and Cyprus – which, he added, 'we intend to defend . . . to the last man and the last round'.[3] He concluded with a short assessment of the current air situation with regard to the recent heavy raids on Britain, and the RAF's response of bombing the French Atlantic ports in the hope of closing them to German warships.[4]

The tone of the meeting became a great deal darker when Hugh Dalton, who was in the chair, invited Leonard St Clair Ingrams – technically attending the meeting on behalf of the Ministry of Economic Warfare, but in reality closely tied to the whole Messrs H deception operation – to speak. Ingrams began by outlining the current state of 'Russo–German relations'. Firstly, he announced, 'the extent to which Hitler could exploit his Balkan successes . . . depended upon the extent to which Russia intended to send supplies to Germany. [The Allied loss of Greece was very serious, for] Russian oil could now be sent via the Black Sea and Greece.' However, he commented, it should be noted that 'Russia had released to Germany very little oil during the last month or so.'[5]

At this point the minutes reveal that the meeting became more animated.

The two trump cards Russia holds against the Germans are the threat of war on two fronts and the trans-Siberian railway, which was Germany's last one outlet to the outside world but the importance of which was daily diminishing as the United States came more and more into the war. The less Hitler could obtain from the outside world, the more important it became for him to draw upon the Russian reservoir [of natural resources and industrial production]. Hitler might therefore become bolder in his demands upon the Kremlin, supporting them with threats of force. Much would depend upon Russian resistance to these demands.

Hitler would have to attack quickly, if he intended to attack . . . since if he left it too long he would be faced with the bogey of war on two fronts but he would also have to wait until the Russian harvests had been brought in. Meanwhile Germany's supplies were lessening and her labour shortage was increasing. If Hitler could gain a quick success over Russia the sixty to eighty divisions on her Eastern Frontiers could be released to supply the labour which her war machine demanded. *We should therefore encourage the Germans to attack Russia by misleading Hitler and by hinting that the large sections both in Britain and the United States, who preferred to see the overthrow of the Russian rather than the German regime, might be prepared to force through a compromise peace between Britain and Germany and combine to destroy the common enemy, Communism.*[6] [Emphasis added.]

This last statement almost exactly mirrored what Rudolf Hess believed, and proposals to bring about which he was planning to bring with him to Scotland later that very day. There was, however, a crucial, devastating difference. Whereas Hess was genuine in his wish for peace with Britain, believing that men like Sam Hoare and Lord Halifax would be prepared to give Nazi Germany free rein in eastern Europe for the sake of peace, in truth the last thing these top Britons were aiming for was a conciliatory armistice with Nazi Germany. No one in the British government was about to agree to a treaty that would see Hitler free to invade Russia, then to possibly turn back on western Europe the moment it suited him.

Finally, at the invitation of Hugh Dalton, Anthony Eden asked a number of pertinent question arising out of what had been said, and after a little more debate the meeting adjourned and everyone went to lunch.

By May 1941 Hugh Dalton was having serious problems with many of those attending that meeting. His relationship with Rex Leeper had deteriorated over the past months to the point of pure animosity, and he was also out of favour not only with Eden, Vansittart and many of Rex Leeper's minions, but most of all with Winston Churchill. His position was becoming untenable.

Dalton had never been popular with Churchill, particularly after the way he'd crowbarred his way in to take over SOE, but following his letter of 28 February indicating his concerns over the true purpose of Messrs HHHH, his standing had deteriorated severely. Churchill had by now let Brendan Bracken off the leash to undermine the Minister for Economic Warfare, and with responsibility for SOE, bringing to mind Vansittart's comment that 'BB has been given the go ahead to reduce him once the operation has reached its conclusion'.[7] The strain of Bracken's bitter and acrimonious campaign, covertly sanctioned by Churchill, to destroy Dalton both politically and psychologically was beginning to tell.

On one occasion, Dalton discovered that Bracken had been loudly and publicly abusing him in the Carlton Grill.[8] Furious,

Dalton went to the lengths of obtaining statements and signatures of witnesses to the incident, and presented this strange document to his party leader Clement Attlee, who in turn was forced to take the matter up with Churchill. The Prime Minister expressed outward anger at the incident and, for Attlee's benefit, gave Bracken 'a ticking off'. However, Robert Bruce Lockhart – ever an insider – soon learned the truth, which Bracken proceeded to dine out on for many months, to Dalton's acute embarrassment. Churchill had privately asked Bracken: 'Is it true that at dinner the other night, you attacked SO2 and Dalton's work?'

'What I said,' an unrepentant Bracken retorted, 'was that Dalton was the biggest bloodiest shit I've ever met!'

Churchill, Lockhart recorded, far from admonishing his faithful friend, had 'roared with laughter'.[9]

Once the Messrs HHHH operation concluded, Churchill would let Bracken off the leash altogether. Hugh Dalton had much to fear from Brendan Bracken.

As the meeting at Woburn Abbey was concluding, six hundred miles to the east two German gentlemen were discussing much the same subject. Reichsleiter Alfred Rosenberg had arrived at Augsburg earlier that morning, courtesy of the special flight laid on for him by the Deputy-Führer, and he and Hess had held a lengthy discussion at Hess's substantial villa on Harthauser Strasse in the suburb of Harlaching. Now, at midday, these two leading men of the Reich also sat down to a private lunch. Exactly what they discussed is not known, and no papers concerning this meeting have surfaced since the end of the war. However, Hess's household staff noticed that something was definitely up, and were given 'strict instructions not to disturb the men's meal'.[10]

It is, however, possible to hypothesise with a fair degree of accuracy what Hess and Rosenberg discussed on that particular Saturday in May 1941. In the preceding week, Hess's time had been almost entirely taken up with his preparations to depart for an important meeting with a British emissary close to King George VI. It will also be recalled that during the mid-1930s, contacts between Rosenberg's Aussenpolitisches Amt and the British monarchy were conducted through the Duke of Kent as intermediary. It is therefore likely that Hess requested this last meeting with Rosenberg to ask his advice about the Duke – whether, for example, there was any particular ploy that could be employed to gain the psychological upper hand, or whether the Duke might be favourably disposed towards National Socialism. These were questions that Rosenberg would have been eminently qualified to answer. That Hess opted to conduct his talk with Rosenberg over an early lunch is also a strong indicator that he was not asking for in-depth or complicated political advice, but merely wanted some final pointers for his imminent mission to Britain.

Intriguingly, after leaving Hess, Rosenberg did not return to Augsburg for a flight back to Berlin. Instead, he ordered his driver to take him the 120 miles from Munich to Berchtesgaden, where Adolf Hitler had arrived forty-eight hours before. It is not known whether Rosenberg took a message to Hitler from Hess, or whether, concerned by Hess's intimations that he was about to fly to Britain, he decided to consult with his Führer immediately. Rosenberg may already have been aware of the secret negotiations, for he had worked closely with Albrecht Haushofer on occasion. Thus it may be that, like Haushofer, Rosenberg had believed Ernst Bohle was the man expected by the British, and had travelled swiftly to the Berghof to warn Hitler against allowing the Deputy-Führer to place himself in such jeopardy.

Whatever the reason for Rosenberg's journey to the Berghof that Saturday afternoon, it made not one iota of difference; nor did Hess seem to be at all bothered by the thought that Rosenberg might reveal all to the Führer. This therefore suggests that Rosenberg travelled to the Berghof with Hess's sanction, perhaps carrying a last private communication from the Deputy-Führer before the big event took place.

Rudolf Hess appeared completely relaxed and at peace with himself after Rosenberg's departure. Knowing he had a long flight and night ahead of him, he retired to bed for a few hours' rest, getting up again in mid-afternoon. He then dressed quietly in a brand-new

Luftwaffe uniform, and went to see his wife and small child before departing.

Hess found Ilse glancing idly through a copy of *The Pilot's Book of Everest*, the Duke of Hamilton's account of flying over the world's highest mountain several years before. It seems unlikely to have been coincidental that she was reading this particular book on this of all days. It is possible that Hess himself had been looking at it prior to retiring for his nap, left it out, and Ilse had subsequently picked it up.

Taking the book from his wife, Hess turned to the front and read the inscription: 'With all good wishes and the hope that out of personal friendship a real and lasting understanding may grow between our two countries.' It was signed 'English friends'. Flicking through to a plate of the Duke of Hamilton, Hess paused contemplatively for a few seconds before remarking to his wife, 'He's very good-looking . . .'[11]

Hess and Ilse then took a little light tea together, chatting about family matters and friends. Then, towards the end of their meal, Ilse asked her husband when he would be returning. It was an unpremeditated, God-tempting question, the answer to which would prove horribly inaccurate, for Hess answered: 'I don't know exactly – perhaps tomorrow, perhaps not, but I'll certainly be back by Monday evening.'

'As early as tomorrow? Or Monday?' Ilse responded in surprise. 'I don't believe it – you won't be back so quickly!'[12]

If everything was as Hess and Hitler imagined it to be, and the Deputy-Führer would soon be secretly in the company of a band of powerful Britons united in a peace faction, he would indeed return in just a few days.

Finally Hess looked in on his young son 'Buzz' to say a light-hearted goodbye, before departing for the forty-mile journey to Augsburg in the company of his Adjutant, Lieutenant Karl-Heinz Pintsch, orderly Joseph Platser, and personal detective Franz Lutz.[13] Before arriving at Augsburg, the fatalist within Hess would determine he had one last task he wished to perform before setting off on his historic mission. Ordering his driver to stop the car at a roadside copse, Hess took himself off for a brief solitary walk through the trees, alone with his thoughts in the German countryside. Had he but known it, he would never again have the luxury of privacy and the right to wander his homeland. His life as a free man had less than six hours left to run.

At 5.45 p.m. exactly, Hess's Me-110, registration VJ-OQ, thundered down the main runway at the Augsburg aerodrome, its twin Daimler-Benz supercharged engines thrusting out their full 1395 horsepower as the aircraft, heavily laden with twin drop-tanks carrying an extra four hundred gallons of fuel, struggled to lift off the ground. First the tail rose, and then as the aircraft reached the necessary speed for the wings to develop lift, the wheels of Hess's plane lumbered off the runway. The aircraft quickly picked up speed and began climbing gently. Those below watched as the undercarriage retracted hydraulically into the engine nacelles, and the hinged doors swung shut behind them. Hess banked his aircraft onto a north-westerly heading, and prepared to switch on the sophisticated guidance systems that would zero in on a German radio beacon stationed near Den Helder on the coast of Holland,[14] broadcasting at a frequency that would guide him towards the North Sea.

Enclosed within an aircraft prepared to the peak of performance, Hess knew he had a long flight ahead of him. He also knew that his powerful twin-engined fighter was totally unprotected, for its nose-mounted twin 20mm Oerlikon cannons and quadruple 7.9mm machine-guns were unarmed and packed with grease. He was about to travel across war-torn western Europe, out over the North Sea, and thence into British – enemy – airspace totally unarmed, as befitted a peace envoy who hoped to end a bitter war.

Ahead of Germany's Deputy-Führer lay an appointment with the Duke of Kent and, he may have believed, the Duke of Hamilton, Lord Steward of the Royal Household. Had Hess expected the Duke of Hamilton to be present at this extraordinary meeting – as would be natural given the use of Dungavel House – he may have been looking forward to a conversation with the man who had flown over Everest, one flying enthusiast to another. However, in this, as in almost everything else, he was to be disappointed.

The whole of SO1's Messrs HHHH operation seems to have been marked by a string of coincidences: Violet Roberts' nephew being a Director of SO1; Albrecht Haushofer's friendship with the Duke of Hamilton; the Duke of Kent–de Ropp/Rosenberg and the Duke of Buccleuch–Ernst Bohle relationships. However, if these apparent coincidences are examined on the basis that the highly accomplished men of SO1 were capable of co-ordinating their operation in such a manner as to make use of a variety of beneficial situations, then what at first appears coincidental may be reassembled to make a great deal more sense. Indeed, the evidence clearly reveals that the Dukes of Kent, Buccleuch and Hamilton were drawn into the operation precisely because of their past connections. It is clear that SO1 consistently introduced, developed and manipulated elements perceived as useful to Messrs HHHH. There was calculated intelligence behind these developments, and extensive use was made of past associations to further the operation's chances of success. Another coincidence was about to occur.

As Rudolf Hess's aircraft streaked in from the North Sea towards its destination in western Lanarkshire, it would pass over the most north-easterly corner of England, thirty miles north of Newcastle, before crossing almost immediately into the Lowlands of Scotland. That section of British airspace fell under the control of No. 13 (Fighter) Group's headquarters at Ouston, near Newcastle upon Tyne. Some ninety miles to the north-east of Ouston, the Duke of Hamilton, in the plot room of RAF Turnhouse near Edinburgh, undoubtedly watched as a WAAF teller began to plot the lone aircraft designated '42J' as it thundered in from the North Sea, crossed the coast near Cheviot, and headed inland. Two Spitfires from RAF Acklington, already on patrol out over the Farne Islands, were ordered by Ouston to engage the mysterious aircraft. A third Spitfire was then scrambled from Acklington to assist them, but none managed to make contact, and the lone Me-110, which had by now ducked under radar cover, continued unmolested on its journey to the Scottish Borders.

Whether the Duke of Hamilton had been contacted by SO1 on the arrival of Albrecht Haushofer's letter in Britain in the autumn of 1940 is not known, although MI5 did dispatch a memorandum to the Foreign Office, dated 22 November 1940, enquiring whether there were any objections to sending the letter on to the Duke.[15] After some consideration of the matter – which may well have included a referral to Lord Halifax, who was still Foreign Secretary at this time – the Foreign Office responded on 7 December that they had no objections.[16] However, they commented, the Duke should receive only a copy of the letter and not the original. It can therefore be seen that Hamilton's involvement in Messrs HHHH, albeit on the periphery, had begun as far back as the autumn of 1940.

On 26 February 1941 Hamilton received a surprise summons from a Group Captain Stammers of Air Intelligence, who requested a meeting at the Air Ministry in Whitehall. The two men duly met, and discussed the Albrecht Haushofer correspondence. On 28 March Stammers again wrote to Hamilton, this time to rebuke him for not sending him Haushofer's letter of July 1939 (which the Duke had taken to Churchill, Halifax and Chamberlain).[17] If Hamilton's involvement had remained this minimal, it might be possible to explain away many of his actions on the night of Saturday, 10 May 1941 after the arrival of Rudolf Hess on British soil. As it was, however, his involvement in the days ahead was to be raised to a much higher level.

Bearing in mind that the Duke of Hamilton, as a Wing Commander serving with Fighter Command, was serving with the RAF in an operational capacity, he must have been surprised to receive a second telegram from Air Intelligence on 18 April, ordering him to return to Whitehall on 25 April for another meeting.[18] That date would become deeply entwined within all the plotting and subterfuge now taking place to rope the Duke of Kent into SO1's machinations.

Having flown down to London from RAF Turnhouse, the Duke of Hamilton found himself ushered into a meeting at the Air Ministry in Whitehall with Group Captain Blackford of RAF Intelligence and Major 'Tar' Robertson of MI5's double-cross organisation, known as 20 (or XX) Committee.

20 Committee was a highly dangerous organ of Intelligence, particularly if one was an Axis agent, and exercised few scruples in its task of achieving ultimate victory over Germany. It had the responsibility of turning captured Axis spies into double-agents, and its operating parameters were both very simple and utterly ruthless. If the captured enemy agent co-operated, then he or she survived; if the agent did not co-operate, he or she very quickly had an appointment with an executioner's bullet or the gallows. 20 Committee was not an organisation to be trifled with, and 'Tar' Robertson's involvement in this affair was a very serious development indeed.

This does not mean that 20 Committee was involved in SO1's plot to undermine Hitler and Hess, but it does indicate that the Messrs HHHH operation, first bandied about in the summer of 1940 as a loose concept for a deception campaign, now ran up the chain of command not only from the experts in subterfuge and political warfare at SO1 to Rex Leeper, Anthony Eden and on to Churchill, but downward from Churchill, through his Air Minister Archibald Sinclair (hence his presence at Ditchley Park on 10–11 May 1941) to a selected few in Air Intelligence and also to the top man at MI5's 20 Committee, Major 'Tar' Robinson. Add to this the fact that the operation had grown to encompass real-life actors on the stage of deception – eminent marionettes such as Sir Samuel Hoare, Lord Halifax, the Duke of Kent and now it seemed the Duke of Hamilton as well – many of whom were pretending to be members of a peace faction poised to oust Churchill from his premiership, and it is clear the scope and range of the operation was very considerable indeed.

The Duke of Hamilton's 25 April meeting at the Air Ministry indicated that SO1 had now called upon the services of 'Tar' Robertson, for the Duke, to his great discomfort, was asked by

Blackford and Robertson if he would be prepared to travel to Portugal for a secret meeting in Lisbon with his old friend Albrecht Haushofer. This request, little more than a fortnight before Rudolf Hess came winging his way across the North Sea, must have emanated from the very heart of SO1's Messrs HHHH operation.

To Blackford and Robertson's surprise they found the Duke distinctly unenthusiastic. His response to their exciting proposal was that he would go, but only 'If I am ordered to.'

'We don't like to order people to do these sort of jobs,' the Intelligence men replied in an effort to be reasonable. 'We like volunteers.'[19]

However, the Duke of Hamilton was not about to be hustled into such a mission. His loose association with SO1 and their use of his home at Dungavel House was one thing, but to become a pawn in British Intelligence's game of high intrigue was quite another. Several days later, having sought the counsel of his old and trusted friend Lord Eustace Percy (who also just happened to be an old acquaintance of Albrecht Haushofer), the Duke responded to Group Captain Blackford. Lord Percy had advised that Hamilton should agree to participate only if ordered to do so, and that was the stance Hamilton adopted. He would consent to go to Portugal, he announced, but only after discussions with the Ambassador to Lisbon and Sir Alexander Cadogan.

There are distinct echoes here of the terms under which the Duke of Kent had agreed to participate in SO1's project, insisting that he too be briefed by either Eden or Cadogan. Reconciled to this annoying ducal caution, Group Captain Blackford wrote to Hamilton on Saturday, 3 May, saying that he understood his position, and that he had discussed the matter with Air Commodore Boyle, the head of Air Intelligence. It appears, however, that by the weekend preceding the German emissary's arrival something must have changed, for Blackford's eagerness to dispatch the Duke of Hamilton to Lisbon for surreptitious talks with Albrecht Haushofer had suddenly cooled. He wrote to the Duke that Boyle 'agrees with you that this might not be the right time to open up a discussion, the nature of which may be misinterpreted'.[20]

These matters may have passed through the Duke of Hamilton's mind as he watched WAAF tellers plotting the course of enemy raid 42J across the large multi-coloured map of northern Britain at 10.30 p.m. on Saturday, 10 May 1941. In his pre-war days as a flying enthusiast, the Duke had ordered an airstrip to be constructed in the grounds of Dungavel House, near what had formerly been the ducal hunt's kennels. These had been converted into an office and maintenance buildings capable of housing several aircraft. With the coming of war the airstrip had been uprated for occasional use by the Air Training Corps, and by the late spring of 1940 Dungavel had become an emergency landing strip for aircraft unable to reach their own bases due to damage or mechanical failure. In consequence of this new role the runway had been uprated for night use by the fitting of landing lights.

As the plot of raid 42J progressed before the eyes of those in the Operations Room at RAF Turnhouse, certain men already gathered at Dungavel House, Woburn Abbey and Ditchley Park must have been contemplating their own roles in the extremely complicated affair that had developed from Leeper's first approach to Churchill the previous August to set in motion a deception on a hitherto unpractised scale. If it worked, Hitler would feel confident enough to turn on Russia, and it would be only a matter of time before the haemorrhaging of whole armies into the endless Russian expanse would prove the Nazis' undoing. If it failed, Britain might well cease to exist. The next twenty-four hours could be among the most important (albeit forever kept secret) of the war, a day that would see Britain securing her survival until the two big players – Russia and the United States – could be sucked into the fray.

The only complication – and it was to be a devastating one – was that everyone was expecting the approaching German aircraft to be carrying the head of the Auslandsorganisation, Gauleiter Ernst Bohle.

Seated in his Messerschmitt's noisy cockpit, Rudolf Hess would have had little time to ponder the events of the past ten months. He may have had the luxury of contemplative thought during his almost three-hour flight over the North Sea, where he had adopted a holding pattern from 8.52 to 9.52 p.m. awaiting dusk to make his approach; but as he had neared the east coast of Britain, he would have had to give his full concentration to flying at nearly four hundred mph in the dark, at heights of only fifty to a hundred feet. This would have been a hair-raising challenge for the most accomplished and highly trained flier, and Hess was a middle-aged politician with a passion for flying, not an operational Luftwaffe pilot. He may have had an almost new aircraft tuned to the peak of performance, a far superior machine to what most Luftwaffe pilots could ever hope to get their hands on, but Hess's flight was extraordinarily difficult, and flying at low altitude in the dark it would have taxed any pilot's skills to ensure that he did not plough into one of the many hills the Me-110 was negotiating at breakneck speed.

Hess had not faced such real personal danger since his time as a fighter-pilot of the Jagdstaffel 35, flying a handful of combat missions in a Fokker Dr-1 triplane in the autumn of 1918. That had been a 110-horsepower, wood-and-canvas triple-winged aircraft, most often associated with the daring escapades of the Red Baron. In 1941, Hess's flying style still reflected his extremely out-of-date training. Whereas most Second World War combat pilots would have sought to avoid the enemy by utilising their aircraft's maximum altitude – thirty-two thousand feet in the case of an Me-110 – Germany's Deputy-Führer adopted the barnstorming tactics of the First World War, thundering in low over the Scottish countryside, skimming houses and trees, hedge-hopping and swinging this way and that through steep-sided valleys. While a Fokker triplane's top speed was a stately 103 miles per hour, Hess's Me-110 screamed in over the remote Lowland villages at almost four times that speed, and he was burning up his remaining fuel at an extremely high rate. Following Hess's flight, the expressions of wonder should have been made not so much at the fact that he flew all the way from Germany to a remote corner of Scotland, but rather that he avoided killing himself in the process. However, Hess's tactics during the flight should not be entirely denigrated, for they took him below Britain's radar cover, and certainly prevented him from being spotted – silhouetted against the sky or horizon – by any patrolling fighter cover.

It was Hess's overwhelming desire for the success of his mission that made him throw caution to the wind. For one weekend only he was playing the star role as the daring adventurer who would fly deep into enemy territory to make peace. However, despite all the outward signs of careless abandon, Hess had spent months meticulously planning his flight, and had ordered several significant technical modifications to his aircraft to improve his chances of success.

In the latter 1930s, while British scientists had been experimenting with radar, their German counterparts had also been studying radio-waves, but their endeavours had taken them down an entirely different path. German scientists had spent considerable resources developing the broadcast of powerful and concentrated radio beams which could be used for aircraft navigation, and they had gone on to create a network of radio beacons. By early 1940, forty-six such beacons existed, criss-crossing the skies above Germany and western Europe in an invisible network of airborne motorways four to five hundred metres wide, named Knickebeins.

RAF Intelligence had long suspected that the Luftwaffe's extremely accurate bombing of Britain's airfields and cities had been assisted by some form of navigational aid, and in June 1940 the capture of a downed Luftwaffe pilot confirmed their fears. During interrogation, the pilot revealed that the Luftwaffe were using Knickebeins as a bomb-dropping aid involving two intersecting radio beams, the beams being picked up by a special aircraft-mounted receiver named a 'Lorenz'.[21] More worrying still, an expert evaluation concluded that a bomber using Knickebeins and a Lorenz receiver could achieve accuracy of within thirty-five to forty feet.[22] This was a new and deadly secret weapon, one that British scientists eventually countered by broadcasting their own radio waves on a similar megacycle frequency to distort the Knickebein beams, a practice known as 'beam-bending' or 'meaconing';

but not before many deadly Luftwaffe raids of unerring accuracy had caused much devastation.

The Germans had maintained their navigational/bomb-ranging system by regularly changing the Knickebein frequencies.[23] By the spring of 1941, Britain and Germany were fighting a continual war of the airwaves that saw Britain increasingly criss-crossed by a network of invisible flight paths.

Rudolf Hess's aircraft was fitted with a Lorenz receiver, which he tuned to a variety of Knickebein frequencies as he navigated his way firstly across western Europe, then the North Sea, and finally the British countryside.

The fitting of a Lorenz receiver was not the only significant improvement that had been made to Hess's Messerschmitt. An Me-110 was really designed for three men: the pilot, a navigator/radio man, and a rear gunner. As Hess was the sole occupant of his plane its radio systems had to be adapted. There was no room in the cockpit for the equipment itself, but after some experimentation the technicians at Messerschmitt managed to fit a set of remote controls so the radio equipment could be worked from the pilot's seat.

One other important modification to Hess's plane reveals a great deal about his attitude to his daring flight. The fuselage of the Deputy-Führer's Me-110 was half a metre longer than that of a normal production machine, and along its top a thin copper tube ran from the cockpit to an added-on half-metre section midway to the tail. Within this tube ran a steel cable connected to a handle near the pilot's seat. Had Hess encountered a major problem and been forced to ditch his aircraft over the sea, pulling this handle would release an inflatable rubber dinghy complete with survival facilities to sustain his life until rescue.

During his flight low over the Scottish countryside, Hess had easily managed to evade the three Spitfires over the east coast, his twin-engined Me-110 possessing sufficient power to outrun the British fighters; but his progress across the Lowlands was now being noted by various listening posts.

At 10.23 p.m. Hess's low-flying aircraft had been heard and

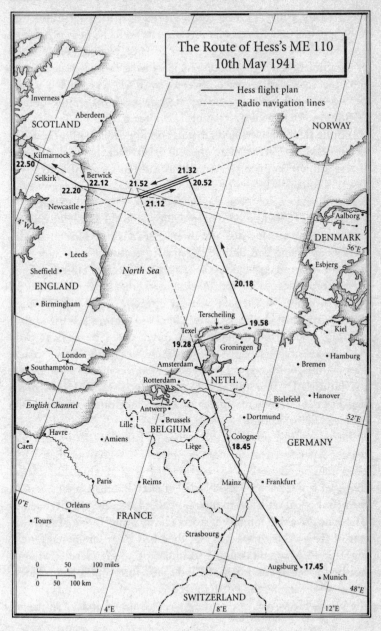

The Route of Hess's ME 110
10th May 1941

—— Hess flight plan
– – – Radio navigation lines

reported by a Royal Observation Corps post based at Embleton, and then, less than fifteen minutes later, by an ROC post at Ashkirk approximately ninety miles to the north-east, placing Hess's speed at this time in the region of 360 m.p.h. Just at this point he crossed into the sector of airspace covered by RAF Ayr, and here the response to the incoming enemy aircraft was a little more potent. A Boulton Defiant was scrambled to intercept it.

To the RAF plotters and air staffs on duty that night, the flight of a lone Me-110 was a most unusual occurrence, particularly since it was known that the Messerschmitt did not carry sufficient fuel reserves to make the return journey home. The response, however, was still fairly paltry. Boulton Defiants like that sent to intercept Hess's Me-110 had initially been deployed in the Battle of Britain, but they were so outdated and their losses against Germany's Me-109s so appalling that despite the gravity of the air war, they were withdrawn from service in the south of England entirely. They were simply too slow to compete with the far more powerful planes of 1940. A Defiant was an effective night-fighter when deployed against the heavy, slow Heinkel 111s, but against a faster and more powerful Me-110 it was outclassed. The Defiant from Ayr never even managed to make contact with Hess's plane. Despite this, within days Britain's Air Minister would stand before the House of Commons and brazenly declare that Hess's plane had been 'in imminent danger of being shot down' prior to the moment he baled out.[24]

Intriguingly, evidence did emerge in late 1999 that there had been a separate effort to intercept Hess's Me-110, but that it had been scuppered on the instructions of RAF Fighter-Command itself.[25] Two Czech pilots, Vaclav 'Felix' Bauman and Leopold Srom (who had returned to their homeland after the war), related to a Czechoslovakian military historian how, whilst flying Hurricanes out of RAF Aldergrove in 1941, they had been scrambled on the night of 10 May and ordered to intercept a lone German aircraft heading towards the Firth of Clyde, just forty miles from Aldergrove. On reaching the Forth in record time, the two pilots spotted the plane. However, just as they were about to attack, an urgent message came through over their radios ordering them to 'Stop action and return.' Believing there had been a mistake, Flight-Sergeant Bauman responded that they were within range, but he was cut short and told, 'Sorry, Felix, old boy. It is not possible. You must return. Now.'[26]

By the time Bauman and Srom spotted Hess's plane, the Deputy-Führer was little more than nine minutes' flying time from Dungavel House. It was at this point that a major oversight began to take on increasing importance. At the time of his approach to Britain's east coast from the North Sea the light had been a major concern to Hess, as he had not wanted to be spotted and perhaps shot down by an enemy unaware of the importance of the pilot or his mission. Now, however, darkness became an increasing problem. Dusk had fallen, and Hess could not make out the ground contours or the road and rail networks he had hoped to use for his final approach. One mistake, and within a mere two minutes he could have been as much as six or seven miles from his anticipated position. Unsurprisingly, Hess did indeed miss Dungavel, over-shooting his destination to find himself on the west coast of Scot-land. He was later to recall that as he neared the coast he had been able to make out 'the glassy sea . . . in the light of the rising moon',[27] but little else. Although he had not known it, Hess's navigational skills had been better than he realised. He had actually overflown Dungavel House at 10.45 p.m. before continuing on to the coast. Those awaiting the arrival of the German leadership's emissary had heard the aircraft passing nearby in the darkness.

Germany's Deputy-Führer turned his plane back inland and began zigzagging in an attempt to locate Dungavel House. By now he had been forced to jettison his empty spare wing-tanks, and his fuel was running dangerously low. He knew he had mere minutes to land his plane safely, or he would have to abandon it.

In 2000 a former WAAF, under the pseudonym of 'Mrs Abbot', as she wished to remain anonymous, recalled that on the night of 10 May 1941 she and a friend had been leaving Dungavel House's kitchen when they were surprised to see that the airstrip's landing lights had been turned on.[28] So unusual was this occurrence, contravening strictly enforced blackout regulations, that they hoped the lighting-up had not resulted from 'some infernal electrical fault that would attract Jerry raiders and get us killed'.

Moments later, the two women were relieved to see the lights blink out, plunging the airstrip back into darkness. But to their surprise they soon heard an aircraft coming in low over the countryside. They had 'half expected the lights to go back on again. But they remained off.' Some ten minutes later 'Mrs Abbot' and her companion, still standing out in the darkness, 'heard an aircraft – presumably the same one – pass over again'.

Quite why the airstrip lights went out and were not relit has never been clearly understood. It may be that the ME-110's pilot had prior instructions to make radio contact with Dungavel as he was making his approach, and that those waiting on the ground suddenly became aware that their visitor was not Ernst Bohle after all. Hess may even have unwisely announced exactly who he was, causing much alarm, for while the SO1 plotters might have expected to be able to stall negotiations with Bohle by raising some point which he'd have to consult Berlin about, Rudolf Hess, as Deputy-Führer, had the power to take executive decisions. There would be no hope of pulling the wool over Hess's eyes, as might have been the case with Bohle.

In the time-honoured fashion of someone wishing to deter an unwelcome visitor, the men at Dungavel's airstrip may have panicked on hearing that it was someone other than Bohle aboard the plane, turned out the lights and pretended not to be in. They would not have minded in the slightest if some Nazi dignitary were killed in a plane crash, which would have served very nicely to stall the Messrs HHHH negotiations further anyway.

'Mrs Abbot' had been curious enough about the 'strange incident' of the landing lights to make enquiries about it. To her surprise, she learned that they had been switched on as the result of a phone call from Bowhill, yet another of the Duke of Buccleuch's country properties, located a mere thirty miles south-east of Dungavel House. Significantly, Bowhill was directly under the flight path of Hess's Me-110. Rudolf Hess had overflown it eleven minutes before his arrival in the airspace over Dungavel House.

There is one more significant piece of evidence. Another WAAF who also wishes to be identified under a pseudonym, as 'Mrs Baker', was also at Dungavel that night. She later recalled that in the late spring of 1941 two packing cases were delivered to the castle, and placed in storage at the airstrip's hangar. The cases caused some curiosity among the personnel based at Dungavel, for they were stamped with markings which indicated that their place of origin had been the Messerschmitt works in Augsburg. 'Mrs Baker' went on to assert that although she had not seen what was in the cases herself, she was told by an acquaintance that they contained 'petrol tanks'. This statement is quite remarkable, not least because it would appear impossible for Britain to have obtained aircraft parts from the Messerschmitt works in time of war.

Or would it? One simple fact must be borne in mind: in the world of Intelligence, anything is possible. Yes, it would have been remarkably difficult for Britain to obtain aircraft parts from Germany. But it should be noted that the Spanish air force was equipped with Me-110s, and the Messerschmitt works at Augsburg continued to supply it with spare parts until the winter of 1943. Samuel Hoare, having discussed with Albrecht Haushofer the technical requirements of the German emissary's visit, may have requested Captain Hillgarth to obtain a pair of drop-tanks from General Vigon. They could then have been dispatched to Britain aboard the weekly flying boat from Lisbon to Portsmouth, and thence shipped to Dungavel.

Such deals were grist to Hillgarth's mill. Within a few months he would be busy paying many millions of US dollars to Franco's generals in a massive bribery deal to keep Spain neutral. It worked. The Generalissimo was supported in his neutral stance by his key men, the Iberian Peninsula remained war-free, and Churchill's faith in Hillgarth continued unbounded. Indeed, Churchill would soon support Hillgarth's pleas for more bribery money with the Chancellor of the Exchequer, writing: 'We must not lose them now, after all we have spent – and gained. Vital strategic decisions depend on Spain keeping out . . . Hillgarth is pretty good.'[29] The acquisition of a few aircraft parts would have been a simple matter for a man such as Hillgarth.

'Mrs Baker' was to make one other interesting statement concerning the night of 10 May 1941 at Dungavel House. She commented that 'the Duke and his people were in the Kennels', adding that this group included a Pole.[30] Pressed by an interviewer concerned that she might be mistaken, for it was known that the Duke of Hamilton was at RAF Turnhouse that night, the elderly lady had responded in annoyance: 'Not the Duke of Hamilton. The Duke of Kent!'

'Mrs Baker's comment about a Pole being present at Dungavel that night is perturbing, but may be erroneous. It should be remembered that in 1941 she was a young woman, and had probably had little or no contact with foreigners. It may be that an officer with a strong north-eastern European accent was identified as Polish for ease of explanation to a curious young WAAF.

There was a man in Britain in May 1941 who was known to the Duke of Kent, the Duke of Buccleuch and Ernst Bohle. Furthermore, he was known to have a strong north-east European accent, and he was an old friend not only of Alfred Rosenberg, but also of Albrecht Haushofer, and of Rudolf Hess too in an indirect manner. He was one of the most important members of covert British intelligence if one wanted to make contact with an important personage in Germany. He was a Balt of former east Prussian stock, whose family had lost all their possessions, land and aristocratic standing at the end of the First World War. His name was Baron 'Bill' de Ropp.

Thus, on the evening of Saturday, 10 May 1941, there were many men gathered in three key places, awaiting developments that might come with the German emissary.

At Dungavel House waited the Duke of Kent, the Duke of Buccleuch and a north European who was almost certainly Bill de Ropp, together with three or four mechanics who were ready to fit twin drop-tanks and refuel the visiting aircraft. Also present, as will appear, was a dark-haired, neatly tailored man named S. Voigt. He was from SO1 Woburn, delegated to report on the emissary's meeting and, perhaps, to keep an eye on the Dukes of Kent and Buccleuch for the duration of Bohle's visit.

At Woburn Abbey the protagonists and co-ordinators of the whole Messrs HHHH operation – Rex Leeper, Anthony Eden, Hugh Dalton, Sir Robert Vansittart, Robert Bruce Lockhart, Brigadier Brooks, Hugh Gaitskell, Leonard St Clair Ingrams, Thomas Barman, Richard Crossman and Con O'Neill – undoubtedly lurked in SOE's operations room, connected to the outside world by teletype, telephone and transmitter. Perhaps they took an occasional stroll outside, where they could not help but see the *raison d'être* for their whole highly dangerous deception operation. To the south, the evening sky glowed red; London was burning.

Winston Churchill, deep in the Oxfordshire countryside, whilst mindful of the developments about to take place in Scotland, was also kept abreast of the situation in London. He was later to write: 'The worst attack was the last. On 10 May the enemy returned to London with incendiary bombs. He lit more than two thousand fires, and, by the smashing of nearly a hundred and fifty water mains, coupled with the low tide in the Thames, he stopped us putting them out . . . it was the most destructive of the whole night Blitz.'[31] With Churchill at Ditchley that night were Sir Archibald Sinclair, the loyal Brendan Bracken, and President Roosevelt's personal representative Harry Hopkins.

However, the news everyone was anticipating – that the German emissary had arrived – was about to take an unexpected twist.

Since the Second World War, much has been published concerning the details of Rudolf Hess's flight to Scotland on that May evening in 1941. Every aspect of his flight, from each twist of his plane to the countermeasures taken by Britain's defences, has been examined time and time again in an effort to discover the truth. However, the technical details behind the flight are not as important as the planned arrival of a German emissary on British soil in the midst of a desperate war, or how such a situation came about. When the truth is known – that certain high-echelon Britons were expecting a German plane, albeit carrying a different emissary – the technical evidence about the flight pales into insignificance.

From the very moment that Hess (undoubtedly in a panic, for it was certainly no part of his plan to kill himself trying to land his plane in the dark while lost) bailed out of his Me-110, the whole of SO1's carefully choreographed Messrs HHHH operation suddenly took off at a tangent. All subsequent events from 11.09 p.m. on Saturday, 10 May 1941 – the instant Hess parachuted from his plane – have to be viewed in the light of the fact that what took place from then on was completely unplanned. From that moment, Britain's reaction to Hess's arrival was almost entirely a damage-limitation exercise, aimed primarily at preventing the Messrs HHHH operation from collapsing before Hitler took the fatal decision to proceed with his attack on Russia; but also to hide the fact that top men of the British government, Secret Service, aristocracy and diplomatic corps had participated in a Machiavellian plot to enter into bogus peace negotiations with the German leadership.

Despite Britain's dire strategic position in early 1941, the unscrupulous use of peace negotiations – particularly undertaken by diplomats on neutral territory – to further British war objectives was anathema, and would have been viewed with acute alarm by Britain's allies and Churchill's political rivals. The revelation that important Britons had been secretly negotiating with Hitler had the potential to cause a catastrophic rift within the alliance, and might have led Russia to decide not to assist the Allied cause. Churchill and SO1's sole objective may have been to assure Britain's survival, but if the means of this survival became public, the nation would pay a terrible price. Her politico-diplomatic integrity would be in shreds, and her many would-be detractors on the international stage would have an excuse to regard Britain's diplomats and politicians as pariahs. Revealing the truth behind Rudolf Hess's arrival in Britain was not an option.

❋   ❋   ❋

'RUDOLF HESS IN GLASGOW – OFFICIAL' blared the head-lines of the *Daily Record* on 18 May, before going on to declare: 'Herr Hess, Hitler's right-hand man, has run away from Germany and is in Glasgow suffering from a broken ankle.'[32] The article went on to dramatically report that Hess, having bailed out of his aircraft in the dark, had the good fortune not only to survive his first-ever parachute jump, but to come to earth within yards of a farm-worker's cottage. No doubt the local ploughman who found him, David McLean, would have been highly offended to discover that Germany's Deputy-Führer believed his home to be 'a goat-herder's hut', but McLean was a keen interviewee, and the *Daily Record* quoted him as saying:

> I was in the house and everyone was in bed late at night when I heard the 'plane roaring overhead. As I ran out . . . I heard a crash, and saw the plane burst into flames in the field about 200 yards away.
>
> I was amazed and a bit frightened when I saw a parachute drop-ping slowly earthwards though the gathering darkness. Peering upwards I could see a man swinging from the harness . . .

Such was the public report of Rudolf Hess's arrival in Scotland. Yet the very fact that the event was so promptly reported is cause for suspicion. Britain at this time operated under the strictest cen-sorship regulations in its history. However, Mr McLean was free to talk, and the *Daily Record* was free to report. Thus the men of the Ministry, be it censorship or intelligence, must have wanted the report released, otherwise it would not have been. There was already a hidden agenda taking place behind the scenes.

Germany's Deputy-Führer had, it was reported, suffered a men-tal aberration and decided to take himself off to enemy territory in time of deepest war. Between the moment that Hess left his plunging aircraft to glide softly to earth, and the appearance of the *Daily Record*'s report, a sea-change had taken place in British Intelligence's attitude to him. In the very act of coming, and so losing his position in Germany, Rudolf Hess had to a great degree lost his usefulness.

Ever since Hess's arrival late on the night of Saturday, 10 May 1941, it has been recorded that he was first held by a local Home Guard unit, who duly (as per their standing orders) telephoned the nearest army unit to come and take charge of the captured enemy airman. In this instance, the Home Guard telephoned the 14th Argyll and Sutherland Highlanders' headquarters at Paisley; but curiously, Sub-Area Command ordered that the Argylls were *not* to be dispatched. Instead, a unit of Cameronian Highlanders was sent from Glasgow to take the downed German pilot directly to Maryhill Barracks in Glasgow.[33] Furthermore, instead of being bundled unceremoniously into the back of an army lorry, as was the usual fate of captured Luftwaffe air-crew, this prisoner travelled by private car 'as [an] extra measure of courtesy'.[34] Thus it was already known that this was no run-of-the-mill PoW.

Despite the officially sanctioned reports of the *Daily Record*, there *were* two other men on the scene at David McLean's farm when Rudolf Hess arrived, but any mention of them was strictly censored from inclusion in the *Daily Record*'s report.

In 1947, one of these two men, Daniel McBride, wrote an article which appeared in the *Hong Kong Telegraph*. This threw considerable new light on what had actually taken place after Hess bailed out of his plane. McBride, a sergeant in the Royal Signals, was based at Eaglesham House, a few miles north of Dungavel House, from where anti-enemy-signals work was undertaken. This work was so secret that no local ever knew what was being done at Eaglesham. In layman's terms 'anti-enemy-signals' work means meaconing, or beam-bending.

A year prior to Hess's flight, No. 80 (Signals) Wing, based at Radlett, just a few miles south of St Albans, discovered that the Germans had set up a powerful Knickebein which was broadcasting on 30 Mc/s (thirty megacycles) from precisely 54°39'N 08°57'E.[35] This positioned the broadcast station at Stollberg, on the west coast of Denmark. By the late spring of 1941 the Stollberg

Knickebein had been directed at Glasgow to guide German bombers to their target, and Hess had undoubtedly followed this beam across the Scottish countryside during the last leg of his journey, for it passed extremely close to Dungavel House. Thus the reason he came to earth midway between Eaglesham (also broadcasting on thirty megacycles so as to bend the Stollberg beam away from Glasgow) and Dungavel House is because his Lorenz receiver told him he was near Dungavel.

After the war, Daniel McBride revealed:

> Now that I am under no further obligation to HM Forces and Rudolf Hess has been sentenced at the Nuremberg Trials, the true story of Hess's apprehension after he landed at Eaglesham, Scotland, can be told for the first time.
>
> The purpose of the former Deputy-Führer's visit to Britain is still a mystery to the general public, but I say, and with confidence too, that high-ranking government officials were aware of his coming. No air-raid warning was given that night . . . nor was the plane plotted at the anti-aircraft control room for the west of Scotland . . .[36]

McBride disclosed that on Saturday, 10 May he had been eagerly awaiting his relief at 6 p.m. from an afternoon stint in the Signals Operations Room at Eaglesham House, when he was annoyed to hear from a colleague that all weekend leave had suddenly been cancelled. He went on:

> Later that night, I was lying in bed . . . when I heard the unmistakable drone of a low flying aircraft increasing rapidly to a nerve-racking roar . . . The sleepers [all] woke, jumped out of bed and were outside in no time. We were standing in various stages of undress as the plane zoomed low overhead. We saw it plainly, but owing to the fading daylight we could not make out its markings. From the noise of the engines and the design of the plane, we guessed it was not one of ours . . . Scarcely had the last man climbed into bed again when the plane was heard returning. Out we dashed and the machine was clearly to be seen. Twice the pilot circled HQ.

As the young men stood on the terrace staring at the night sky they spotted the plane, which suddenly appeared to climb steeply before its engines cut out. The plane rolled on its back and began to dive, and a lone figure was thrown clear. His parachute opened, and the man drifted gently to earth. McBride commented: 'I thought it must be one of our own boys come to grief while trying out a German machine, more especially as there had been no anti-aircraft fire directed at him and no sirens sounded.'

From here onward, Daniel McBride's evidence clashes with the official story of a lone farmer who stumbled from his cottage one dark night to find a German airman coming to earth mere yards from his back door. McBride was to assert that *he* had been the first to reach the prone figure, it had been he who helped the pilot indoors, and during a brief conversation the German airman stated that his name was Alfred Horn.

Hess's use of this name for his first eighteen hours in Britain suggests that it must have been agreed back in Germany that if something went wrong, if the Deputy-Führer fell into the wrong hands, he would use the name 'Alfred Horn' in the first instance. That the name was pre-arranged, and not made up off the cuff, is evident because the following day Hess asked if he could let his family know he was safe by sending a telegram to 'Rothacker, Herzog Str. 17, Zürich, stating that Alfred Horn was in good health'.[37] Frau Emma Rothacker, of Herzog Strasse 17, Zürich, was one of Rudolf Hess's aunts. A prior arrangement must have been made that in the event of her receiving a message concerning 'Alfred Horn' she was to notify the appropriate authorities in Berlin.

The name Alfred Horn was not picked at random either. While Alfred was the name of Rudolf Hess's younger brother, Ernst Bohle's assistant at the Auslandsorganisation, Horn was a name few people, except a few very close friends and relations, would associate with Hess. His wife Ilse's maiden name was Pröhl; however, what was not widely known, unless one was close to the Hess family, was that Ilse's widowed mother had remarried – a Munich businessman by the name of Carl Horn. Thus Rudolf Hess's mother-in-law was now called Frau Horn.

The Deputy-Führer would persist in the charade of maintaining that his name was Alfred Horn until the middle of Sunday, 11 May. In the meantime people like Daniel McBride had no cause to doubt that this was the lone pilot's real name. It was not part of Hess's plan to reveal his true identity to the wrong people too soon, for he undoubtedly hoped he would still be delivered to the safety of the important Britons awaiting him at Dungavel House.

Following the briefest of introductions between the lone Luftwaffe pilot named Alfred Horn and Daniel McBride, the young British sergeant asked: 'Did you come to bomb us?'

'My plane was not fitted to carry bombs,' the German retorted indignantly. 'I came to see the Duke of Hamilton.'

Hess, according to McBride, then asked him 'to take him to the Duke [of Hamilton]'s home, which, he said, was not far away. To this I could only reply that I had no power to do so but my superiors would probably do so later on.'

Shortly afterwards there was a commotion outside. The door was flung open and a Home Guard officer rushed in, followed by a number of men. The German pilot said to the officer: 'I wish to see the Duke of Hamilton. Will you take me to him?'

'You can save all that for the people concerned,' said the officer. 'At present you are coming with me.'[38]

During his time in Home Guard custody and his journey to Maryhill Barracks in Glasgow, Germany's Deputy-Führer persisted in his demand to see the Duke of Hamilton. However, to his undoubted concern, rather than being taken to Dungavel House, where he must have hoped the matter of his arrival might yet have been kept out of the public domain, Hess found himself among unfriendly natives, being carried off towards Glasgow – the opposite direction to that which he wished to be taken.

Just nine hours before, Rudolf Hess had been a cosseted, high-ranking German politician, attended by servants, adjutants and even his own personal detective. Now he was being bundled into the local Home Guard headquarters, a damp and dusty Scout hut in the scruffy Glaswegian suburb of Giffnock, where indignity was heaped on indignity. He was stripped of all his personal possessions and thoroughly searched, then subjected to a gruelling two-hour interrogation by an unfriendly and uncompromising Pole named Roman Battaglia, who worked at the Polish Consulate in Glasgow.

Battaglia's presence that night at the Scout hut in Giffnock is as curious as it was alarming to MI5, considering their undoubted knowledge of the true circumstances behind the German emissary's arrival, and they immediately launched an investigation into the Battaglia incident. Within a few days the head of MI5 in Edinburgh reported with some consternation to his superior in Oxford: 'How on earth he [Battaglia] got to know of Hess's arrival, and, further-more, went out and interrogated him for over two hours, I simply cannot conceive.'[39]

Roman Battaglia was duly interrogated by MI5 at Glasgow's Police Headquarters. Yet despite MI5's suspicion that he had been tipped off that something strange was afoot that Saturday night, the interrogating officer, John Mair, was forced to concede in his report that Battaglia denied knowing the true identity of the strange airman. However, Mair noted that Battaglia had declared, 'the circumstances [of his arrival] were so fantastic, that the prisoner must have come on some special mission'.[40]

Regardless of MI5's concern that others had attempted to inter-vene in the events surrounding the German's arrival, Rudolf Hess had been allowed to remain in the hands of the local Home Guard until 2 a.m. There was evidently much to worry Whitehall. What had he said? And to whom had he said it? The only reassuring certainty British Intelligence possessed was that from 2 a.m. onwards, the mysterious Alfred Horn had been in the custody of professional soldiers. Men who obeyed orders and did as they were told – first taking Hess to a local hospital to check the ankle he had hurt on landing, then whisking him off to Maryhill Barracks in the north of Glasgow; taking Hess ever further from his intended destination, Dungavel House, and his desire to meet the Duke of Hamilton.

Despite repeated assertions since the war that the Duke of Hamilton's first meeting with Hess occurred on the morning of

Sunday, 11 May, remarkable new evidence emerged in the 1990s which indicated that the Duke almost certainly undertook a secret car journey in the middle of the night of Saturday, 10 May, to meet the captured German emissary.

Ever since 10 May 1941, the Duke of Hamilton asserted that he came off duty at RAF Turnhouse at 11.15 p.m., as soon as he heard that the mysterious lone raider – '42J' – had crashed. He then took the very short journey to the house he and his wife had rented near the air base for the duration of his posting. Then, he maintained, he had gone to bed.

Yet within six days of the Hess landing a report was to appear in the *Glasgow Herald* which appeared to indicate that something very different had occurred during that Saturday night. It suggested that the Duke of Hamilton had not been as lax about raid 42J as might at first have appeared, and reported that late on Saturday night a 'meeting between the Duke and Hess took place at a point on the road to the hospital [en route to Maryhill Barracks] to which Hess was removed, and it is understood that representatives of the Intelligence Service and Foreign Office were present'.[41]

If this article was accurate – and there is no reason to assume that so precise a report did not have a basis in fact – it would indicate that a great deal more activity went on in the hours immediately after Hess landed than has ever been admitted. It is known that members of the Intelligence Service, certainly, as will appear, Mr Voigt of SO1, and quite probably Bill de Ropp, were present at Dungavel House on 10 May, awaiting the visiting emissary. Who the reported representative of the Foreign Office was is a little less clear, but it may have been that one of the men in the know at the Foreign Office, such as William Strang or Frank Roberts, was at Dungavel that night. It was Strang, after all, who had enlisted the Duke of Kent to meet the visiting German emissary, and it is therefore likely that a Foreign Office adviser would have been made available to support the Duke during the meeting itself.

Other evidence concerning the Duke of Hamilton's movements

that night emerged many years later, and the nature of its source suggests that there can be little doubt that the Duke did indeed, contrary to every subsequent denial made by him, drive the forty-five miles from RAF Turnhouse to Glasgow. In 1991 the Duke's widow, the present-day Dowager Duchess of Hamilton, was to reveal that after her husband returned from RAF Turnhouse at 11.15 on the night of Saturday, 10 May, he received two telephone calls.[42] At that time the Duke was not aware that the lone Messerschmitt 110 had carried anyone other than the expected emissary, a Nazi Party functionary named Ernst Bohle.

At 2 a.m., Major Graham Donald of the Royal Observation Corps (who had arrived at the Giffnock Home Guard's Scout hut after viewing the crash site) put an urgent telephone call through to the Duke of Hamilton. He told the Duke that he had just met an extremely strange German pilot, a man who insisted his name was Alfred Horn, but who bore a remarkable resemblance to Rudolf Hess. Furthermore, Donald reported, Horn only had one topic of conversation: to repeatedly insist that he had a message for the Duke of Hamilton, which was of 'the highest interest to the British Air Force'.[43]

The Duke's immediate reaction was to remain aloof, and it may well be that, given what is known of SO1's orchestration of the whole event, he had been instructed not to become directly involved. However, not long after Donald's call, the telephone rang again. It is not known who was on the other end of the line, but it may have been someone at either Dungavel House or Woburn Abbey, and it appears that Hamilton was instructed he was needed to meet the mysterious pilot, who evidently was *not* the expected Mr Bohle. Whatever was said, it must have been of major importance, for the Duke immediately roused himself. 'I'll have to go,' he told his wife. 'It's something to do with the crashed plane.'[44] The Duchess had no recollection of her husband returning that night, or indeed the next morning, and was to remark that 'the next time she saw him was the following afternoon'.

There are two other lines of evidence to support the fact that things were far from what they seemed on that night of Saturday,

10 May 1941. They reveal that the Duke of Hamilton's participation was not that of a man uninformed about what was taking place.

In 1991 a former Squadron Leader named Hector MacLean, who was the Duty Section Controller at RAF Ayr in 1941, revealed that he too had telephoned the Duke that Saturday night concerning the German pilot's request to meet him. He recalled that Hamilton had seemed taken aback, apparently unnerved by this request. 'What do you think I should do?' he had asked tentatively.

'I think,' MacLean responded, 'you should go and see him.'

There was a pause, the ducal brain obviously clicking though his options. Eventually the response came: 'Yes, I think I will . . .' With that the Duke rang off, leaving MacLean to order that the Glasgow police be notified that the Duke of Hamilton was coming.[45]

The second piece of evidence concerning the Duke of Hamilton's reaction to the unfolding events on that night is perhaps the most telling of all. Perhaps, too, it reflected the reaction of those waiting at Dungavel House, Woburn Abbey and Ditchley Park.

A WAAF named Nancy Moore, who had been on duty at RAF Turnhouse on the night of Hess's arrival, was to recall that at 11.45 p.m. the Duke of Hamilton, having gone off duty at 11.15, following the reported crash of raider 42J, suddenly returned to the Operations Room to take a telephone call. The call concerned the arrival of a German pilot named Horn, and Nancy Moore noticed with curiosity that the Duke appeared to be wearing his pyjamas under his uniform.

What was to happen next so piqued Miss Moore's interest that she retained ever after the image of her pyjama-clad commanding officer, the Duke of Hamilton, 'standing, hunched over the phone, holding it to his shoulder, looking extremely horrified'.[46] She could not hear what was said, but one of the other WAAFs on duty that night, who had initially taken the call for the Duke, told her that 'the CO had been called to speak to the pilot of the crashed plane'.[47] If the Duke of Hamilton had indeed suddenly found himself talking on the telephone to no mere German pilot or diplomat, but rather a very prominent German politician, he had every right to look 'extremely horrified'.

This was as clear an indication as possible that SO1's carefully choreographed plan for high political deception had been thrown completely off its tracks. It was a disaster that had the potential to blow all SO1's hard work of the previous ten months to smithereens at the very last moment, unless some quick thinking was undertaken to shore up the operation.

In the days and weeks ahead, great efforts would be undertaken to ensure that Rex Leeper's carefully organised Messrs HHHH operation attained its full potential. There was however a problem that occurred within just a few hours of Hess's arrival that needed immediate attention.

Early on the morning of Sunday, 11 May, the Duke of Kent, with the Duke of Buccleuch as a passenger, was driving along the Douglas to Lanark road, away from the entrance to Dungavel House. The Duke of Kent, tired after a night's wakefulness, or perhaps distracted in the process of lighting a cigarette, suffered a lapse of concentration that resulted in his car having a collision. Within a few hours, Leonard Ingrams at SO1 HQ Woburn passed on an enquiry to Mr Voigt at Dungavel 'concerning the accident . . . on the Douglas to Lanark road between a car driven by HRH the Duke of Kent, and a coal lorry'.[48]

On Monday, 12 May, thirty-six hours after Hess had landed on British soil, Voigt dispatched a memorandum, headed 'MOST SECRET', directly to Rex Leeper, reporting: 'I can confirm that neither the Duke, or his passenger, Buccleuch, were injured, and in view of Lanark's close proximity to the events of last weekend, steps have been taken to ensure the accident remains unreported by the press . . .'[49]

Over the following weeks SO1 would redouble its efforts to ensure that Hitler made the right decision – as far as British interests were concerned – and opened up a second front, turning the German war machine on Soviet Russia. The main problem in the immediate future was what to do with Hess.

CHAPTER 8

A Fatal Decision

At Hitler's Berghof on the morning of Sunday, 11 May 1941, all was peace, alpine tranquillity and, according to Walter Hewel, the Führer's liaison to the Auswärtiges Amt, 'great excitement'.[1]

Ever since that eventful weekend it has been believed that on learning of his Deputy's precipitate departure for Britain, Hitler went berserk, ranting and raving up and down the corridors of the Berghof, screaming for his closest confederates, ordering arrests and terrible retribution on anyone who had assisted Hess in his heinous betrayal of trust. However, that was not the case.

On that May morning at the Berghof, Adolf Hitler was full of optimism for the future, undoubtedly expecting that his and Hess's efforts to negotiate an armistice with Sir Samuel Hoare and Lord Halifax would be successful. His Deputy's flight to meet a British VIP had been undertaken as part of the inexorable progress towards that deal – a deal that was about to see Winston Churchill suddenly and rudely unseated from his premiership. When Hess's Adjutant, Karl-Heinz Pintsch, arrived at the Berghof at 9 a.m. to officially hand Hitler a letter that notified him of his Deputy's flight to Britain, the Führer already knew that Hess's take-off from Augsburg the previous evening had gone ahead without a hitch.

After the war, Pintsch would reveal that following Hess's departure he had taken the night train from Munich to Berchtesgaden to deliver Hess's letter. However, his journey had been delayed while he had been forced to wait for Hess's private carriage to be hitched to the overnight Salzburg express. He had therefore only arrived at Berchtesgaden at 7.30 a.m., and had then had to wait a further hour while a car was sent down from the Berghof to collect him. His journey had therefore taken nearly fifteen hours. Rosenberg, travelling the previous afternoon by car, had managed the same journey in just three hours.

The letter Pintsch handed to Hitler undoubtedly echoed the discussion between Hess and Hitler in the privacy of the Führer's office at the Chancellery the previous week. It ended: 'and if, my Führer, my plan ... should fail, if fate should decide against me, it can have no evil consequences for you or Germany. You can drop me at any time – say that I am mad . . .'[2]

There is, however, clear evidence that Hitler was already aware by the evening of Saturday, 10 May that Hess had successfully taken off from Augsburg. This evidence also clearly reveals Hitler's fear of the reaction of his fellow Nazi leaders if it were discovered he had been secretly negotiating with the British. To make an announcement after an agreement had been reached was an entirely different matter. Thus Hitler's actions over the forty-eight hours from Saturday evening were undertaken with the specific intention of protecting his reputation.

The first piece of evidence concerns a telephone call made at 10 p.m. on Saturday evening by Reichsmarschall Hermann Göring to fighter-ace Adolf Galland, the commanding officer of the Luftwaffe's Fighter Command over the English Channel. In some amazement, Galland had listened as Göring proclaimed that the Reich's Deputy-Führer, Rudolf Hess, had gone mad, and had flown off from Augsburg with the objective of flying to Britain. Galland was therefore ordered to shoot him down. Galland recalled that when he received Göring's call it was 'about ten minutes to darkness'.[3] Although Galland did not know it, by then Hess was far from the reach of any Luftwaffe fighters, having just crossed over the coast of northern Britain more than four hundred miles away.

The second piece of evidence which proves that Hitler was aware of Hess's flight concerns Hess's personal detective Franz Lutz and chauffeur Rudolf Lippert. Following Hess's departure from Augsburg, Lippert was ordered first to return the Deputy-Führer's

Mercedes to Munich, take a Kübelwagen from the NSDAP's motor-pool and drive with Lutz to the small Austrian village of Gallsprach. There they were to remain with an old friend of Hess's until the heat of his departure had died down.[4] Having driven most of the night to reach Gallsprach, Lippert and Lutz had not even had a chance to unpack when, at 5.30 a.m. (over three and a half hours before Hitler received Hess's letter from Pintsch), they were arrested and taken into custody for questioning regarding the sudden departure of their boss.[5] Pintsch was later to claim it was he who had ordered Lippert and Lutz to stay out of sight in Gallsprach, probably on the instructions of Hess, who feared widespread arrests would be made to preserve the illusion that Hitler had not known about his flight beforehand.[6]

The inference is clear. Pintsch's delivery of Hess's letter to Hitler at 9 a.m. on Sunday, 11 May was a performance put on for the benefit of the leadership of the Reich, with the sole objective of protecting Hitler's reputation should the Hess–Haushofer–Hoare–Halifax peace negotiations collapse. Given Hitler's close involvement throughout the whole affair, it is improbable that he would have been kept in ignorance overnight about whether his Deputy's take-off had been successful and on schedule.

It has frequently been suggested since the war that Hess's Senior Adjutant, Alfred Leitgen, travelled to see Hitler at the Berghof immediately after Hess's take-off at 5.45 p.m. on the evening of 10 May, to unofficially report Hess's successful departure. This would have given him an arrival time at Berchtesgaden of about 9 p.m., leaving Hess's Junior Adjutant, Karl-Heinz Pintsch, to deliver the *official* notification the following morning, in front of witnesses.[7] After the war, Leitgen and Pintsch kept to the story that Hitler had not known about Hess's flight. To have revealed the truth could have prejudiced the former Deputy-Führer's chances of release from Spandau prison, as any involvement in the plan to invade Russia would have been very damaging to him in Soviet eyes.[8]

If Hitler really had found himself presented on the morning of Sunday, 11 May with a devastating political crisis – that his Deputy had flown off to make peace with the enemy – one might expect that he would have given his full attention to the problem, cancelling everything that day in an attempt to counter a looming political disaster. In fact, far from ranting and raving, ordering arrests and retribution for anyone who had betrayed his trust, the Führer did not alter his schedule by one iota.

Following a brief vegetarian lunch, Hitler spent the afternoon in conversation with Admiral Darlan, the Vice President and Foreign Minister of Vichy France, and the designated successor to the aged Marshal Pétain. In the comfort of the Berghof's vast main reception room, seated on sofas scattered with cushions decorated with tiny swastikas, and overlooked by a vast tapestry of the Emperor Charlemagne, these two former enemies – now suspicious confederates – discussed the progress of the war.

Jean-François Darlan had no love for the British. He had, Churchill noted in a memorandum the previous November, been 'mortally envenomed by the injury ... [Britain had] done to his fleet',⁹ which was sunk at Mers-el Kebir on Churchill's orders in July 1940, with great loss of French life. Had he expected a typically virulent Hitler tirade against the perfidiousness of the British, and outrageous proclamations about the great Reich that would soon swamp all Allied resistance, he was to be very surprised. Rather than being in a belligerent mood, Hitler pragmatically confided to Darlan that

he [still] did not understand why France and England had declared war on Germany ... The tremendous disaster involved in a war such as the present one was out of all proportion to the colonial revision for which Germany was striving.

Moreover, Germany had never presented these colonial demands in an urgent form or in a manner that would in any way have threatened the honour or the existence of France or England.

As late as September 1, 1939 [Hitler informed Darlan,] he (the Führer) had implored [French] Ambassador Coulondre ... that France should not make the mad decision to go to war. The Polish conflict could easily have been localised. The German demands on

Poland had been very moderate. The German city of Danzig was to have been returned to Germany, and as for the rest a vote had been planned under international supervision . . .[10]

These were placatory words indeed. The all-conquering master of occupied Europe went on to insist that

> he did not have the ambition to be a great military leader but was interested rather, as the leader of his nation, in assuring the cultural and social advance of the German nation. Others had forced him to be a military leader. He would have been happy if the war had ended in June or July of last year [i.e. 1940], just as he had striven for peace after the Polish campaign. All nations would have benefited by such a peace . . .
>
> If the English had not fanatically insisted on continuing the war, there would have been peace long since and all European countries could devote themselves to repairing the misfortunes of war and to reconstruction . . .

Hitler continued: 'It was not Germany's fault, at any rate, that this [restitution of peace] could not be done. The question now was whether, in the greater European interest of ending the war, one should not jointly oppose the incendiaries who constantly wished to feed the flames of war in Europe with new objects.' He then referred to the prospect of American involvement in the war if it continued much longer, dourly commenting: 'If little England had developed such a big appetite as to incorporate a quarter of the territories of the world into her Empire, how big would be the land hunger of the much larger United States!'[11]

The conversation eventually turned to Franco–German matters, the purpose of Darlan's visit. But the Admiral must have been disconcerted by the general tone of the meeting. It was almost as if Hitler were preparing the rabidly anti-British Darlan for some sudden and astonishing change in the war's direction.

*　　*　　*

Despite Hitler's outwardly calm demeanour, put on for Admiral Darlan's benefit, he must have been deeply concerned that there was still no news of Hess. There had been no notification from the International Red Cross in Geneva that he had arrived safely at Dungavel House. Nor had there been a telegram from Hess's aunt Emma Rothacker in Zürich that the British authorities had notified her of 'Alfred Horn's' capture. Something must have gone badly wrong. Either Hess was lying dead at the bottom of the North Sea, or – infinitely worse – he had been captured.

In March 1945, as the Reich fell in ruins about him, Hitler would be approached by one of the top SS men in Italy, Karl Wolff (who by coincidence was yet another old friend of Albrecht Haushofer's), who revealed that he had managed to open a line of communication to President Roosevelt. Hitler told Wolff to proceed with his attempt to open a peace dialogue, but added, 'Should you fail, I shall have to drop you exactly like Hess.'[12]

Now, on the evening of 11 May 1941, as the sun began to sink over the mountains behind the Berghof, Hitler visibly grew more and more concerned. What had gone wrong? More importantly, where was Hess? Hitler knew he had to act to protect his political integrity. He ordered Karl-Heinz Pintsch (whom he'd happily invited for lunch six hours previously) to be arrested. In mounting panic, and possibly real rage that all the months of hard peaceable negotiations may have been for nothing, Hitler summoned his Foreign Minister Joachim von Ribbentrop and Hermann Göring to the Berghof, and ordered that Albrecht Haushofer come the following day, to write a report for him on the peace avenues in Britain. (This report, it should be noted, would make no reference to the Hoare–Halifax situation, or to the peace offer passed by the Papal Nuncio to Hoare in Madrid the previous November.)

Interestingly, Hitler did not call for the two men in Germany with the real power to control the developing situation: Josef Goebbels, the Nazis' high priest of propaganda, controlling press, radio and public relations; and Heinrich Himmler, who as master of the SS could quell any dissent or political unrest through sheer terror.

Instead, the Führer placed his reliance on two men who had been party to earlier peace initiatives. Göring undoubtedly knew of the Hess–Haushofer–Hoare attempt. He had after all been connected to Hitler's previous secret peaceable attempts in 1940, via Dahlerus, and it was he who had telephoned Adolf Galland the evening before, almost certainly at Hitler's suggestion, concerning Hess's flight. He and, to a lesser degree, Ribbentrop would understand the Führer's dilemma more clearly than Goebbels or Himmler, and would at the same time be unlikely to use the situation to further their own ambitions to supplant him. The same could not necessarily be said of Himmler.

Walter Hewel was later to record that there was much anxiety that evening at the Berghof, and a very heated and protracted discussion between Hitler, Ribbentrop, Göring and Martin Bormann in the Berghof's main hallways, with 'a lot of speculation'.[13]

In distant Berlin, Albrecht Haushofer received his summons to report to Hitler at the Berghof the following morning, and heard for the first time the astonishing news that Ernst Bohle had not been the emissary dispatched to Britain to meet the eminent representative of King George VI. In his stead had gone his old friend Rudi Hess. It must have been a very bitter blow to Haushofer that Hess had not trusted him enough to tell him his real plans. Had he known, Haushofer would undoubtedly have tried to deter Hess from making such a trip. Showy acts of that type were not the way to peace. Diplomacy proceeded in a sequence of careful moves of great complexity, carried out in a slow and methodical manner. Haushofer must have realised that all his work to negotiate a peace with a political faction in Britain had been squandered. 'With fools such as this,' he was heard to remark bitterly, 'what can you expect?'[14]

Albrecht Haushofer must also have understood that he had been kept in the dark on Hitler's instructions, and probably suspected that Hess had always intended to travel to Britain himself. He would also have known, unlike the more naïve Hess and Hitler, that the last thing one should do when engaged in deep and critical negotiations with an enemy is to spring a dramatic surprise. In such circumstances anything at all can happen, usually something counter-productive.

Meanwhile, in Britain, there was also much concern and speculation. At Ditchley Park, Churchill was being kept abreast by telephone of events back in London, following the appallingly heavy air raid the previous night. Ditchley Park was no mere country residence. It had been transformed into an extremely well-equipped command centre, complete with communications rooms kitted out with numerous secure telephone lines, deciphering equipment, teletypes and a transmitter powerful enough to communicate with the farthest reaches of the globe. If German troops ever reached London, Churchill would have temporarily retreated to Ditchley, from where he was as fully in command as if he had been in the Cabinet War Rooms deep beneath Whitehall.

Churchill first heard *official* news of the mysterious German emissary's arrival while he and a select band of guests were watching a private showing of a Marx Brothers film. 'Whilst the merry film clacked on,' he would later write, 'a secretary told me that somebody wanted to speak to me on the telephone on behalf of the Duke of Hamilton . . . [and] I asked Mr Bracken to hear what he had to say.'[15]

The identity of the person delegated to speak on behalf of Hamilton has never been revealed, but what he had to say caused Bracken to pale in surprise. 'After a few minutes,' Churchill went on, 'Mr Bracken told me that the Duke . . . had an amazing piece of information to report. I therefore sent for him. On arrival he told me that a German prisoner whom he had interviewed alone said he was Rudolf Hess. "Hess in Scotland!" I thought this was fantastic.'

Such was Winston Churchill's official version of the events of Sunday, 11 May. Yet it is disingenuous, for he certainly knew a great deal more than he ever let on. It should be realised that Churchill's literary works after the war occasionally deviated from precise fact. He was after all the victor writing his version of history for posterity. Rex Leeper's deception plan was far from the only such secret British operation during the Second World War, and Churchill deliberately excluded many of them from his multi-volume history of the war.[16]

Several hours before Churchill received notification of Hess's arrival, the Duke of Hamilton, in the company of a German-speaking RAF interrogation officer, Flight Lieutenant Benson, had gone to Glasgow to officially interview Hess. However, as soon as the Duke was ushered into Hess's presence, the first thing he did was to surprise Benson by announcing that he would interview Hess in private, promptly dismissing both Benson and the officer of the guard from the room.

What Hess and Hamilton talked about is not known, but towards the end of their discussion Hess asked Hamilton if he could assemble leading members of his faction 'to talk over things with a view to making peace proposals'.[17] He also repeated his request for Emma Rothacker in Zürich to be notified that 'Alfred Horn' was in good health. Then, curiously, the Deputy-Führer of a nation engaged in a bitter war with Britain asked Hamilton if it might be possible for King George VI to grant him parole – freedom to come and go as he wished – on the understanding that he would not run away.

Hess, it seemed, was unaware that his chain of peaceable intent had been inexorably broken. In fact, he was unaware that it had never really existed to start with. There was in actuality no peace faction, no politico-constitutional *coup d'état* in the offing, and no line connecting the King with the presumed intriguings of Sam Hoare and Lord Halifax.

The only action the British authorities undertook in response to Hess's request for parole was to remove him from the danger of being accidentally killed by a German raid on Glasgow, and take him under strong guard to Drymen Military Hospital in Buchanan Castle, on the banks of Loch Lomond several miles to the north of Glasgow.

Several years later the Duke of Hamilton described the chain of events that led to Brendan Bracken taking his call at Ditchley Park. As soon as he left Maryhill Barracks Hamilton tried to get in touch, by telephone, to report the matter to the Permanent Secretary, Sir Alexander Cadogan. I got through to his secretary and asked for an interview with Sir Alexander himself. I was informed that Sir Alexander was an extremely busy man ... and I got into a tremendous argument with the Secretary ...

Suddenly, in the midst of this rather acrimonious discussion a strange voice said, 'This is the Prime Minister's secretary ['Jock' Colville] speaking. The Prime Minister sent me over to the Foreign Office as he is informed that you have some interesting information.'[18]

According to Hamilton, Colville then asked him, 'Has somebody arrived?'[19]

After confirming that 'somebody' had indeed arrived, Hamilton was immediately ordered to fly straight down to Oxfordshire to brief the Prime Minister. After a complicated journey from Glasgow back to Edinburgh, from Edinburgh to London, and thence out to deepest Oxfordshire, an exhausted Duke of Hamilton eventually arrived at Ditchley Park late on Sunday evening. Churchill immediately waved across to the ducal Wing Commander as he was ushered into a room, heavy with the smoke of after-dinner cigars, where the Prime Minister was holding court among his friends and colleagues. 'Now,' Churchill insisted, 'tell us this funny story of yours!'[20]

Mindful of the sensitivity of his news, Hamilton responded that the matter was extremely sensitive and important, and endeavoured to impress upon the Prime Minister that he thought it best if he initially gave his report in private. Eventually everyone left the room, Hamilton recorded, except Churchill and the Secretary of State for Air, Sir Archibald Sinclair. It is likely that Brendan Bracken also remained to hear the extraordinary news.

When Hamilton revealed exactly *who* had perilously arrived the previous night, Churchill's good mood suddenly vanished, and it was obvious that he was 'rather taken aback'. He undoubtedly realised the possibly disastrous consequences of such an act by one of the top leaders of Nazi Germany, a close friend of Hitler,

and a man pivotal to Rex Leeper's Messrs HHHH deception operation. Rudolf Hess's appearance in Bohle's stead was not the harmless act of a madman; it had the potential for disaster.

'Do you mean to tell me,' Churchill said very deliberately, 'that
the Deputy-Führer of Germany is in our hands?'

Hamilton confirmed that this was so, and produced photographs
of Hess from his wallet. Both the Prime Minister and the Air
Secretary were forced to agree that the man did indeed look 'rather
like Hess'.

Suddenly the Prime Minister's mood changed again. He no
longer wished to talk with the man who had flown all the way
from Scotland to see him. 'Well, Hess or no Hess,' he growled, 'I
am going to see the Marx brothers!'

This famous remark has always been attributed to Churchill's
belief that Hess's arrival in Britain was the act of a madman. However, in reality it reveals a man who, confronted with an important
and dangerous situation, chose not to enter into complex debate
with his minions, but rather withdrew into himself to ponder the
intricacies of the situation before making any comment or taking
any decisions.

While his guests enjoyed the antics of Groucho, Chico and
Harpo Marx on the big screen, Churchill's mind was playing to
an entirely different tune. His decision to postpone his discussion
with Hamilton had been taken so that he could sit in the dark,
largely oblivious to the chuckles of amusement around him, ponder
the implications of Hess's arrival and consider his next move. It
had most definitely not been any part of SO1's plans to capture a
top Nazi. Would Rudolf Hess's unexpected arrival affect the outcome of the Messrs HHHH operation? Was it still possible to
manoeuvre Hitler towards the original objective of an attack on
Russia?

Later that night, after all the other guests had retired to bed,
Churchill, Sinclair, Bracken and the Duke of Hamilton sat down
to debate this new and highly dangerous development. The details
of what was discussed have never been revealed. All that is known
is that the meeting continued until 3 a.m., and that at dawn on

Monday, 12 May the Duke of Hamilton and Winston Churchill were driven 'very rapidly', ignoring all speed limits, back to London in the prime ministerial limousine. It was evidently imperative that whatever action was needed had to be undertaken immediately.

Once they reached Downing Street another discussion took place between Hamilton and Churchill, this time in the presence of Anthony Eden. By now Churchill's primary concern seems to have been that the man being held in Buchanan Castle might not be Hess at all, but a 'double'. That would have been a very serious development indeed, for it would reveal that it was German Intelligence, rather than SO1, which had the upper hand in the deception campaign against Hitler; that the Germans were engaged in a dangerous deception of their own, and had sent a nobody to negotiate with the representative of Britain's 'man of influence'. This would also mean, horrifyingly, that Hitler's Hess–Haushofer peaceable attempt was a sham, that Hitler had given up attempting to make peace with the British, and quite possibly changed his mind about invading Russia in the immediate future. That would leave only one possibility for the latter half of the fighting season of 1941 – the Middle East. With the loss of Britain's oil would also go any chance she had of emerging victorious from the war.

The meeting with Churchill concluded, Hamilton and Eden walked quickly along Whitehall to the Foreign Office, where they met Sir Alexander Cadogan to discuss what should be done next. Soon Stewart Menzies, the head of SIS, was summoned to advise on how best to verify whether or not it really was the Deputy-Führer of Nazi Germany who was cooling his heels in Buchanan Castle. It was decided to dispatch Ivone Kirkpatrick with Hamilton to vet the prisoner.

Kirkpatrick was a sound choice. He had been First Secretary at the British Embassy in Berlin through much of the 1930s, and had thus met Hess many times, in both an official and a private capacity. He had also participated in Leeper's deception operation over the past nine months.

Robert Bruce Lockhart, out at Woburn, was soon to comment:

'Immense excitement over Hess ... Ivone Kirkpatrick has been sent to see him and talk with him.'[21] However, Bruce Lockhart went on to observe that Kirkpatrick was 'not the man I should have chosen, for he has no knowledge or understanding of psychology'. This may indicate that a subtle behind-the-scenes struggle was already taking place between SO1 on the one hand, and the more generalised body of British Intelligence (MI5 and MI6), the Foreign Office, or even the upper echelons of government about who would to take control of Hess. SO1 may have had its own notions about how it wanted to use Hess to further Rex Leeper's stratagem of covert political warfare.

'Meanwhile,' Bruce Lockhart went on, 'the Prime Minister who hopes (perhaps too wishfully) to obtain valuable military information out of Hess has taken complete control. No ammunition for the propagandists. Valentine Williams and Sefton Delmer not allowed to go to Glasgow.'

The Duke of Hamilton and Ivone Kirkpatrick, meanwhile, were driven to Hendon aerodrome, from where the Duke piloted a De Havilland Rapide back to RAF Turnhouse. There they were greeted with the news that while they had been airborne, a communiqué had been broadcast over the German home stations announcing that: 'Party member Hess, who has been expressly forbidden by the Führer to use an aeroplane because of a disease which has been becoming worse for years, was in contradiction of this order able to get hold of a plane recently. Hess started on Saturday, 10 May at about 1800 hours from Augsburg on a flight from which he has not returned ...'[22]

There was no mention of the facts that for months 'Party member Hess' had not only been flying regularly all over Germany, and indeed to foreign countries as well, but had been well enough to commission improvements to a powerful military aircraft placed at his personal disposal. Hitler, it seemed, was rapidly covering his tracks. The communiqué concluded: 'The Führer at once ordered the arrest of Hess's adjutants who alone knew of his flight and who, in contradiction of the Führer's ban ... did not prevent the flight nor report it at once. The National Socialist movement has unfortunately in these circumstances to assume that Party Comrade Hess has crashed or met with a similar accident.'

It was already late by the time Hamilton and Kirkpatrick received this news, but any thought of rest vanished when the Duke received an urgent call from Sir Archibald Sinclair, almost certainly at Churchill's behest. Sinclair insisted that he and Kirkpatrick proceed post-haste to Buchanan Castle. It seems that Churchill needed to know that very night whether or not it was the real Hess who had arrived in Scotland the previous evening. Hamilton and Kirkpatrick immediately set off on the long and tortuous drive to Buchanan Castle, where they would attempt to probe Hess's mind, and in so doing try to discern whether Messrs HHHH was still on track.

At Woburn Abbey, Rex Leeper ordered his secretary, Mr Foss, to type up a memorandum. It was a note of few words, but it spoke volumes about the level of disquiet fluttering through Woburn Abbey: 'The Director has asked me to say that he does not wish Minutes to be kept of the Saturday 12 o'clock meeting in future. He feels that, even as an informal record, it is not desirable that an abbreviated report of statements made by, for instance, Brigadier Brooks or Mr Ingrams, should be made . . .'[23]

Back in Scotland, meanwhile, the Duke of Hamilton and Ivone Kirkpatrick were not having a comfortable time interviewing Hess; the Deputy-Führer, for his part, also had his problems. He could not reveal the real reason he had appeared on British soil, for fear of compromising what he still believed to be an anti-Churchill faction about to enact a democratic usurpation of power. Behind his brave façade, however, Hess must have suspected that, to use a favoured expression of his own, everything had 'gone to smash'.[24]

Hess was inclined to talk peace, but would say nothing that might compromise the imaginary political clique. He could name no names; could indicate a willingness to negotiate with the British government, but not *which* British government. Along with Germany's Deputy-Führer, the British had also acquired the papers Hess had brought with him for his meeting at Dungavel House.

These almost certainly included detailed proposals for a peace treaty, undoubtedly one of the documents Hess and Hitler had drafted together, which Ernst Bohle had been instructed to translate the previous weekend. From Churchill's point of view it was also almost certainly the case that it would be better for these papers to vanish completely, which indeed they did.

The first meeting between Hess, Kirkpatrick and Hamilton began at midnight on Monday, 12 May, and lasted more than three and a half hours. It soon became apparent to Kirkpatrick that the man seated before him really was Rudolf Hess. The Deputy-Führer, drawing upon notes he had spent much of the previous day drafting, began a lengthy monologue on Anglo–German relations, detailing the *entente* promoted by Edward VII in 1904.

As Hess droned on, Hamilton and Kirkpatrick must have realised it was going to be a very long night indeed. At 1 a.m. they were given a brief respite when they were summoned to the telephone. It was Anthony Eden, asking on Churchill's behalf whether the prisoner was the real Hess. To Eden and Churchill's undoubted relief, Kirkpatrick confirmed that it was.

On Kirkpatrick and Hamilton's return, Hess resumed his monologue, repeatedly emphasising the injustices he believed Germany had suffered at the hands of the Allies in 1919, and the worthy cause she was now applying herself to: reorganising Europe on more efficient lines that would promote peace long into the future. He even claimed that Hitler had delayed launching the horrors of the Blitz on Britain 'partly out of a sentimental regard for English culture and English monuments'.[25] On he went for hour after hour, declaring Germany's sincere wish for peace, how the war with Britain was an unmitigated disaster for all concerned, how the hand of friendship should be grasped and the prospect of peace held on to. Hamilton fell asleep at one point, waking some time later to find Hess still talking, and a mesmerised Kirkpatrick staring at him with eyes that were glazing over. Kirkpatrick would later record that he had not interrupted Hess, or contradicted any of the points he raised, 'since I realised that argument would be quite fruitless and would certainly have deprived us of breakfast'.[26]

It is strange that Hess, now that he finally had a chance to put Germany's case before *real* representatives of the British government, did not say anything about the peaceable intent of his mission. Nor did he give vent to the lapel-grabbing offers he had previously made via the Papal Nuncio and Albrecht Haushofer to Sam Hoare, such as Germany's withdrawal from occupied France, Holland and Belgium, or that Hitler would accept some form of autonomy for Poland and national identity for Czechoslovakia.

It may be that Hess did not want to say anything that might compromise all the hard work of the previous months of negotiation. His three-hour monologue was therefore largely a stalling tactic. He would have realised that he could not remain silent, which would have made the British authorities *really* suspicious. It might even have prompted Churchill to order the Intelligence Services to investigate the true reasons for his arrival. He therefore had no choice other than to talk, to give Kirkpatrick something to think about, while not going into sufficient detail to undermine his and Haushofer's negotiations with Hoare.

A clue that Hess was stalling came at the very end of his meeting with Hamilton and Kirkpatrick, when he commented that it was known in Germany that Churchill had been planning a war with the Reich since 1936, and thus the Prime Minister and his confederates were not men with whom the Führer could negotiate.[27] In covert language, Hess was laying his cards on the table: We won't talk with Churchill and his clique, but we *will* negotiate with another party. Hess may even have been subtly asking Kirkpatrick whether he was a supporter of the anti-Churchill faction. Unfortunately for Hess, he was not.

However, next morning, Tuesday, 13 May, Kirkpatrick telephoned Sir Alexander Cadogan and suggested that 'in view of the reservation that Germany could not negotiate with the present government', Hess might talk more freely to 'some member of the Conservative Party who would give him the impression he was tempted by the idea of getting rid of the present government'.[28]

Before the end of the week, another meeting took place between Hess, Kirkpatrick and Hamilton. It became clear that the Deputy-

Führer had reformulated the conditions under which he was prepared to talk to the British government, and he requested that two particular German prisoners of war he knew should be appointed as his assistants if peace talks were opened.[29] The precise details of this discussion have remained secret, however, for as was noted in the margin of a statement Churchill was preparing to make to the House of Commons, Hess had 'also made other statements which it would not be in the public interest to disclose'.[30]

There is, though, one clue which both indicates the direction of Hess's pronouncements and reveals much about the British government's concern that the whole matter should remain completely under wraps. Following his second meeting with Hess, the Duke of Hamilton flew back to London, where, after visiting Sir Alexander Cadogan to discuss the situation, he had lunch with the King at Buckingham Palace.[31] Within a few days, Hess was transferred from Scotland to Mytchett Place, a large house near Aldershot in Surrey. Here the Deputy-Führer would be within easy reach of a select band of Intelligence personnel who intended to interrogate him with any means at their disposal. There was a second reason for moving Hess: in the unlikely event that the Germans decided to target him, he would be more secure near Aldershot than in the wilds of Scotland.

The week following the loss of Hess had been an uncomfortable one for Adolf Hitler as the public-relations exercise to distance him from his Deputy was set in motion. On Monday, 12 May he gave the order for official communiqués about the Deputy-Führer's disappearance to be issued. He summoned his Reichsleiters and Gauleiters – his loyal conduit to the German people – to explain the embarrassing situation. Many of them were alarmed by the broken look of their Führer, who seemed to have aged overnight. The Governor-General of Poland, Hans Frank, noted that Hitler, looking completely shattered, 'spoke to us in a low, halting voice, expressing an underlying depression beyond words'.[32]

The extent to which this depression was caused by the loss of

Hess is impossible to tell. Its primary cause may rather have been Hitler's realisation that all his peaceable endeavours of the past nine months, through Hess, Haushofer, Papal Nuncios, British Ambassadors and a multitude of lesser middle-men, had been for nothing. At the very moment when a peace deal had seemed so close, it had all suddenly gone wrong. Hitler may even have wondered if the disaster had been caused by his agreement to Hess's suggestion that he, rather than Ernst Bohle, was the best man to attend a meeting with a British VIP. It may be that Hitler suspected that some deep perfidy by the British had cost Hess his freedom, and that all the offers of peaceable negotiations had merely been a subterfuge of British Intelligence.

Regardless of Hitler's depression and uncertainties during those first days of Hess's incarceration in Britain, what happened next was a sure indicator that he had not entirely abandoned his old friend.

On Tuesday, 20 May, Sir Samuel Hoare in Madrid wrote a letter headed 'PERSONAL AND SECRET' to Anthony Eden:

> ... I have just written Winston a short personal note in view of the fact that he took so much interest last year in agreeing to our secret plans. I thought that he would like to known that during the last two or three weeks they have worked out very much as we hoped ...
>
> I am enclosing a curious and very secret note that has just been sent me from Beigbeder. The suggestions in it bear a remarkable resemblance to what I imagine Hess has been saying in England. You will therefore no doubt wish to take it into account in connexion with anything that you get out of Hess.[33]

The 'curious and very secret note' from Beigbeder long ago vanished from its appropriate place within the Foreign Office archives. However, it is known that Albrecht Haushofer had been in contact with both his old friend at the German Embassy in Madrid, Eberhard von Stohrer, and Beigbeder over the previous year, and it is likely that Hoare had been contacted by Beigbeder on Haushofer's behalf in an attempt to discover what was really going on. Much depended on whether, regardless of the loss of Hess, the Hoare–Halifax faction still intended to try to oust Churchill. Hoare commented to Eden: 'I feel sure that in each case our reply will be a very definite negative ... That is why I should much like your definite instructions as to the form of any answer that you may wish me to make to Beigbeder. He is sure to return to the charge and I must then either say that we do not intend to make any answer or that our answer is such and such.'[34]

It is not known what Eden responded, or whether Hoare subsequently contacted Beigbeder to impart a message for German ears – although it is extremely likely that he was instructed to do so. What is known, however, is that Hitler was still desperately clinging to his hopes of peace with Britain, rather than allowing the loss of Hess to cause its abandonment, which would result in him sinking into a maelstrom of total and unremitting war.

The many complex strands of Operation Barbarossa were by now coming together with relentless speed. Hitler's initial plan had been to attack Russia in the middle of May, but because of Germany's unplanned commitments in the Balkans, and the flooding in the Pripet Marshes, he had had to delay the invasion until the second half of June. Given what is now known about Hess and Hitler's plotting behind the scenes with a British clique they believed was about to oust Churchill from power, it is possible that there was also a secret political element in Hitler's decision to delay Barbarossa. Had he been hoping to see a new British government in place before he opened a new and terribly costly second front?

The decision to attack the Soviet Union raised issues well beyond mere military strategy. Russia was still providing a vast range of resources to the Reich: over two hundred thousand tons of grain and ninety thousand tons of petrol in April 1941 alone. Even as Hitler planned the invasion and subjugation of Russia, a heavy cruiser was being built for the German navy in Leningrad, and the trans-Siberian railway was shipping over two thousand tons of raw rubber into the Reich every month.[35]

With the launching of Barbarossa, Hitler knew that Germany would suffer an immediate, and possibly critical, shortage of previously imported supplies. He therefore had to be extremely sure that he was not about to bite off more than he could chew by attacking Russia before he had done as much as he could to remove the threat posed by Britain. Added into this complicated calculation was the fact that any Russian campaign had to take place within a small weather window of opportunity: after the draining of rivers and marshes swollen by the previous winter's snow, but before the next winter set in. Churchill, like Hitler, was also fully aware of the situation, and a German attack on Russia could give Britain a unique opportunity to strike at Hitler.

Several years after the war, Churchill would write: 'Nemesis personifies the Goddess of Retribution, who brings down all immediate good fortune, checks the presumption that attends it ... and is the punisher of extraordinary crimes.'[36] It would be natural to assume that that Churchill was referring to Hitler's Germany, but in fact he was writing about Russia, stating with much truth that throughout the disasters of 1940, the Soviet government 'had shown a total indifference to the fate of the Western Powers'.[37] However, by late 1940 it had become obvious to many in Britain's government and Intelligence Services that while Stalin had undoubtedly been rubbing his hands in glee as he watched western Europe implode, he was also aware that it would not be long before Hitler began contemplating his stated ambition of creating a Greater German Reich, by slicing off a vast swathe of western Russia.

After the war Churchill would write that 'up till the end of March [1941] I was not convinced that Hitler was resolved upon mortal war with Russia', and he remained extremely fearful about the fate of the Middle East. Nor were his concerns eased by British Intelligence's persistent fence-sitting in their assessment of which direction the war would take in the fighting season of 1941 – north-east into Russia, as per Hitler's ambitions for territorial expansion into the Ukraine and Caucasus; or south-east into the

Middle East, as strategic expediency dictated, to remove the dangers posed to the Reich by continued war with Britain.

A 'most secret' strategic assessment of 26 May 1941 did not help resolve these fears. In many ways it made extremely grim reading, for it declared that 'the German General Staff does not believe that Germany can achieve her aims by threats or by peaceful penetration of the Ukraine'. Pessimistically, it went on: 'rumours of an imminent German attack on Russia have given place to reports ... that Russo–German discussions are in progress and even that an agreement has been reached, more particularly for the delimitation of spheres of influence in the Middle East, and that German troops assembling at Lvov are to move through the Soviet Union to Iran with Russian consent'.[38]

There was much cause for concern in this report, particularly when Churchill read an intelligence submission from Romania which alleged not only that 'German troops are preparing to embark from a Romanian port for Beirut', but also that, incredibly, 'Many German tourists are said to be going to Iraq through Iran, and it is reported that war materials are being sent to Iraq, through Turkey.'

The implication was clear. These German tourists were in reality troops – special forces – dispatched to Iraq to foment unrest and revolution. Even this paled into insignificance when compared with the report's comment that: 'The Germans are stated to be bringing pressure to bear on Iran to hamper the movements of British warships in the Shatt-el-Arab. They are also reported to be urging Iran to cancel British oil concessions and take over the oilfields.'[39]

SO1's efforts to make Hitler feel confident enough to attack Russia seemed to have fallen flat; and Rudolf Hess's shocking arrival in Britain had only served to confuse the issue still further.

On Tuesday, 27 May, a little over a fortnight after Hess had come drifting out of the Scottish night sky, Air Vice Marshal Trafford Leigh-Mallory summoned an old acquaintance of his, a young army officer named John McCowen, to a meeting. Major McCowen had served with the Territorial Army during the inter-war years, and had spent over a year in Hanover during the 1930s, becoming a fluent German-speaker. By May 1941 he was an intelligence officer serving on the General Staff. His duties included gathering intelligence on the head of the Abwehr, Admiral Canaris, and Professor Willy Messerschmitt; he also assisted with the interrogation of prisoners of war and captured enemy agents.

Expecting his linguistic skills to be called upon once again, McCowen was surprised when Leigh-Mallory revealed to him that he had received important information concerning a recent coded message broadcast from Germany. This decrypt probably emanated from Bletchley Park, whose codebreakers by 1941 had completely broken the Luftwaffe Enigma code, and were thus able to read virtually every single Luftwaffe communication. Leigh-Mallory informed McCowen that the Germans intended to drop several SS parachutists in the Luton area that very night, and he was ordered to accompany an anti-aircraft unit to assist in the capture of these dangerous men.

Later that evening, four 40mm anti-aircraft guns, together with two searchlights of the 73rd Light Anti-Aircraft Regiment,[40] were deployed at Chalton, several miles north-west of Luton,[40] and Home Guard units and armed police were put on full alert. It is doubtful if many of those on the ground realised the importance of the area they were guarding. A mere five miles to the north-west stood Woburn Abbey, with its panoply of deep and covert thinkers dreaming up ingenious ways to politically wrongfoot, undermine and sabotage the enemy. Five miles to the west lay Bletchley Park, Britain's priceless code-breaking facility that daily decrypted the Reich's top secrets. Churchill would later call Bletchley the 'goose that had laid golden eggs', and he would not lightly forgive anyone whose lax security put such a valuable facility in jeopardy.

A little after 3 a.m., the distant boom-boom-boom of anti-aircraft fire alerted those waiting on the ground that a wave of German planes had arrived over Luton, dropping several sticks of bombs over the town and its environs. The men immediately went on full alert, for it was known that the Germans often sent a parachute plane to accompany a bombing raid.

That was the case on this particular night: a Luftwaffe He-111, seconded to the Abwehr and piloted by Hauptmann Gartenfeldt, was tailing the raid.[41] During the previous months Gartenfeldt had developed a very successful stratagem for dropping agents over enemy territory. His ploy was to tail the raid into British airspace, and then, just before the bombers commenced their attack, break away from the formation, banking his aircraft to quickly lose altitude before levelling off to drop his parachutists as low as possible (an absolute necessity, as agents were more likely to evade capture if they reached the ground as quickly as possible). After dropping his charges, Gartenfeldt would quickly regain his original altitude, endeavouring to join the raid formation for the flight home.

As soon as the raid began, it was reported by the local military command centre: 'Parachutist agent believed to have dropped immediately after bombs, is armed and will have parachute marks. Probably making for the road Dunstable–London.'[42] A thorough search of the area failed to locate any enemy agents, but at 4 a.m. a second urgent report was issued to the anti-aircraft unit, Home Guard and armed police units, stating: 'Parachutists believed down one mile east of Sundon [four and a half miles south-east of Woburn Abbey]. May have travelled some miles or may be lying up. Do not withdraw patrols. Have country searched.'[43] Still no traces of any parachutists were found, and the patrols were withdrawn at 8.45 a.m.

However, hiding out in the English countryside during wartime, with every farmer, Home Guard and policeman – and, in this case, armed police and officers of MI5 – on the lookout for suspicious characters, was well-nigh impossible. Later that day (Wednesday, 28 May) three parachutists were spotted, cornered and captured 'not many miles away, but in another county [, destined] never to return to the Fatherland'.[44]

Many years later, in 1996, the then eighty-nine-year-old John McCowen was to reveal that he had participated in the interrogation of these three enemy agents at Ham Common, an interrogation centre run by MI5's double-cross specialists, 20 Committee.

McCowen maintained that he had forgotten the men's names, but said they had been dropped in Britain with the intention of murdering Hess, in order to prevent him revealing details about Barbarossa. According to McCowen, the agents believed Hess was being held at Cockfosters on the outskirts of London, thirty-five miles south-east of Woburn Abbey, where Luftwaffe prisoners were normally interrogated. Finally, McCowen stated that after they had been interrogated, all three were executed by firing squad at the Tower of London.[45]

The historian who interviewed McCowen in 1996 was to comment that 'these assassins could not have expected to burst into the cage at Cockfosters and gun down Hess in his cell'.[46] Cockfosters was an intermediate detention centre, consisting of just a few barrack buildings and an administration block, surrounded by a security fence and guard posts. If there really was a desperate German need to prevent Hess revealing details about Barbarossa, it is by no means beyond the realms of possibility that Hitler would have ordered the Cockfosters camp completely destroyed by a concerted and well-targeted raid. If he wanted Hess dead, that would be the only means to assure such an end.

There is however, another aspect of this story that John McCowen, as a relatively junior Intelligence officer, was unaware of. On 8 June 1941, George Hill, based at Woburn Abbey, wrote a letter, headed 'SECRET', to his old friend Rex Leeper. Hill was one of the old gang who had participated in Churchill's endeavours via Bruce Lockhart, Leeper and Sidney Reilly to destabilise the Bolshevik state in 1918. He was thus one of the trusted few. He began his short missive by revealing that '[Con] O'Neill has now finished his liaison with MI.5 over the matter of the parachutists. He attended several of the interrogations, but they are astutely sticking to their story of being sent to rescue our recent acquisition, in the vain hope, I suspect, of believing such a tale will save their skins.'[47]

Thus, far from intending to assassinate Hess, the agents revealed, after what was undoubtedly a drawn-out and possibly unpleasant interrogation, that their real objective had been to rescue him. This raises a further problem: How did they hope to find a single prisoner held deep in enemy territory?

There was another alternative, which might explain the particularly hard line taken with these agents. What if their orders from Berlin had not been to kill or rescue Hess, but rather to find out what was taking place in Britain with regard to him? Their true objective is revealed by Hill's comment to Leeper: 'However, as we all know their intentions were significantly different [from the purported rescue of Hess], we must be thankful that Mr E[den] was saved from their obvious intentions.'[48]

This becomes clearer when it is understood that the young, good-looking and capable Foreign Secretary, who acted as a very effective foil to Churchill's elder-statesmanlike presence in British politics, was widely regarded as the Prime Minister's most loyal lieutenant. The truth is a little more complicated, but that is certainly what would have been believed by Hitler, who since the Anglo–German diplomatic shutdown of 1939 had increasingly lost touch with the subtleties of the British political scene.

Hill's comment to Leeper suggests that the three parachutists had been sent to Britain with the intention of kidnapping Anthony Eden. This does not however, necessarily present us with the slightly ludicrous picture of trench-coated German agents pouncing on the Foreign Secretary in Whitehall; the whole matter becomes a great deal more serious and deadly when other factors are taken into consideration.

Firstly, there is the location where the men were parachuted into Britain: less than five miles from Woburn Abbey, a large estate deep in the Bedfordshire countryside. Secondly, they arrived during the early hours of Wednesday, 28 May.

The significance of these two factors is that on virtually every Saturday morning between the summers of 1940 and 1941, including that of Saturday, 31 May 1941, Anthony Eden would leave London by car, accompanied only by his driver and, occasionally, a plain-clothes policeman, to attend the lunchtime meeting of SO1 at Woburn Abbey. Eden's journey took him north-west out of London along the old A5 Watling Street road. At Hockliffe, a small market town four miles beyond Dunstable, his car would turn right onto the much narrower road to Woburn, the A4012. Just a mile along this country lane is a sharp left bend, surrounded by hedges and high trees – the only real place for an ambush on the whole road. It is also a mere two miles cross-country from Chalton, where the parachutists landed.

Eden was fortunate that the German agents were apprehended, for there is little doubt that they would have killed both his driver and the policeman, before attempting to make off with him to some hidden and secure spot where they would interrogate him about the truth concerning Hess's situation, and perhaps also about the peaceable intent emanating from Woburn. It may even have been part of the parachutists' orders that they were to hold Eden hostage until Hess was delivered safely to neutral territory, such as Ireland, Spain or Sweden.

All this must, to a certain degree, be speculation; but it has a basis in the known documentation, combined with our knowledge of SO1's endeavours over the previous nine months. It is therefore certainly within the realms of possibility, particularly if undertaken by very determined men with everything to play for.

However, Woburn Abbey contained equally determined men. George Hill wrote to Rex Leeper: 'Mr O'Neill is of the opinion that they [the parachutists] have no useful information and can now be duly dispatched. I do not believe that these man can be turned or otherwise used, and agree with Mr O'Neill, but if you have any other wishes, please let me know.'[49]

As it happened, Leeper did not have any contrary wishes, which sealed the fate of the three agents. He duly scrawled across the bottom of Hill's letter: 'I see no reason to keep these men. Yes – MI-5 can conduct their usual services but notify Sir Robert Vansittart first. R. Leeper.'[50]

Following Hess's arrival, some of the more radical members of the House of Lords began making statements that indicated a lack of stomach for continuing the war. Some were even openly suggesting that Britain would have to sue for peace by the autumn.[51]

One of the most dangerous of these peers was the Duke of Bedford, who by strange coincidence was the owner of Woburn Abbey. On the very day of Hess's arrival he had written to a political acquaintance suggesting that now was the time for David Lloyd George to make his stand for a peaceable accord with Germany. Lloyd George, the Duke wrote, should issue a public statement setting out Britain's terms for peace, to which Germany could respond. The Duke went so far as to comment that Lloyd George was 'obviously the one man who could save the country'.[52]

Churchill would had been well aware of this rising tide of anti-war sentiment, and he must have wondered whether SO1 had unintentionally created a many-headed Hydra that would destroy his premiership before Hitler attacked Russia and Britain could broach the tide of war.

Time was what it came down to. Was there time for Hitler to launch his greatest folly, the committing of Germany to war with Russia, before the frightened peers and politicians of Westminster gained sufficient impetus to challenge Churchill's leadership, and force through a compromise peace with Germany? Or would Hitler, suspecting that something was seriously amiss with the supposed Hoare–Halifax peace faction, lack sufficient confidence at the last moment to launch his invasion of the Soviet Union?

On Tuesday, 3 June 1941, Churchill's confidence received a substantial boost from Military Intelligence's most optimistic assessment to date. Headed 'Recent German Activities and Possible Intentions', the two-page report commented: 'A continued advance through North Africa into Egypt combined with a pincer movement from the north on Suez must certainly be tempting, but there have been no signs of the recent reinforcement of German troops in North Africa.'[53]

Military Intelligence believed it was much more likely that Russia would soon be subjected to aggressive German attention:

During May there was first of a spate of rumours, many of which could be traced to German sources, announcing an imminent German attack on Russia . . .

Germany undoubtedly wants certain food-stuffs and raw materials from the Ukraine and oil from the Caucasus . . . There is said to be a difference of opinion between the political and the military leaders in Germany as to whether these aims should be achieved by persuasion or by force, and it is probable that Hitler has not yet taken a decision on the point.

The assessment ended with a brief handwritten afterthought: 'Meanwhile reports of train movements suggest that Germany intends to be in a position to implement her threats if the Soviet [Union] should prove obdurate.' This last comment was more important than much of the prior document, giving as it did the first clear indication that things were definitely afoot in the east. Unbeknownst to many at the War Office, Churchill was already beginning to learn this from his highly secret daily caseload of Bletchley Park decrypts.

At the very time MI14's appreciation of 3 June was being disseminated in Whitehall and Downing Street, Hitler's interpreter, Paul Schmidt, was writing his notes on a meeting which had taken place the previous day between his Führer and Benito Mussolini at the Brenner Pass, which links Austria and Italy. Much had been discussed by the two dictators during their day-long meeting, ranging from Axis relations with Japan to the military situations in North Africa and the Middle East.

During the course of the conversation, the subject of Churchill had come up, and what Hitler told the Duce revealed something of his understanding of the political situation in Britain: 'If Churchill resigned, [Hitler said, he felt that] . . . perhaps Lloyd George or Sir Samuel Hoare would take over the government; in any event, the English would not fight to the last ounce of their supplies.'[54] In fact this analysis was far from the truth, but so long as Hitler believed it there was every chance that he would take the catastrophic decision to attack Russia while still committed to war with Britain and her allies.

On Saturday, 14 June, Hitler attended a conference with his military high command to discuss the final details of Barbarossa, which was destined to be launched the following weekend. This would be a war like no other, Hitler told his generals, not only as a fight to the finish between two totally opposing political ideologies, but also in terms of the Reich's expansion to make living space for its peoples at the expense of the sub-humans to the east. General Franz Halder, chief of the army General Staff, concerned by Hitler's tone, noted that the Führer 'said that the struggle between Russia and Germany was a Russian struggle. He stated that since the Russians were not signatories of the Hague Convention, the treatment of their prisoners of war did not have to follow the Articles of the Convention.'[55]

This was one of the first ominous notes to be sounded about the campaign to come, a murderous war that would see millions die, as a result of direct military action, or of disease and starvation as the Red Army struggled to hold Hitler's forces at bay. Stalin's only advantage would be the same one that had defeated Napoleon 130 years before – the vastness of Russia, and the appalling severity of her winters.

On the day following Hitler's meeting with his high command, Churchill dispatched a ciphered telegram to President Roosevelt informing him:

> From every source at my disposal, including some most trustworthy [Ultra], it looks as if a vast German onslaught on Russia is imminent . . . Should this new war break out we shall of course give all encouragement and any help we can spare to the Russians, following the principle that Hitler is the foe we have to beat. I do not expect any class political reactions here, and trust a German–Russian conflict will not cause you any embarrassment . . .[56]

Later that week, Robert Bruce Lockhart was invited down from Woburn Abbey to Downing Street. After dining with the Prime Minister and a few other select guests, he noted in his diary: 'Arthur Yencken [was] there – sent by Sam Hoare . . . I cramp Yencken's style. Brendan [Bracken] comes in ... [and he is] very anti-Dalton ...'[57]

Why Arthur Yencken, Minister Plenipotentiary based out at the Madrid Embassy with Captain Hillgarth and therefore Sam Hoare's second-in-command, had been sent all the way to Britain by Hoare is not clear. It is known that he reported on Serano Suñer's gastric ulcer, and had some criticisms of SO2 to pass on, but these were all items that could have been conveyed in a ciphered telegram. There must have been an additional reason for his presence at 10 Downing Street.

During the period between Rudolf Hess's surprising appearance in Britain and the dispatch of Arthur Yencken to London, Sam Hoare had been visited by another friend of Albrecht Haushofer's, Don Joachim Bar. In a 'most secret' memorandum, headed 'Subsequent Note on the Candid Proposals of DJB', Hoare reported to London that Bar had revealed that he had recently been visited by Ribbentrop's agent in Paris, Hans Gardeman, yet another old friend of Albrecht Haushofer, who had helped Gardeman secure his much-coveted posting to Paris. Gardeman, Hoare reported, had asked Bar to act as an intermediary between himself (Hoare) and the German government.

Hoare must have blanched at the thought of resuming his extremely difficult and distasteful role as make-believe peace envoy for a non-existent political force poised to topple his own government. He deftly fended Bar off, reporting to London that once again Germany was wielding her 'big stick', intimating that Britain should make peace soon, or she would suffer the consequences, 'with new destructive methods so terrible ... that anything done hitherto will seem mere child's play'.[58] The men in London were not impressed. Germany had done her worst for nearly a year, and the 'big stick' had been found wanting.

On Monday, 16 June, Bletchley Park issued its analysis of the latest decrypts, reporting to Churchill their belief that a German attack on Russia was imminent, and could come at any time after 19 June – only three days away.[59]

Despite this heartening sign that Hitler was about to make his fatal blunder, there was still much cause for concern. The Foreign Office was not convinced that 'Germany intended to attack Russia', and believed it was not beyond the bounds of possibility that Hitler was conducting a potentially war-winning bluff of his own, and that Germany's tremendous military build-up might be a ruse to force Stalin to accept Hitler's territorial and economic demands.[60] This belief was strengthened on 19 June, when the Foreign Office received information from the Swedish government that it expected Germany to issue economo-territorial demands to Russia within the next week.[61]

Despite these concerns, Winston Churchill, who received much from Bletchley Park that the Foreign Office was completely ignorant of, was absolutely convinced that the latter half of June would see Hitler take the plunge into probable disaster. On Friday, 20 June, Churchill withdrew to Chequers to await developments, convinced that 'the German onslaught upon Russia was a matter of days, or it might be hours', away.[62]

On Saturday, 21 June, Churchill's Private Secretary 'Jock' Colville arrived at Chequers. As the two men took an evening stroll around the croquet lawn after dinner, Colville tentatively asked the Prime Minister 'whether for him, the arch anti-Communist, this [inevitable need to support and join forces with Russia] was not bowing down to the House of Rimmon'. Churchill was in a good mood that evening, and had chuckled, replying: 'Not at all. I have only one purpose, the destruction of Hitler, and my life is much simplified therein. If Hitler invaded Hell I would make at least a favourable reference to the Devil in the House of Commons.'[63]

He did not have long to wait, for Hitler was about to invade a Hell of his own making. Even as Colville and Churchill strolled around the grounds of Chequers that Saturday evening, in eastern Europe, along a front nearly 450 miles long, Axis corps commanders were receiving their final orders, and tanks, armoured cars and footsoldiers numbering nearly four million were dispersing to their jumping-off points for an attack that would be launched at dawn the next morning. Operation Barbarossa was about to begin.

'When I awoke on the morning of Sunday, the 22nd,' Churchill would later recall, 'the news was brought to me of Hitler's invasion of Russia. This changed conviction into certainty.'[64] It was the event that Churchill had long hoped for. Ever since the debacle of Dunkirk, and through the Battle of Britain, he had known that Britain could not defeat Germany on her own. Yes, she had the support of the dominions, the Free French, and a few exiled Czechs, Poles, Dutch and Belgians. However, Nazi Germany was a prodigious foe, which now had most of occupied Europe to supply her war needs. It was, as Rex Leeper had commented during one of SO1's Saturday meetings in February 1941, becoming increasingly clear that Britain was probably unable to win in Europe.[65] The Axis was just too big, the territorial losses just too vast for Britain to recover from. Yet this had not meant that Nazi Germany was invincible, and the men of Whitehall had come to the conclusion that Britain, with the help of the United States and the Soviet Union, *could* win a world war.[66] That high-risk formula had eventually won through little more than twenty years before, when Germany had found herself in the fatal situation of fighting a two-front war. Now, it seemed, Hitler had made exactly the same mistake.

Later that evening, having spent much of the day writing his speech, Churchill broadcast to the nation:

> The Nazi regime is indistinguishable from the worst features of Communism. It is devoid of all theme and principle except appetite and racial domination. It excels all forms of human wickedness in the efficiency of its cruel and ferocious aggression. No one has been a more consistent opponent of Communism than I have for the last twenty-five years ... But all this fades away before the spectacle which is now unfolding. The past, with its crimes, its follies, and its tragedies, flashes away ...
>
> I see advancing [upon Russia the] hideous onslaught of the Nazi

war machine, with its clanking, heel-clicking, dandified Prussian officers ... the dull, drilled, docile, brutish masses of the Hun soldiery plodding on like a swarm of locusts ... [And] behind all this storm, I see that small group of villainous men who plan, organise, and launch this cataract of horrors upon mankind ...

We have but one aim and one single, irrevocable purpose. We are resolved to destroy Hitler and every vestige of the Nazi regime. From this nothing will turn us – nothing.

Perhaps allowing himself a little private irony, Churchill went on:

We will never parley, we will never negotiate with Hitler or any of his gang. We shall fight him by land, we shall fight him by sea, we shall fight him in the air, until ... we have rid the earth of his shadow and liberated its peoples from his yoke ... if Hitler imagines that his attack on Soviet Russia will cause the slightest divergence of aims or slackening of effort in the great democracies who are resolved upon his doom, he is woefully mistaken. On the contrary, we shall be fortified and encouraged in our efforts to rescue mankind from his tyranny ...,[67]

During the autumn of 1941, Hitler was to comment to his guests over dinner one evening: 'On the 22nd of June, a door opened before us, and we didn't known what was behind it. We could look out for gas warfare, bacteriological warfare. The heavy uncertainty took me by the throat. Here we were faced by beings who are complete strangers to us. Everything that resembles civilisation, the Bolsheviks have suppressed it.' In a chilling portent of the horrors to come, he commented: 'I have no feelings about the idea of wiping out Kiev, Moscow or St Petersburg.'[68]

On Tuesday, 16 December 1941, one of Albrecht Haushofer's assistants at Berlin University, Frau Irmegard Schnuhr, was alarmed to receive a sudden and discreet summons to the Reich Chancellery.

In the months following the collapse of the Hitler–Hess–Hoare–Halifax negotiations, Albrecht's fortunes had waxed and waned in accordance with the progress of the war. At times his position would seem secure, and the leaders of the Reich would actively seek his counsel; at others, top Nazis such as Goebbels would snipe at his racial background. At one low point he lost his prestigious post as Secretary-General of the Society of Geography. But Albrecht Haushofer remained in Germany, and did not flee to the safety of Switzerland although he could easily have done so.

Haushofer moved quickly to realign himself with several new and powerful champions. The first was Rudolf Hess's replacement within the chain of command at the Chancellery, Martin Bormann. Within a short space of time Haushofer was busily writing reports for Bormann. However, these were not on foreign affairs, but rather pandered to Bormann's personal ambitions. They were Haushofer's secret assessments of the top personalities in Nazi Germany, such as Göring, Ribbentrop, Goebbels, Ley and others. Appraisals of their standing in internal and foreign politics, and whether or not they might one day pose a threat to Bormann.

Haushofer's other new alliance was an altogether more sinister and dangerous one, with the Reichsführer-SS, Heinrich Himmler. Himmler had been a political ally of Hess's – which was curious, for the two men were opposites in many ways. Despite being head of the quasi-mystical Schutzstaffel, sworn to the service of the Führer, Himmler had no intention of going down with the Nazi Party should Germany lose the war, and he too began to use Haushofer to further his own ends of negotiating a peace settlement with the Allies. It was an alliance that would protect Haushofer's life, even after he became involved in the July 1944 plot to kill Hitler, but only until the exact moment he outlived his usefulness to Himmler.

In the meantime, in the autumn of 1941 Albrecht was still in favour, and in November he had written a twenty-page report for Hitler on the possibilities of still negotiating a peace agreement with Britain.[69] This was a far-reaching and complex document. It not only explored the failings of the prior peaceable attempts (primarily that of 1940–41, which Haushofer had participated in with Hess) and made suggestions for the conditions under which future discussions should take place, but went into great depth on matters such as American influence in the Pacific, Japanese influence in the Far East, the dangers posed by a unified Anglo–American power-base, and Germany's future role in Europe, the Middle East, Russia and the Indo-Pacific regions.

Thus, despite the unmitigated catastrophe Rudolf Hess had brought upon himself and upon Hitler's desire for peace before embarking upon his eastern war of conflict, Hitler and the other leaders of the Reich clearly regarded Albrecht Haushofer as blameless. To a degree they were correct: Haushofer personally was blameless – but he had unintentionally been the key to unleashing a multitude of disasters upon Germany's war strategy. Had Hitler ever realised Haushofer's true role in British Intelligence's plot to undermine Germany – to reap the rewards of a Führer 'ripe for exploitation' – had he suspected that the H negotiations were anything but real, Albrecht Haushofer would have found himself stood against a wall and shot faster than he could have comprehended what was happening. This therefore means that no one in Germany suspected SO1's involvement in Messrs HHHH.

Many things had changed in Germany during the latter half of 1941 – since the loss of Hess to the British. The stunning early successes of Barbarossa in the summer had given way to the clinging Russian mud in the late autumn, and now, in the last days before Christmas, even as the Führer awaited Frau Schnuhr's arrival in his Chancellery office, he knew his troops were facing the appalling severity of a Russian winter. In the act of delaying Barbarossa for five weeks had lain the seeds of disaster, and the army in the east had failed to reach its primary objective. Moscow was in sight on the horizon, was being pummelled by howitzers, but still the German troops could not get into the city. Allied to that failure was the significant fact that Stalin was still in the Kremlin issuing orders. Had he been forced to flee (and at one crucial point his train was ready and waiting to whisk him away to the Urals), there was every chance that the Soviet government would have wobbled, and with its loss of face Russian armed resistance may well have collapsed. As it was, the ill-equipped German troops were now exposed to the Russian winter. Just three weeks later Hitler would comment bitterly over dinner: 'The supplying of the front creates enormous problems ... Amongst the unforeseen matters in which we've had to improvise was the catastrophe of the temperature's falling, in two days, from 2° below zero to 38° below. That paralysed everything, for nobody expected it ... On the front at Leningrad, with a temperature of 42° below zero, not a rifle, a machine-gun or a field-gun was working, on our side.'[70]

There was, however, an even more worrying situation which had developed in the first week of December 1941. Churchill's long-term strategy of seeing Germany pitted against Russia, Britain and the United States had finally come to pass. On 7 December the Japanese had attacked Pearl Harbor, and in support of her Japanese Axis partner, Germany found herself at war with America four days later.

Now, on Tuesday, 16 December, after a weekend contemplating this new and potentially catastrophic situation, Adolf Hitler determined to act. He would sound out Albrecht Haushofer's assistant before committing himself to a conversation with the man he had known for twenty years.

Ushered into the daunting surroundings of Hitler's enormous office, Irmegard Schnuhr was shown briskly across to a sofa and seated before the Führer. Frau Schnuhr found Hitler businesslike and polite, yet at the same time at pains to impress upon her that this was an absolutely confidential conversation. He told her that he had a 'special interest' in Albrecht Haushofer, and 'was interested to know whether he [Albrecht] thought there was [still] a possibility of making peace with Britain'.[71]

It seemed that, despite the complete failure of Hitler's 1940–41 peaceable attempt, which had seen him lose Rudolf Hess, he had not entirely given up the idea of a negotiated conclusion to the war, particularly now that it was taking a new and very dangerous direction. A war with the democratic western Europe states and Britain had been bad enough – and had warranted many covert attempts to negotiate a peace – but the involvement of America was a different matter altogether.

Six weeks later, in early February 1942, Frau Schnuhr once again found herself invited to meet the Führer in the formal yet confidential surroundings of his Reich Chancellery office. Having evidently spoken at length about the matter to Albrecht, she reported that he believed that 'to the best of his knowledge neither Britain nor Germany had any intention of being the first to put out a peace feeler'. However, she commented, Albrecht had also said that 'if Hitler did desire to negotiate with Britain, the very fact that the German Foreign Minister was Ribbentrop would make it impossible for any negotiations to get off the ground'.[72]

It appears that Albrecht was determined to convey that he would only assist Hitler on the condition that a signal was given to the British that Germany was prepared to make deep changes in foreign policy. Hitler responded in a manner that indicated he was not about to change his objectives merely on Albrecht's insistence. He did not, after all, want to change his expansionist policies; he just wanted peace with the British – and now the Americans too – before all his plans were thrown completely out of kilter.

Hitler, his patience evidently wearing thin, testily told Frau Schnuhr that Albrecht Haushofer 'was not as clever as he thought he was, and that it would be easy to sack Ribbentrop if the British first sacked their Foreign Minister, Anthony Eden'. Frau Schnuhr then asked Hitler whether he desired a face-to-face meeting with Albrecht. No, Hitler responded, 'he would not dream of it'. His temper now up, he openly called Albrecht a '*Mischling*' – a half-breed – and declared that the outcome of the war would be settled on the battlefield. However, Hitler was never a man to completely close a door, and Frau Schnuhr would later comment that despite his belligerent stance, she had the distinct impression that he still wanted to keep an avenue open to Albrecht Haushofer, 'should peace negotiations with Britain ever become a possibility'.

In the end Hitler never did summon Haushofer into his presence again. As the disasters of war, such as Stalingrad, El Alamein, the Allied invasion of Italy and D-Day, made a compromise peace ever more unlikely, so Hitler's intransigence and increasing isolation made the prospect of total defeat for Germany ever more certain.

From the winter of 1941 onward, many in Germany secretly began to harbour the belief that defeat was certain. Over the next two and half years, Albrecht Haushofer increasingly found himself in the company of those who believed that the war was turning into the greatest disaster that had ever befallen their country, and that the only way to stop it before Germany lost everything would be to oust Hitler and his fellow Nazis. Through the auspices of the diplomat and leading member of the anti-Nazi resistance Ulrich von Hassell, Albrecht found himself sucked into the company of such eminent Germans as General Beck, Admiral Canaris, General Oster, Johannes Popitz, Field Marshal Erwin Rommel, General Stuelpnagel and Field Marshal Witzleben. Haushofer's role, had they succeeded, would have been to become Germany's post-war Foreign Minister.

The plot to remove Hitler from the political equation culminated at the Führer's military headquarters at Rastenburg, east Prussia, on 20 July 1944, when Lieutenant Colonel Claus von Stauffenberg planted a bomb that blew up Hitler's conference room while a meeting was in progress. Four men were killed, and most of those present were severely injured, several being blown clear through the building's wooden walls. Hitler survived, although the blast set his hair alight, partially paralysed his right arm, burnt his right leg and damaged his eardrums. His injuries were kept from the German people.

Hitler's vengeance was terrible. Some of the conspirators were summarily shot on the very first day, and all the others were tracked down and handed over to the Gestapo for thorough interrogation before swift National Socialist justice was dispensed by the Volksgericht, the dreaded people's court. It is estimated that between 180 and two hundred people were killed as a direct result of the July Plot. There was, however, one exception.

As soon as he heard of the plot's failure, Albrecht Haushofer fled to Bavaria, believing his intimate knowledge of the region's forests, hills and lakes would be his best protection against the endeavours of the Gestapo to find him. He managed to evade capture throughout the summer and autumn of 1944, hoping that the swiftly moving Allied advance might soon result in the removal of Bavaria from Hitler's sphere of influence, at which time he would give himself up to the Allies. However, on 7 December, disaster struck, when the Gestapo discovered Albrecht hiding in a hayloft on a friend's country retreat. It was the cold weather that betrayed him – his breath had caused a cloud of mist that was noticed.

Albrecht may have expected imminent execution at the hands of the Gestapo or the SS, but instead he was whisked away to Berlin, where he was incarcerated in Moabit prison, a grim red-brick edifice on Lehrterstrasse. There he was extensively question by the Gestapo. They were not brutal – their prisoner was after all an important man – but they were extremely insistent. They wanted to know the names of the plotters behind the Stauffenberg bombing, who their associates were, and whether there were any other plots still in the offing. Albrecht revealed as little as he could get away with.

Within a few weeks of his arrival at Moabit, Albrecht found himself contacted by the Reichsführer-SS, Heinrich Himmler, who had not forgotten Albrecht's previous assistance in his endeavours to contact American Intelligence, conducted through the auspices of SS-General Wolff. Himmler wanted advice on how to conduct a peaceable approach to the Allies, and after considering Albrecht's comments, asked whether he would be willing to mediate between him and the Americans sweeping northwards through Italy.

To begin with, this potentially dangerous relationship protected Albrecht, as Himmler wished to keep his foreign affairs expert alive, in case an opportunity arose to cut a deal with the Americans. However, just at the point when Albrecht's expertise might have prompted Himmler to order his release so that he could contact the Americans, the fickle Reichsführer-SS met the Swedish representative of the Red Cross, Count Folke Bernadotte. Bernadotte was suave, urbane and, most importantly, an eminent neutral – which made him a more acceptable peace emissary than Albrecht Haushofer. In absolute secrecy from Hitler, Himmler asked Bernadotte to contact the Americans in the second week of April 1945, offering to capitulate to the Western Allies, but not to the Russians.

On the evening of Monday, 23 April 1945, as Russian troops battered their way into the outskirts of Berlin, Albrecht Haushofer and fifteen other political prisoners, many of whom had been involved in the Stauffenberg plot, were led away from Moabit. The purpose of their journey, they were told, was for them to be evacuated from Berlin by train. In fact, they had an appointment with an executioner's bullet in the ruins of the Ulap Exhibition Centre.

Two days later, on Wednesday, 25 April, word came through to Himmler from Count Bernadotte. Churchill and the new US President, Harry S. Truman, had rejected his peace offer.

Later that same week, on the night of Saturday, 29 April, as Russian T34 tanks prowled the Tiergarten, and Soviet troops began ransacking and firing Germany's offices of government, reducing the capital of the thousand-year Reich to rubble and scratching their names upon the very walls of the Reichstag, Adolf Hitler, ensconced in a bunker beneath the ruins of the Reich Chancellery, put a gun to his head, pulled the trigger, and Nazi Germany effectively ceased to exist.

Epilogue

Despite the vast scale of the Second World War, on a political level it was essentially a conflict between two gigantic personalities: Winston Churchill and Adolf Hitler.

Throughout the 1930s, Churchill had been Britain's prophetic voice of doom, decrying the folly of appeasement, proclaiming the evils of Nazism and the threat to European democracy posed by an expansionist Germany led by Adolf Hitler. With his attainment of the premiership in May 1940, Churchill's condemnations of Hitler became even more forthright; he compared the German Führer to Satan incarnate. Hitler, in return, likened Churchill to a drunken ogre, a stooge of world Jewry and capitalism, a man willing to drag his people down to satisfy his own ambitions.

In the end, Hitler's doomed secret peaceable appeals only revealed a deep flaw to certain top men within the British government, Foreign Office and Intelligence Services, and presented them with a devastating weapon against which the might of the Reich was powerless to protect him. Hitler had entered into a devious political battle which he hoped would see Churchill rudely ousted from the British premiership; but in the event he was devastatingly outwitted by his arch-enemy's experts in political warfare.

As a result of SO1's secret endeavours, Hitler saw his dream of peace in the west – and with it a free hand to conquer in the east – shattered. Yet it was a failure he had to keep to himself, for he could trust no one. The loss of face could have been fatal, even for the Führer himself, and he increasingly withdrew from the public stage to the Wolf's Lair in the years ahead. As the signs began to multiply that Germany would lose the war, so too did cracks begin to appear in the Reich. Hitler had been safe from internal dissent while Germany had been winning the war, but by mid-1944 his promises of victory to the German people were beginning to sound hollow, and for the first time he was beginning to appear vulnerable. Who could he trust? Who had been party to the plot to kill him? The Wehrmacht? The party itself? Perhaps even elements within the SS? There was a reason for the Führer's fury and terrible vengeance on all those who had plotted against him: anything less would have shown weakness, and that would court disaster.

Before losing the Second World War itself, Adolf Hitler lost the war of wits against Winston Churchill, and with it his peace of mind. He then made the mistakes that cost him everything else as well. His failure was total, for he not only failed to achieve peace in the west before embarking on his great eastern adventure, but in the very act of being outwitted by SO1 he was tricked into the one thing he had sworn he would never be so foolhardy as to do – undertake a two-front war which he knew Germany could not win.

Thus the seeds of Nazi Germany's destruction were planted in 1941 by Winston Churchill, Sir Robert Vansittart, Sir Samuel Hoare, Rex Leeper and the men of SO1. All the vast domains Hitler had gained by conquest – from the Arctic Circle to the Sahara, and from the Atlantic to the Black Sea – were pushed back, until his glorious thousand-year Reich extended only to a few wrecked and smoking blocks of central Berlin, defended by old men and children.

In the end, Hitler's defeat was absolute.

Given the extremely important contribution to the war effort that SO1 (renamed the Political Warfare Executive and placed under Brendan Bracken within just a few weeks of concluding the successful operation against Hitler) performed, it may be wondered why the decision was taken to keep the facts about Messrs HHHH forever secret. The repercussions were terrible indeed. Hitler's invasion of the Soviet Union would cost over twenty million Russian lives. It may well be that Hitler would ultimately have attacked Russia anyway, but British Intelligence certainly helped give him the mindset to take that decision in 1941. The disclosure of that fact would have given Britain's enemies an opportunity to decry British perfidy, tainting her post-war standing in the world of foreign affairs.

The manner in which the Second World War concluded created a new and extremely dangerous situation, with Soviet forces occupying half of Europe and showing every sign that they intended to stay. Britain, meanwhile, was in almost as bad a condition as Germany. With the uncertainties and fears of the Cold War came the very real concern that any form of disclosure would give Stalin an excuse to accuse the Western powers of treachery, scoring a very strong propaganda point and racking up the tension even more.

The first ominous signs that Stalin knew something about SO1's secret operation became evident in the autumn of 1944, while Churchill was on a visit to Moscow. As Churchill sat down to supper in the Kremlin, Stalin raised his glass and proposed a toast to the British Intelligence Services, which he said had 'inveigled Hess into coming to England'. Eyeing Churchill closely, he went on: 'He could not have landed without being given signals. The intelligence service must have been behind it all.'[1]

An unsettled Churchill immediately protested that the British government had known nothing about Hess's arrival beforehand. Stalin responded with a broad and knowing smile, and said that Russian Intelligence often did not inform the Soviet government of its intentions either, until an operation came to fruition.

The implication was clear. Stalin was letting Churchill know that he did not believe the yarn about the mad Deputy-Führer who had suddenly taken it upon himself to fly to Scotland in an attempt to make peace with the British. It is known that Stalin had already been briefed by the NKVD head Lavrenti Beria on the more secret aspects of British Intelligence's operation, which had been gleaned from the Czechs and the French in the months following Hess's arrival in Britain; but the Russians also possessed more accurate information from a source deep in the heart of British Intelligence. A British operative working in Spain and Portugal, a man well known to Sir Samuel Hoare and Captain Hillgarth, had long ago sold his soul to the Soviets. His name was Kim Philby.

With the end of the war came much apprehension and uneasiness in Britain at what might be revealed at the Nuremberg Trials. The main concern was about what Alfred Rosenberg and, more particularly, Rudolf Hess might say. Both men were on trial for their lives, and had nothing to lose by spilling the beans to an international tribunal, complete with an audience of the world's press. That they did not declare exactly what had taken place emanated from their political pedigree, their understanding of the new balance of power and the expediency of maintaining secrecy.

In the end, what could Hess have said anyway? He could hardly admit that he had not been negotiating for peace with the British government, but rather with a political faction that had intimated its willingness to topple Churchill, so that Germany would be free to attack Russia. Despite his acts of apparent lunacy, Hess was an intelligent man, and he had a politician's instinct for survival. To have revealed the truth in open court before four Allied judges, one of whom was Russian and another British, would not have aided his cause in the slightest. Better to stick to the official British and German proclamations of 1941. Better to feign madness in the hope that he would be judged less culpable, than to be found guilty of the intent to wage an eastern war of conquest that had cost twenty million lives. That would have guaranteed a death sentence, as would befall Rosenberg, Ribbentrop, Göring and nine other defendants. Hess may have hoped to receive a lesser custodial sentence, like Albert Speer, Admiral Doenitz, Neurath and von Schirach, who were jailed for terms ranging from ten to twenty years.

Hess's bizarre behaviour at Nuremberg did not make the British authorities any less paranoid that evidence might come to light which would reflect a different version of events from that promulgated by the British government ever since 1941.

One such cause for disquiet occurred during the very first days of Hess's trial. On 5 January 1946 Britain's Ambassador in Paris, Duff Cooper, an old friend of Churchill's who had been Minister of Information during 1940–41, sent an urgent telegram to London stating that a release of documents at Nuremberg had resulted in a French newspaper article which 'alleges that British officials were preparing to negotiate with Hitler in 1941. The first paragraph of the ... story reads "A high Foreign Office official, several Conservative M.P.s, Five Lords, Three under-Secretaries of State and an English Ambassador were ready to negotiate with Hitler in 1941." '[2]

Anyone in the know about what had really taken place would have realised immediately that this was too close for comfort, and the matter was immediately passed to an eminently appropriate Whitehall official to respond. Sir Alexander Cadogan, still serving as Permanent Under-Secretary at the Foreign Office, first sought the counsel of Con O'Neill (formerly of SO1), who commented: 'I think we must issue some form of brief statement to the Press to-day. This should be done here, not in Paris ... There is some advantage in not having the text [of the article] at the moment. Our preliminary statement can be more non-committal ...'[3]

Accordingly, Cadogan promptly drafted a statement for immediate dispatch to Duff Cooper, with copies to Washington, Berlin and Moscow, that declared: 'His Majesty's Government have not yet received or examined the text of the document in question. But it may be stated at once that no person in a responsible position in this country ever took any initiatives for the opening of negotiations with Germany in 1941 or at any other time during the war ...'[4] The extreme sensitivity of the British officials, their absolute refusal to concede that the slightest contact with the German government had taken place during the war, was emphasised by the heading at the top of the document. It stated: 'This telegram is of particular secrecy and should be retained by the authorised recipient and not passed on.'

It would be a mistake to assume that the desire for secrecy of these British officials was motivated solely by concern for their nation's standing on the world stage. There was also a substantial degree of personal fear behind their actions – fear that the trial of Nazi Germany's leaders at Nuremberg could suddenly become refocused on the conduct of certain top Britons, and *their* conduct during the war.

Such a fear definitely existed in Whitehall on the morning of 10 January 1946, when an official at the Foreign Office recorded a memorandum to his superior that disclosed:

> Colonel Phillimore [British representative at Nuremberg] telephoned at 7.15 last night to say that the Americans had put in and released to the Press another somewhat embarrassing document. It was a Memo by Rosenberg entitled 'A short report on the activities of the Foreign Policy Office (Aussenpolitisches amt) of the NSDAP'...
>
> Despite the obvious stupidity of the article, it is for consideration whether we should not draw attention of the American prosecution (or possibly the [US] State Department) to the fact that the Americans are not living up to the Agreement by which they are bound to notify us in advance of any material which they put in *which may lead to counter-charges which we shall be called to answer*...[5] [Emphasis added.]

In the event the British government had little to fear, for despite certain mildly embarrassing documents coming to light during the trial, Rudolf Hess did not blurt out the truth behind why he had really flown to Britain, or any details about the secret Anglo–German peace negotiations conducted during the nine months preceding his flight.

At the end of the trial, on the day the sentences were handed out by the Nuremberg judges on the former leaders of the Third Reich, Hess maintained his feigned diminished responsibility to the very last, standing in the dock, swaying aimlessly, with his eyes fixed on the ceiling. Despite this act, however, he undoubtedly clearly heard Sir Geoffrey Lawrence, the British judge on the panel of the International Military Tribunal, proclaim: 'The tribunal sentences you to imprisonment for life . . .'

In the forty-one years of Rudolf Hess's incarceration that followed the Nuremberg Trials, many theories have been explored in an attempt to uncover the truth behind his flight to Britain. Many of those who were connected to the events of 1941 at some time made their own pronouncements about what had taken place. Some were true, but most were not. By a strange quirk of fate the man at the very apex of this intrigue, Rudolf Hess, almost the only one who (as far as we know) never talked, was to outlive virtually every other participant, in some cases by many years.

In the latter 1960s, after twenty years' imprisonment, Hess began to hope that the Four Powers might relent and release him along with the last of the other political prisoners still remaining in Spandau prison. He was to be bitterly disappointed. In Rudolf Hess's case, life meant life, and there he remained into extreme old age, a stoic reminder of Germany's darker past.

By the 1980s, many people began to regard it as an outrage that such a frail old man should remain a lone prisoner in the vast confines of Spandau. However, it should not be thought that, with the passing of the years, Britain's political secrets became any less important or dangerous. Behind closed doors, it was not in the British government's interests ever to see Rudolf Hess released. A free Hess, at liberty to give press conferences and, perhaps, to write his memoirs, would have much locked away within his mind that could cause Britain extreme embarrassment.

Furthermore, it is almost certainly the case that Hess never realised that he had been totally deceived by SO1, and that he spent more than four decades of incarceration believing that his actions alone – his decision to replace Ernst Bohle as the emissary – had caused such disaster to Germany. Had a freed Hess ever talked, and, as a consequence of his disclosures, had he been confronted by the evidence that no British peace party had ever existed, he might in a blinding flash of revelation have realised that he, Hitler and Albrecht Haushofer had all been tricked by the machinations of British Intelligence.

Hess's pedigree should be remembered here. He had been the Deputy-Führer of a National Socialist totalitarian state. If he discovered that Hitler's fatal blunder – the invasion of Russia before concluding the war in the west – had been engineered by the British, out once again would come the terrible cry of 'betrayal', of '*Dolschtoss*' – the stab in the back – that had fertilised latent German nationalism following the First World War.

Despite Hess's frailties in extreme old age, he was still a man whose knowledge of the true events in 1941 was incredibly dangerous, not only to the prestige of the British government, but to the future of Europe. His revelations could have caused much bitterness in Germany, and much distrust throughout Europe of the British government, resulting in political repercussions that would echo into the twenty-first century. Hess's knowledge was a secret best banished to the past. He was never to be released. He was never to talk freely about the tumultuous events of 1941, when the outcome of the war hung so delicately in the balance.

Thus the ninety-three-year-old Rudolf Hess took his terrible secret to his grave in August 1987. Whether intentionally or not, his forty-year silence has prevented much bitterness, discord and danger for Europe in the future.

Postscript

Having devoted two years of my life to researching the machinations of the British Foreign Office, Winston Churchill and his closest confederates to save Britain in her darkest hours of 1940–41, I was left with several unanswered questions when I eventually completed my investigations into the circumstances of Rudolf Hess's arrival on a lonely Scottish hillside in 1941. A nagging little voice at the back of my mind persisted in asking: Did Hess ever realise in the subsequent years that he, Adolf Hitler and his old friend Albrecht Haushofer had not been negotiating with a real peace faction? Did he ever suspect that he had been tricked by British Intelligence? Did he go to his grave believing that his deep yearning for a peace agreement with Britain, for which he would receive the credit, had ultimately caused the collapse of any possibility of peace, and with it Germany's strategy for the conduct of the war? In an effort to answer these questions, I determined to engage in one last piece of research, one last investigation, that I would conduct on my own account.

On a quiet Sunday morning in late September 2001, I sat down on the sofa in my drawing room in Dorset, the sound of distant church bells in the air, picked up the telephone on the coffee table before me, and proceeded to dial a long number, one that would connect me with an unremarkable detached house in the quiet suburbs of Hindelang, a town a few miles south of Munich.

My intention was to hold one last conversation with perhaps the only man alive who might know whether Rudolf Hess ever realised that his peaceable endeavours had ended in disaster because he had unwittingly been negotiating with British Intelligence, rather than with a political faction intent on unseating Churchill. The man I telephoned was the godson of both Albrecht Haushofer and Adolf Hitler: Rudolf Hess's son, Wolf Rüdiger.

After some brief introductory conversation – we had corresponded in the past, and shared several acquaintances – I began to edge towards the real object of my call, without revealing the nature of what I had discovered. Finally I asked Wolf Rüdiger Hess whether his father had ever mentioned any suspicion that British Intelligence had interfered with his and Albrecht Haushofer's correspondence with the Duke of Hamilton, or ever disclosed a feeling that his peace mission to Britain in 1941 had failed because of the machinations of the Churchill government?

There was a resigned sigh. Had I, I wondered, asked the wrong sort of question, that would result in a swiftly concluded conversation? But no, there was an answer forthcoming, and it confirmed some of my own conclusions about what had occurred in the post-war years.

'You have to remember,' Hess's son began, 'that I didn't meet my father, as an adult, until the late 1960s. Until he was left alone at Spandau when the others were released, he had kept us all at a distance. The other prisoners had received their monthly visits, but my father kept himself hidden away.'

There was a long pause, then he continued. 'In the years since I first started to visit him, I only ever met him – oh, some 250 times. He was only allowed monthly visits. At those times, our discussions were strictly monitored. We sat either side of a large table, and present within the room were two representatives of the Governing Powers. We had no private conversation. We were only really free to discuss family matters. We were not allowed to talk about the war. We were not allowed to talk about National Socialism. We were not allowed to talk about the events that led to his flight.'

That was it. Even had Hess senior known the whole truth, he had not been allowed to talk about it. What harm could there have been in allowing a frail, nonagenarian prisoner to talk freely to his son – unless he held secrets that were so dangerous they had to be kept out of the public domain forever.

Thus the continuing secrecy *had* been inspired by post-war fears of what had been done in 1941. It was not just about a secret British Intelligence operation, but a political secret that still had the potential to cause much unrest if taken up by neo-Nazis who wished to make political mileage out of the fact that Germany had in part lost the war because of British subterfuge. To condemn Germany's Nazi government of 1933–45 as monstrous and inept is an easy way of writing off an unsavoury regime; if, however, they had failed largely through British trickery, that presents an infinitely more complex situation.

Just four weeks later, I was staying in a substantial and imposing hotel in the Schorfheide, the extremely pretty forested and lake-dotted countryside thirty miles north of Berlin. I was there to deliver a lecture on the events of 1939 to a group of German historians, academics and retired military.

The hotel had once been one of the Third Reich's official guest-houses, set in the vast grounds of Karinhall, Hermann Göring's magnificent country estate. In the 1930s, Lord Halifax, Mussolini and Russia's Foreign Minister Molotov had all stayed here, and in the years following the fall of the Reich, when the Schorfheide had been in East Germany, it had become DDR leader Erich Honecker's country retreat.

It was there, after dinner on my last evening at the hotel, that I heard the news that Wolf Rüdiger Hess had died. I knew he had been ill for a long time, but still it was a shock. Yet another link to the past gone.

Later that evening I slipped discreetly from the hubbub in the lounge, letting myself out through the french doors to walk across the terrace and then down through the heavily wooded gardens towards the lake. Soon I was standing in the darkness by myself on a jetty at the lake's edge. The broad wooden jetty had once been part of Göring's boating house. On the far side of the lake rose a heavily wooded ridge where Göring's mansion, Karinhall, had stood before it was blown up by Göring himself and then bulldozed into oblivion by the conquering Russians at the war's end. The call of ducks echoed across the still water, and in the mist made luminescent by the full moon, half a dozen greylag geese flapped in frantic unison before taking off to fly across to the deep reed-beds at the far end of the lake.

As I leant on the rail at the end of Göring's jetty, I pondered the many complexities of German political life in the late 1930s and early 1940s. They had been powerful men all – Göring, Hitler, and Hess too – but in the end their abilities had proven inadequate when put to the test by men like Churchill's, Cadogan, Vansittart, Halifax and Hoare; men trained to run the vast British Empire at the height of its power. When it came down to it, the top Nazis had simply not been good enough politicians. If they had been, I wondered, would Karinhall still have stood on the far side of the lake? Would the trees still have twinkled with light from brightly-illuminated windows? Or would it all have gone by now anyway, imploded just like that other totalitarian state, Soviet Russia?

A mist was thickening on the lake, and a cloudbank high in the star-filled sky suddenly chose that moment to drift across the bright full moon, plunging Göring's ridge – his former home – into darkness. Blotted out, just like the past. Behind me, in the Third Reich's former guest-house for visiting foreign dignitaries, someone was playing the grand piano in the lounge. As its haunting strains drifted towards me through the hotel grounds they became faint and disjointed, the trees and distance masking the tune, just as the passage of time masks the tune of past events, the machinations of leaders, and the hopes and fears of a nation.

I turned and walked very quietly away from Hermann Göring's lake, the only sound that of a tinkling piano and my feet on dead leaves. I knew I would never return. There are some things one must eventually leave to the past.

Martin A. Allen
Autumn 2001

Source Notes

PROLOGUE
1 David Irving, *Hess* (London, 1989)
2 Doc. No. RG226 XL22853 – National Archives, Washington DC.
3 Ibid.
4 Doc. No. 840.414/11–2745 – Confidential File, State Department Archive, Washington DC.
5 Ibid.
6 Ibid.
7 Doc. No. FO 371/60508 – Public Records Office, Kew.

CHAPTER ONE – AN UNLIKELY TRIUMVIRATE
1 Ilse Hess, *Gefangener des Friedens* (Druffel Verlag, 1955), p.17.
2 Doc No. 100–45499, Report of 12 February 1944. Federal Bureau of Investigation, Washington DC.
3 Ibid.
4 Hugh Trevor-Roper, 'The Mind of Adolf Hitler', Introduction to Hugh Trevor-Roper (ed.), *Hitler's Table Talk: Hitler's Conversations Recorded by Martin Bormann* (Oxford, 1953), p.xix.
5 H.J. Mackinder, 'The Geographical Pivot of History' in *Geographical Journal*, XXIII (April 1904).
6 Ibid.
7 Wolf Rüdiger Hess, *My Father Rudolf Hess* (London, 1986), p.33.
8 Ibid.
9 Article by E.A. Walsh, *Life* Magazine, 16 September 1946.
10 Doc. No. WO 208/4467 – Public Records Office, Kew.
11 Ibid.
12 Ibid.

13 Ilse Hess, op. cit., p.24.

14 Wolf Rüdiger Hess, *Rudolf Hess: Briefe 1908–1933* (Langen Muller, 1987), p.310.

15 Ibid, p.311.

16 *The Times*, 12 December 1923.

17 Doc. No. RG226 T253, Roll 59, Notes 21 June 1939 – National Archives, Washington DC.

18 Doc. No. FO 645 Box 157 – 5.10.45 – Imperial War Museum, London.

19 *Hitler's Table Talk*, op. cit., pp.5, 16, 42.

20 Ibid.

21 *N-S Jahrbuch*, pp.188–9.

22 Wulf Schwarzwäller, *Rudolf Hess* (London, 1988), p.76.

23 Doc No FO 371/55672 – Public Records Office, Kew.

24 Doc. No. RG226 T253, Roll 59, Fm 1500069 – National Archives, Washington DC.

25 Schwarzwäller, op. cit., p.120.

26 Ibid.

27 Ibid.

28 James Douglas-Hamilton, *The Truth about Rudolf Hess* (Mainstream, 1988), p.46.

29 F. Taylor (ed.), *The Goebbels Diaries* (London, 1982), entry 22 March 1935.

30 Doc. No. RG226 T253, Roll 59, Notes 26 March 1935 – National Archives, Washington DC.

31 David Irving, *Goebbels* (London, 1996), p.201.

32 Doc. No. RG226 T253, Roll 59, Fm 1500066 – National Archives, Washington DC.

33 Ibid.

34 Doc. No. Folder I, Memo 21 November 1937 – Lord Halifax Papers, Borthwick Institute, York.

35 Martin Gilbert, *Winston Churchill: The Wilderness Years* (London, 1981), p.211.

36 *Hitler's Table Talk*, op. cit., p.202.

37 James Douglas-Hamilton, *Motive for a Mission* (London, 1971), p.54.

38 Robert Rhodes James (ed.), *The Diary of Sir Henry 'Chips' Channon* (London, 1957), pp.185–6.

39 Andreas Mayor (ed.), *Ciano's Diary 1937–38* (London, 1952), pp.44–5.

40 HMSO, Documents on German Foreign Policy, Ser. D, Vol. I, 'The Hossbach Memorandum', pp.29–30.

41 Martin Allen, *Hidden Agenda* (London, 2000), p.66.

42 'The Hossbach Memorandum', op. cit.

43 Douglas-Hamilton, *The Truth about Rudolf Hess*, op. cit., pp.94–9.

44 Ibid.

45 HMSO, *The International Military Tribunal: Trial of German Major War Criminals* (HMSO, 1946–51), Vol. 38, pp.172–3.

CHAPTER TWO – PEACEABLE ATTEMPTS

 1 Doc. No. FO 371/24408 – Public Records Office, Kew.

 2 Author's conversation with Joachim von Ribbentrop's former Private Secretary, Herr Reinhardt Spitzy, 14 May 2001.

 3 HMSO, Documents on German Foreign Policy, Ser. D, Vol. VIII, Doc. No. 384.

 4 Schwarzwäller, op. cit., p.123.

 5 HMSO, Documents on German–Polish Relations, Doc. No. 120, Miscellaneous No. 9 (1939).

 6 Albert Speer, *Inside the Third Reich* (London, 1970), p.165.

 7 Ibid.

 8 Ibid.

 9 HMSO, Documents on German Foreign Policy, Ser. D, Vol. VIII, 'Dahlerus Memorandum', pp.140–5.

10 Ibid.

11 William Shirer, *The Rise and Fall of the Third Reich* (London, 1964), p.772.

12 *Völkischer Beobachter*, 7 October 1939.

13 Shirer, op. cit., pp.773–5.

14 Doc. No. FO 371/26542 – Public Records Office, Kew.

15 Ibid.

16 Ibid.

17 Ibid.

18 Rhodes James (ed.), *The Diary of Sir Henry 'Chips' Channon*, op. cit., p.210.

19 Ibid, p.222.

20 Doc. No. FO 371/24405 – Public Records Office, Kew.

21 Ibid.

22 Ibid.

23 André Brissaud, *Histoire de Service Secret Nazi* (Paris, 1972), p.239.

24 Ibid, p.241.

25 Doc. No. FO 371/23107 – Public Records Office, Kew.

26 Ibid.

27 Brissaud, op. cit., p.244.

28 Ibid, p.249.

29 Doc. No. FO 371/26542 – Public Records Office, Kew.

30 Malcolm Muggeridge (ed.), *Ciano's Diary* (London, 1947), Vol. II, p.455.

31 Douglas-Hamilton, *The Truth about Rudolf Hess*, op. cit., p.203.

32 For further details concerning the Duke of Windsor/Bedaux relationship, and events at this time, see Allen, op. cit., Chapters 2 and 4.

33 Doc. No. 10505–27, Military Intelligence Division, US National Archive, Washington DC.

34 Dossier No. 100–49901, FBI Archive, Washington DC.

35 Ibid.

36 HMSO, Documents on German Foreign Policy, Ser. D, Vol. VIII, Doc. No. 203.

37 Ibid., Doc. No. 235.

38 Allen, op. cit., pp.148–52.

39 Doc. No. WO 202/3/25A – Public Records Office, Kew.

40 Doc. No. FO 371/28741 – Public Records Office, Kew.

41 Ibid.

42 Ibid. Extract from British Intelligence Report of 21 February 1940: 'Saw Walbach [British agent in Germany's Hague Embassy] again this evening. He informed me that Bedeaux [*sic*] is visiting Z[ech]-B[urkesroda – German Ambassador in The Hague] on an almost fortnightly basis...W[albach] has had an opportunity to see the transcribed information that B[edaux] brings verbally, and says it is of the best quality – defence material, strengths, weaknesses, and so on. There is little doubt from what W[albach] has told me that B[edaux]'s source is with the B.E.F., for he was recently in London to attend an A[llied] W[ar] C[ouncil] meeting.'

43 Ibid. Extracts from British Intelligence Report of 4 April 1940: 'W[albach] has said the Z[ech] B[urkesroda] accidentally referred to B[edaux]'s source as "Willi", and thinks this might be part of the man's name. Also Z-B has on more than one occasion hinted that B[edaux]'s source is an important person with the BEF!!. B[edaux] should be stopped.' 'Willi' was the German code-name for Edward, the Duke of Windsor.

44 HMSO, Documents on German Foreign Policy, Ser. D, Vol. IX, Docs No. 378, 456.

45 Rhodes James (ed.), *The Diary of Sir Henry 'Chips' Channon*, op. cit., p.252.

46 Doc. No. FO 797/19 – Public Records Office, Kew.

47 Doc. No. B15/B002545 – Bundesarchiv, Koblenz.

48 Walther Schellenberg, *Memoirs* (London, 1956).

49 HMSO, Documents on German Foreign Policy, Ser. D, Vol. X, Doc. No. B15/B002655.

50 Ibid, Doc. No. 152.

51 Josef Wulf, *Die SS* (Bonn, 1956).

52 Allen, op. cit., p.277.

53 Doc. No. FO 371/24408 – Public Records Office, Kew.

54 Ibid.

55 Ibid.

56 Doc. No. FO 837/593 – Public Records Office, Kew.

CHAPTER THREE – FLAG-WAVING

1 Peter Calvocoressi, Guy Wint and John Pritchard, *Total War* (Harmondsworth, 1972), pp.140–1.

2 'The British Act [of bombing German civilian targets], though a logical development of their strategy, was itself a retaliation for bombs dropped on London on 24 August. The German pilot concerned had dropped them against orders.' A.J.P. Taylor, *English History 1914–1945* (Oxford, 1965), p.499.

3 Doc. No. FO 371/24408 – Public Records Office, Kew.

4 B.H. Liddell Hart, *History of the Second World War* (London, 1970), p.150.

5 F.W. Winterbotham, *The Nazi Connection* (London, 1978), p.151.

6 Doc. No. FO 837/593 – Public Records Office, Kew.

7 Doc. No. FO 371/24408 – Public Records Office, Kew.

8   HMSO, Documents on German Foreign Policy, Ser. D, Vol. XI, Doc. No. 12.
9   Ibid.
10 Ibid.
11 Doc. No. RG226 T542, Roll 59 – National Archives, Washington DC.
12 Ibid.
13 Ibid.
14 Ibid.
15 Ibid.
16 Ibid.
17 Ibid.
18 Ibid.
19 HMSO, Documents on German Foreign Policy, Ser. D, Vol. XI, Doc. No. 12.
20 Ibid., Doc. No. 46 (C109/C002188–89).
21 John Harris, *Hess: The British Conspiracy* (London, 1999), p.249.
22 F.H. Hinsley et al., *British Intelligence in the Second World War* (HMSO, 1979), Vol. I, p.49.
23 Nigel West, *Secret War* (London, 1992), p.12.
24 Ibid, p.14.
25 Ben Pimlott, *Hugh Dalton* (London, 1985), p.305.
26 Gilbert, op. cit., p.153.
27 Dr Michael Stenton, *Radio London and Resistance to Occupied Europe* (Oxford, 2000), p.7.
28 Bruce Lockhart Diaries, 15 June 1940, House of Lords Library.
29 Sefton Delmar, *Black Boomerang* (London, 1962), p.37.
30 Doc. No. FO 898/0009 – Public Records Office, Kew.
31 Ibid.
32 Doc. No. FO 837/593 – Public Records Office, Kew.
33 Doc. No. FO 898/0009 – Public Records Office, Kew.

CHAPTER FOUR – NEGOTIATION
1   Doc. No. FO 371/55672 – Public Records Office, Kew.
2   HMSO, Documents on German Foreign Policy, Ser. D, Vol. XI, Doc. No. 76 (Enclosure 1).
3   Ibid.

4   Doc. No. C109 D002194 – Foreign and Commonwealth Office Library, London.

5   File No. NKVD 20566/24.10.42 – The KGB Archive, Moscow.

6   Ibid.

7   HMSO, Documents on German Foreign Policy, Ser. D, Vol. XI, Doc. No. 103.

8   Doc. No. C3084D613500 – Foreign and Commonwealth Office Library, London.

9. Doc. No. C3084D613511 – Foreign and Commonwealth Office Library, London.

10 Cabinet note 06.05.40 – The Halifax Papers, Borthwick Institute, York.

11 Ibid.

12 Doc. No. FO 371/26991 – Public Records Office, Kew.

13 Doc. No. FO 371/26542 – Public Records Office, Kew.

14 Doc. No. FO 371/26945 – Public Records Office, Kew.

15 David Stafford, *Roosevelt and Churchill* (London, 1999), pp.52–96.

16 Ibid, p.96.

17 Ibid, p.107.

18 Doc. No. FO 371/26991 – Public Records Office, Kew.

19 Ibid.

20 Ibid.

21 Doc. No. F5/0458–0462 – Auswärtiges Amt, Bonn.

22 Doc. No. FO 898/00009 – Public Records Office, Kew.

23 Doc. No. FO 371/26199 – Public Records Office, Kew.

24 Doc. No. FO 371/26542 – Public Records Office, Kew.

25 Ibid.

26 Ibid.

27 Doc. No. FO 645, Box 155 – Imperial War Museum, London.

28 Ibid.

29 Ibid.

30 Ibid.

31 Gita Sereny, *Albert Speer: His Battle with the Truth* (New York, 1995), p.242.

32 Doc. No. FO 645, Box 155 – Imperial War Museum, London

33 Roy Conyers-Nesbit, *Failed to Return* (Patrick Stephens Ltd, 1988), p.63.

34 HMSO, Documents on German Foreign Policy, Ser. D, Vol. XI, Doc. No. 532.

35 Andrew Roberts, *Holy Fox* (London, 1991), p.273.

36 *Who's Who* (London, 2000).

37 Doc. No. WO 190/893 – Public Records Office, Kew.

38 Doc. No. FO 371/26542 – Public Records Office, Kew.

39 Ibid.

40 Doc. No. FO C109 002203 – Foreign and Commonwealth Office Library, London.

41 David Irving, *Hess: The Missing Years* (London, 1987), p.97.

42 James Leasor, *Rudolf Hess: The Uninvited Envoy* (London, 1962), pp.73–81.

43 Nesbit, op. cit., p.63.

44 Doc. No. WO 190/893 – Public Records Office, Kew.

45 Doc. No. FO 371/26145 – Public Records Office, Kew.

46 Roberts, op. cit., p.267.

47 Ibid.

48 Doc. No. FO 898/306 – Public Records Office, Kew.

49 Doc. No. FO 898/14 – Public Records Office, Kew.

50 *Who's Who* (London, 2000).

51 Wolf Rüdiger Hess, op. cit., pp.185–6.

52 Ibid.

CHAPTER FIVE – A TENSE SPRING

1 Doc. No. WO 190/893 – Public Records Office, Kew.

2 Winston Churchill, *The Second World War* (London, 1952), Vol. III, p.86.

3 Ibid, p.91.

4 Doc. No. FO 371/26542 – Public Records Office, Kew.

5 HMSO, Documents on German Foreign Policy, Ser. D, Vol. XI, Doc. No. 680.

6 Ibid, Doc. No. 93.

7 Doc. No. WO 190/893 – Public Records Office, Kew.

8 Ibid.

9 William Shirer, *The Nightmare Years* (Boston, 1964), p.407.

10 Doc. No. FO 794/19 – Public Records Office, Kew.

11 Documenti Diplomatici Italiani, 1939–43, Ser. 9, Vol. I, Lequio to Miny, 14 March 1941.

12 Doc. No. FO 645, Box 155 – Imperial War Museum, London.
13 Churchill, op. cit., Vol. III, p.169.
14 Ibid, p.170.
15 Ibid.
16 Ibid.
17 Ibid, p.191.
18 Ibid, p.207.
19 Nigel Nicolson (ed.), *Harold Nicolson: Diaries and Letters 1939–45* (London, 1967), p.149.
20 Memorandum by D. Lloyd George, 11 September 1940 – Liddell Hart Papers, Kings College, London.
21 Peter Padfield, *Hess: Flight for the Führer* (London, 1991), p.168.
22 *Who's Who* (London, 2000).
23 Churchill, op. cit., Vol. III, p.197.
24 Oliver Harvey's Diary, entries 17–18 April 1941 – British Library, London.
25 *Nicolson Diaries*, op. cit., pp.162–3.
26 Doc. No. WO 190/893 – Public Records Office, Kew.
27 Padfield, op. cit., p.177.

CHAPTER SIX – SOMEONE IS EXPECTED

1 Nesbit, op. cit., p.63.
2 Ibid.
3 Ibid.
4 Doc. No. FO 371/26971 – Public Records Office, Kew.
5 Doc. No. FO 371/26945 – Public Records Office, Kew.
6 Ibid.
7 Ibid.
8 HMSO, Documents on German Foreign Policy, Ser. D, Vol. XII, Doc. No. 422.
9 Doc. No. FO 371/26945 – Public Records Office, Kew.
10 Ibid.
11 Doc. No. FO 898/14 – Public Records Office, Kew.
12 Ladislas Farago, *The Game of Foxes* (London, 1956), p.100.
13 F.W. Winterbotham, *Secret and Personal* (London, 1969), p.81.
14 Audrey Whiting, *The Kents* (London, 1985) p.97.
15 Professor Scott Newton *Profits of Peace* (Oxford, 1996), p.153.
16 Ibid., p.142.

17 Doc. No. FO 371/26542 – Public Records Office, Kew.

18 Ibid.

19 Ibid.

20 Doc. No. FO 898/14 – Public Records Office, Kew.

21 File No. FO 645, Box 155 – Imperial War Museum, London.

22 Ibid.

23 Ibid.

24 Doc. No. RG 319 IRR00887 – National Archives, Washington DC.

25 Doc. No. FO 898/14 – Public Records Office, Kew.

26 Ibid.

27 Douglas-Hamilton, *The Truth about Rudolf Hess*, op. cit., p.195.

28 Klaus Scholder, *Die Mittwochs-Gesellschaft. Protokolle aus dem geistigen Deutschland 1932 bis 1944* (Berlin, 1982), p.79.

29 Ibid.

30 Doc. No. 1504/371076 23.6.40 – Foreign and Commonwealth Office Library, London.

31 HMSO, Documents on German Foreign Policy, Ser. D, Vol. XII, Doc. No. 500.

32 Karl Haushofer interviewed by E. Mann, *Glasgow Evening Citizen* (1945); Padfield, op. cit., p.179.

33 Doc. No. FO 645, Box 155 – Imperial War Museum, London.

34 Churchill, op. cit., Vol. III, p.53.

35 Ilse Hess, op. cit.

36 Geheime Staatspolizei Records: Questioning of Gunther Sorof and Franz Lutz, 22 May 1941. Located at Archiv RSHA Protokolle, Institute für Zeitgeschicht, Munich.

37 Ibid.

38 Ibid.

39 Adolf Hitler (ed. R. Roussy de Sales), *My New Order* (London, 1942), pp.754–65.

40 Ibid.

41 Irving, *Hess: The Missing Years*, op. cit., p.64.

42 Ivan Maisky's Memoirs, p.637, quoting Byorn Prytz, Swedish Ambassador, 30 April 1941.

43 Schwarzwäller, op. cit., p.218.

44 Doc. No. RG266 XL22853 – National Archives, Washington DC.

45 A. Jacobsen, *Karl Haushofer* (Boppard, 1979), p.508.

46 *Stars and Stripes*, January 1946.

47 L. Picknett, C. Prince, S. Prior and R. Brydon, *Double Standards* (London, 2001), p.286.

48 Rhodes James (ed.), *The Diary of Sir Henry 'Chips' Channon*, op. cit., p.302.

49 Michael Smith, *Station X* (London, 1998), p.72.

50 Doc. No. WO 190/893 – Public Records Office, Kew.

51 Churchill, op. cit., Vol. III, pp.51–2.

52 Rhodes James (ed.), *The Diary of Sir Henry 'Chips' Channon*, op. cit., pp.302–3.

53 Ibid.

54 Ibid., pp.303–4.

55 Anne Chisholm and Michael Davie, *Beaverbrook* (London, 1992), p.328.

56 Kenneth Young (ed.), *The Diaries of Sir Robert Bruce Lockhart* (London, 1980), p.97.

57 *Hitler's Table Talk*, op. cit., p.7.

58 HMSO, Documents on German Foreign Policy, Ser. D, Vol. XI, Doc. No. 532.

59 *Hitlers politisches Testament. Die Bormann-Diktat vom February & April 1945* (Hamburg, 1988)

60 J. and S. Poole, *Who Financed Hitler?* (London, 1979), p.100.

61 Ibid.

62 Padfield, op. cit., p.191.

CHAPTER SEVEN – AN EMISSARY COMES

1 Doc. No. FO 898/00009 – Public Records Office, Kew.

2 Young (ed.), *The Diaries of Sir Robert Bruce Lockhart*, op. cit., Vol. II, p.98.

3 Doc. No. FO 898/00009 – Public Records Office, Kew.

4 Ibid.

5 Ibid.

6 Ibid.

7 Doc. No. FO 898/14 – Public Records Office, Kew.

8 Pimlott, op. cit., p.325.

9 Bruce Lockhart Diaries, entry 8 August 1941, House of Lords Library, London.

10 Picknett, Prince, Prior and Brydon, op. cit., p.177.
11 Ibid.
12 Wolf Rüdiger Hess, op. cit., p.17
13 Ibid, p.18.
14 Laurie Brettingham, *Beam Benders No. 80 (Signals) Wing 1940–45* (Midland Publishing, 1997), p.17.
15 Doc. No. FO 1093/11 – Public Records Office, Kew.
16 Ibid.
17 Doc. No. Bundle 5011, Hamilton Papers/28.03.41 – Public Records Office, Scotland.
18 Doc. No. Bundle 5011, Hamilton Papers/18.04.41 – Public Records Office, Scotland.
19 Leasor, op. cit., p.59.
20 Douglas-Hamilton, *The Truth about Rudolf Hess*, op. cit., p.63.
21 F.H. Hinsley, *British Intelligence During the Second World War* (HMSO, 1979), Vol. I, p.553.
22 Ibid., p.557.
23 Brettingham, op. cit.
24 Hansard (House of Commons), Vol. 371, col. 1591, 22 May 1941.
25 Picknett, Prince, Prior and Brydon, op. cit., p.186.
26 Andrew Rosthorn, *Sunday Telegraph*, 21 February 1999.
27 Ilse Hess, *England* (Druffel Verlag, 1955), p.34.
28 Picknett, Prince, Prior and Brydon, op. cit., pp.268–9.
29 Stafford, op. cit., p.96.
30 Picknett, Prince, Prior and Brydon, op. cit., p.269.
31 Churchill, op. cit., Vol. III, p.51.
32 *Daily Record*, 18 May 1941.
33 Doc. No. WO 199/3288A – Public Records Office, Kew.
34 Douglas-Hamilton, *Motive for a Mission*, op. cit., p.283.
35 Doc. No. AIR 41/46 – Public Records Office, Kew.
36 Daniel McBride, in *Hong Kong Telegraph*, 6 March 1947.
37 Doc. No. KV 235 17.5.41 – Public Records Office, Kew.
38 Ibid.
39 Doc. No. FO 1093/11 30.5.41 – Public Records Office, Kew.
40 Ibid.
41 *Glasgow Herald*, 16 May 1941.
42 Padfield, op. cit., p.354.
43 Ibid.

44 Ibid.
45 Hector MacLean, *Fighters in Defence* (privately published, Glasgow, 1999), p.138.
46 Padfield, op. cit., p.200.
47 Ibid.
48 Doc. No. FO 898/14 – Public Records Office, Kew.
49 Ibid.

CHAPTER EIGHT – A FATAL DECISION

 1 Walter Hewel's Diary, 11 May 1941 – Bundesarchiv, Koblenz.
 2 Wolf Rüdiger Hess, op. cit., p.86.
 3 Adolf Galland, *The First and the Last* (London, 1955), p.108
 4 Leasor, op. cit., pp.96–7.
 5 Wolf Rüdiger Hess, op. cit., p.343.
 6 Padfield, op. cit., p.220.
 7 Ibid, p.219.
 8 Ibid, p.220.
 9 Churchill, op. cit., Vol. II, p.419.
10 HMSO, Documents on German Foreign Policy, Ser. V, Vol. XII, Doc. No. 491.
11 Ibid.
12 Joachim v. Lang, *Der Adjutant* (Druffel Verlag, 1985), p.252.
13 Walter Hewel's Diary, 11 May 1941 – Bundesarchiv, Koblenz.
14 Scholder, op. cit., p.150.
15 Churchill, op. cit., Vol. III, p.53.
16 Stafford, op. cit., p.82.
17 Padfield, op. cit., p.214.
18 Doc. No. INF/912 – Public Records Office, Kew.
19 Douglas-Hamilton, *Motive for a Mission*, op. cit., p.178.
20 Ibid., p.180.
21 Young (ed.), *The Diaries of Sir Robert Bruce Lockhart*, op. cit., Vol. II, p.99.
22 Doc. No. INF 1/912 – Public Records Office, Kew.
23 Doc. No. FO 898/00009 – Public Records Office, Kew.
24 Speer, op. cit., p.150.
25 *International Military Tribunal*, op. cit., Vol. 38, pp.116–17.
26 Schwarzwäller, op. cit., p.220.
27 *International Military Tribunal*, op. cit., Vol. 38, pp.116–17.

28 Doc. No. PREM 3 219/7 – Public Records Office, Kew.
29 *International Military Tribunal*, op. cit., Vol. 38, p.183.
30 Doc. No. PREM 3 219/4 – Public Records Office, Kew.
31 Douglas-Hamilton, *Motive for a Mission*, op. cit., p.194.
32 Brigitte Frank, *Im Angesicht des Galgens* (Neuhaus b. Schliersee, 1955), p.401.
33 Doc. No. FO 371/26542 – Public Records Office, Kew.
34 Ibid.
35 HMSO, Documents on German Foreign Policy, Ser. D, Vol. XI, Doc No. 521.
36 Churchill, op. cit., Vol. III, p.286.
37 Ibid.
38 Doc. No. WO 190/893 – Public Records Office, Kew.
39 Ibid.
40 Doc. No. WO 166/1260 – Public Records Office, Kew.
41 Farago, op. cit., p.280.
42 Doc. No. WO 166/1260 – Public Records Office, Kew.
43 Ibid.
44 *Luton at War, 1947* (reprinted by Home Counties Newspapers, 1982).
45 Roy Conyers-Nesbit, *The Flight of Rudolf Hess* (Sutton Publishing, 1999), p.100.
46 Ibid, p.105.
47 Doc. No. FO 898/14 – Public Records Office, Kew.
48 Ibid.
49 Ibid.
50 Ibid.
51 Dr Hugh Dalton's Diary, 12 May 1941 – London School of Economics.
52 Doc. No. G/19/3/27 – Lloyd George Papers, House of Lords Library.
53 Doc. No. WO 190/893 – Public Records Office, Kew.
54 HMSO, Documents on German Foreign Policy, Ser. D, Vol. XII, Doc. No. 584.
55 *International Military Tribunal*, op. cit., Part IV, p.310.
56 Churchill, op. cit., Vol. III, p.298.
57 Young (ed.), *The Diaries of Sir Robert Bruce Lockhart*, op. cit., Vol. II, p.104.

58 Memorandum 31 May 1941 – Templewood Papers, Cambridge University Library.

59 Doc. No. AI/JQ25 – Public Records Office, Kew.

60 HMSO, Documents on British Foreign Policy, Ser. 4, Vol. I, p.620.

61 Hinsley, op. cit., p.480.

62 Churchill, op. cit., Vol. III, p.298.

63 Ibid.

64 Ibid, pp.300–1.

65 Doc. No. FO 837/593 – Public Records Office, Kew.

66 Ibid.

67 Churchill, op. cit., Vol. III, pp.300–1.

68 *Hitler's Table "alk*, op. cit., pp.71–2.

69 Doc. No. RG226 T253, Roll 59 – National Archives, Washington DC.

70 *Hitler's Table Talk*, op. cit., pp.200–2.

71 Douglas-Hamilton, *Motive for a Mission*, op. cit. p.202.

72 Ibid.

EPILOGUE

1 Doc. No. PREM 3 434/7 (6.11.44) – Public Records Office, Kew.

2 Doc. No. FO 371/55672 – Public Records Office, Kew.

3 Ibid.

4 Ibid.

5 Ibid.

Bibliography

Allen, Martin: *Hidden Agenda*, Macmillan, 2000

Allen, Peter: *The Crown and the Swastika*, Robert Hale, 1983

Ashbee, F.: *The Thunderstorm that was Hess*, Aeroplane Monthly, 1987

Bolmus, Reinhard: *Das Amt Rosenberg und seine Gegner*, Deutsche
   Verlags Anstalt, 1970

Brettingham, Laurie: *Beam Benders No.80 (Signals) Wing 1940–45*,
   Midland, 1997

Brisaud, André: *Histoire de Secret Service Nazi*, Plon, 1972

Bullock, Alan: *Hitler: A Study in Tyranny*, Odhams, 1952

Calvocoressi, P., Wint, G. and Pritchard, J.: *Total War*, Penguin, 1972

Charmley, John: *Duff Cooper: The Authorised Biography*, Weidenfeld
   & Nicolson, 1986

Chisholm, A. and Davie, M.: *Beaverbrook*, Hutchinson, 1992

Churchill, W.S.: *The Second World War*, vols I–V, Cassell, 1948–52

Clark, Alan: *Barbarossa: The Russian–German Conflict 1941–45*,
   Macmillan, 1985

Clydesdale, Marquess of, and McIntyre, D.F.: *The Pilot's Book of
   Everest*, London, 1936

Conyers-Nesbit, Roy: *Failed to Return*, Patrick Stephens, 1988

Conyers-Nesbit, Roy, *The Flight of Rudolf Hess*, Sutton Publishing,
   1999

Costello, John: *Ten Days that Saved the West*, Bantam, 1991

Cruickshank, Charles: *SOE in the Far East*, Oxford University Press,
   1983

Day, D.: *Menzies and Churchill at War*, Angus & Robertson, 1986

Delmar, Sefton: *Black Boomerang*, London, 1962

Dilkes, D. (ed.): *The Diaries of Sir Alexander Cadogan, O.M.,
   1938–45*, Cassell, 1971

Documents on British Foreign Policy, Series 4, Vol. I, HMSO, 1949

Documents on German Foreign Policy, Series D, vols IX–XII, HMSO, 1961

Douglas-Hamilton, James: *Motive for a Mission*, Macmillan, 1971

Douglas-Hamilton, James: *The Truth about Rudolf Hess*, Mainstream, 1988

Eade, Charles (ed.): *Churchill, by his Contemporaries*, Hutchinson, 1953

Farago, Ladislas: *The Game of Foxes*, London, 1956

Frank, Dr Hans: *Im Angesicht des Galgens*, Neuhaus b. Schliersee, 1955

Gabel, Charles: *Conversations interdites avec Rudolf Hess*, Plon, 1988

Galland, Adolf: *The First and the Last*, Methuen, 1955

German Library of Information, *The War in Maps*, 1941

Gilbert, Martin: *Winston Churchill: The Wilderness Years*, Macmillan, 1981

Gilbert, Martin: *Churchill: A Life*, Heinemann, 1991

Hanfstaengl, Ernst: *15 Jahre mit Hitler*, Piper, 1980

Hansard, Vol. 371

Harris, J. and Trow, M.J.: *Hess: The British Conspiracy*, André Deutsch, 1999

Hassell, Ulrich v.: *Vom Andern Deutschland*, Atlantis, 1946

Haushofer, Albrecht: *Allgemeine politisches Geographia und Geopolitik*, Vowinckel Verlag, 1931

Haushofer, Albrecht: *Handbuch der Amerikakunde*, Diesterweg, 1931

Haushofer, Albrecht: *Englands einbruch in China*, Junker & Dünnhaupt, 1940

Haushofer, Albrecht: *Sonnets of Moabit*, Blavalet, 1946, and W.W. Norton & Co., 1978

Haushofer, Karl: *Dai Nihon*, Berlin, 1913

Haushofer, Karl: *Geopolitik des pazifisches Ozeans*, Vowinckel Verlag, 1925

Haushofer, Karl: *Bausteine zur Geopolitik*, Kurt Vowinckel Verlag, 1928

Hess, Ilse: *England*, Druffel Verlag, 1955

Hess, Ilse: *Gefangener des Friedens*, Druffel Verlag, 1955

Hess, Ilse: *Ein Schicksal in Briefen*, Druffel Verlag, 1971

Hess, Wolf Rüdiger: *My Father Rudolf Hess*, W.H. Allen, 1986

Hess, Wolf Rüdiger: *Rudolf Hess: Briefe 1908–33*, Langen Muller, 1987

Hildebrandt, Rainer: *Wir sind die letzten; aus dem Leben des Widerstandkämpfers Albrecht Haushofer und seiner Freunde*, Michael Verlag, 1949

Hill, Leonidas (ed.): *Die Weizsäcker Papiere*, Vol. II, Ulstein Verlag, 1974

Hinsley, F.H. et al.: *British Intelligence in the Second World War*, vols I–III, HMSO, 1979

Hitler, Adolf: *My New Order*, Angus & Robertson, 1942

Hitler, Adolf: *Mein Kampf*, Zentralverlag der NSDAP, 1943

Hoare, Sir Samuel: *The Fourth Seal*, Heinemann, 1930

The International Military Tribunal: Trial of German Major War Criminals, HMSO, 1946–51

Irving, David: *Churchill's War*, Hutchinson, 1987

Irving, David: *Hess: The Missing Years*, Grafton Books, 1987

Irving, David: *Goebbels*, Focal Point Publications, 1996

Italiaander, Rolf: *In Memorian Albrecht Haushofer: Gedenkworte von Adolf Grimme, Carl F. von Weizsäcker, und Walter Stubbe*, OEtinger v. Hamburg, 1948

Jacobsen, A.: *Karl Haushofer*, Boppard, 1979

Kershaw, Ian: *Hitler, 1889–1936*, Penguin, 1998

Kershaw, Ian: *Hitler, 1936–1945*, Penguin, 2000

Kersten, Felix: *The Kersten Memoirs 1940–1945*, Hutchinson, 1956

Kirkpatrick, Ivone: *The Inner Circle: Memoirs of Ivone Kirkpatrick*, Macmillan, 1959

Kuusisto, Seppo: *Alfred Rosenberg in der National-Socialistischen Aussenpolitik 1933–1939*, Societas Historica Finlandiae, 1984

Laack-Michel, Ursula: *Albrecht Haushofer und der National-Sozialismus*, Ernst Klett, 1974

Lang, Joachim: *Der Adjutant*, Druffel Verlag, 1985

Leasor, James: *Rudolf Hess: The Uninvited Envoy*, Allen & Unwin, 1962

Liddell Hart, B.H.: *History of the Second World War*, Cassell, 1970

LIFE Magazine, edition of September 1946

Loewenheim, F., Langley, H. and Jonas, M. (eds): *Roosevelt and Churchill: Their Secret Wartime Correspondence*, Barrie & Jenkins, 1975

Ludecke, Kurt: *I Knew Hitler*, Jarrolds, 1938

McBride, D.: *Hong Kong Telegraph* article, 6 March 1947

McDermot, Geoffrey: *The Eden Legacy*, Leslie Frewin, 1969

Mackinder, H.J.: *The Geographical Pivot of History*, London, 1904

Maclean, H.: *Fighters in Defence*, Glasgow, 1999

Masterman, J.C.: *The Double Cross System*, Yale University Press, 1972

Mayor, Andreas (ed.): *Ciano's Diary 1937–1938*, Methuen, 1952

Moran, Lord: *Winston Churchill: The Struggle for Survival*, Sphere, 1968

Muggeridge, Malcolm (ed.): *Ciano's Diary 1939–1943*, Heinemann, 1947

Newton, S.: *Profits of Peace*, Clarendon Press, 1996

Nicolson, N. (ed.): *Harold Nicolson: Diaries and Letters 1939–45*, Collins, 1967

N-S Jahrbuch, editions 1938–1940

Overy, Richard: *Why the Allies Won*, Jonathan Cape, 1995

Padfield, Peter: *Hess: Flight for the Führer*, Cassell, 1991 (revised edn, *Hess: The Führer's Disciple*, Cassell, 2001)

Picknett, L., Prince, C., Prior, S. and Brydon, R.: *Double Standards*, Little, Brown, 2001

Pimlott, Ben: *Hugh Dalton*, Jonathan Cape, 1985

Poole, J. and S.: *Who Financed Hitler?*, Macdonald & James, 1978

Rees, J.R. (ed.): *The Case of Rudolf Hess*, Heinemann, 1947

Rhodes James, Robert (ed.): *The Diary of Sir Henry 'Chips' Channon*, Weidenfeld & Nicolson, 1957

Roberts, Andrew: *The Holy Fox*, Weidenfeld & Nicolson, 1991

Schellenberg, Walter: *Memoirs*, André Deutsch, 1956

Scholder, Klaus: *Die Mittwochs-Gesellschafts. Protokolle aus dem geistigen Deutschland 1932–44*, Berlin, 1982

Schwarzwäller, Wulf: *Rudolf Hess*, Quartet, 1988

Sereny, Gita: *Albert Speer: His Battle with the Truth*, Knopf, 1997

Shirer, William: *The Nightmare Years*, Little, Brown (Boston), 1964

Shirer, William: *The Rise and Fall of the Third Reich*, Pan, 1964

Smith, Michael: *Station X*, Macmillan, 1998

Speer, Albert: *Inside the Third Reich*, Weidenfeld & Nicolson, 1970

Speer, Albert: *Spandauer Tagebücher*, Ullstein Verlag, 1975

Stafford, David: *Roosevelt and Churchill*, Abacus, 1999

Stars and Stripes, edition of January 1946

Stenton, Dr Michael: *Radio London and Resistance to Occupied Europe*, Oxford University Press, 2000

Taylor, F. (ed.): *The Goebbels Diaries*, Hamish Hamilton, 1982

The Times, edition of 12 December 1923

Trevor-Roper, H.R. (ed.): *Hitler's Table Talk*, Oxford University Press, 1953

Trzebinski, Errol: *The Life and Death of Lord Erroll*, Fourth Estate, 2000

Vansittart, Lord: *The Mist Procession: The Autobiography of Lord Vansittart*, Hutchinson, 1958

Völkischer Beobachter, editions from 1937 to 1941

West, Nigel: *Secret War: The Story of SOE*, Hodder & Stoughton, 1992

Whiting, Audrey: *The Kents*, Hutchinson, 1985

Winterbotham, F.W.: *Secret and Personal*, William Kimber, 1969

Winterbotham, F.W.: *The Nazi Connection*, Weidenfeld & Nicolson, 1978

Winterbotham, F.W.: *The Ultra Secret*, Weidenfeld & Nicolson, 1974

Wulf, Josef: *Die SS*, Bonn, 1956

Young, K. (ed.): *The Diaries of Sir Robert Bruce Lockhart*, Vol. II, Macmillan, 1980

Zeitschrift für Geopolitik, editions from 1934 to 1940, Vowinckel Verlag, Heidelberg

Index